W9-AMJ-866

67 SHOTS

67 SHOTS

KENT STATE
AND THE END OF
AMERICAN INNOCENCE

HOWARD MEANS

Da Capo Press
A Member of the Perseus Books Group

Designed by Trish Wilkinson
Set in 11.5-point Adobe Garamond Pro by The Perseus Books Group

Library of Congress Cataloging-in-Publication Data

Names: Means, Howard B., author.
Title: 67 shots : Kent State and the end of American innocence / Howard Means.
Other titles: Sixty seven shots
Description: Boston : Da Capo Press, 2016. | Includes bibliographical
    references and index. | Description based on print version record and CIP
    data provided by publisher; resource not viewed.
Identifiers: LCCN 2015045123 (print) | LCCN 2015044809 (ebook) | ISBN
    9780306823800 (e-book) | ISBN 9780306823794 (hardcover) | ISBN
    9780306823800 (ebook)
Subjects: LCSH: Kent State Shootings, Kent, Ohio, 1970. | Student
    movements—Ohio—Kent—History—20th century.
Classification: LCC LD4191.O72 (print) | LCC LD4191.O72 M43 2016 (ebook) |
    DDC 378.771/37—dc23
LC record available at http://lccn.loc.gov/2015045123

Published by Da Capo Press
A Member of the Perseus Books Group
www.dacapopress.com

Da Capo Press books are available at special discounts for bulk purchases in the U.S. by corporations, institutions, and other organizations. For more information, please contact the Special Markets Department at the Perseus Books Group, 2300 Chestnut Street, Suite 200, Philadelphia, PA 19103, or call (800) 810-4145, ext. 5000, or e-mail special.markets@perseusbooks.com.

10 9 8 7 6 5 4 3 2 1

32018 2957

For Persephone and Forest

CONTENTS

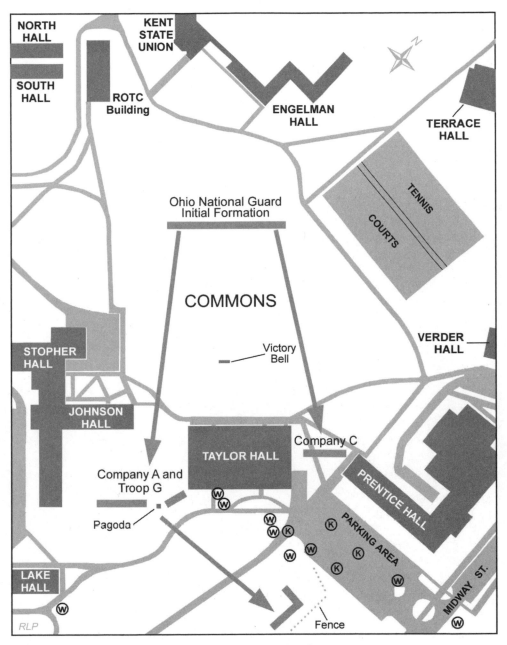

Kent State Campus, May 4, 1970

Prologue

May 4, 1970—South Vietnam

On May 4, 1970, twenty-four American servicemen died while serving their country in South Vietnam.

Ronald Chisholm was killed in Quang Tri province, in the very north of the country, and Larry Lance Watkins in Thua Thien, the next province to the south. James Gerald Anderson and Floyd Watsel Lamb Jr., known as Jason, died in Quang Tin, more than a hundred miles below the line of demarcation between the two Vietnams. Eddie Gean Terrell lost his life in Quang Nam, while Leon Garnett and Theodore Irwin Roberts were killed in Tay Ninh, stuck like a closed thumb into southeastern Cambodia.

Michael Anthony Vancosky died of multiple fragmentation wounds; Richard Walter Paquette, of small-arms and rocket fire. Robert Vincent Thompson was killed in a vehicle wreck in Phong Dinh, in the south of the country, below the Mekong River. James Frederick Hopkins died of burns sustained in an electrical shop fire in Bien Hoa, the joint operating base for both US and South Vietnamese forces.

Two of the twenty-four died on patrol in Cambodia: Major George Ellery Hussey and Army Staff Sergeant Albert Charles Smith.

1

A West Point graduate, Hussey was the highest-ranking officer killed that day.

The dead of May 4 lost their lives in small acts of bravery and large ones. James Edward "Doc" Rimmer, an army medic, was killed trying to save his platoon leader's life. The platoon leader, Stephen Bradford Emery, died as well. Wayne Louis Torsiello—Company B, First Battalion, Seventh Marines, First Marine Division—was leading a counterattack when he "was mortally wounded by enemy fire as he valiantly rushed through the tree line at the forefront of his squad," in the words of his Bronze Star citation.

On average, seventeen US servicemen died daily throughout 1970, down dramatically from the forty-six deaths per day in the peak war year of 1968. Save for a single incident, May 4 would have hit the average on the nose.

Between eleven and eleven thirty that night, a flare malfunctioned catastrophically aboard a UH-1 (Huey) helicopter being used to illuminate a battlefield in Thua Thien. As the Huey raced to ground, it came in on top of an AH-1 Cobra helicopter flying without anti-collision lights on a practice red alert over Firebase Nancy. All seven crewmembers manning the two copters were killed.

Aboard the Huey flare-ship were Sergeant Thomas Oliver Ahlberg, age nineteen, from Idaho Falls, Idaho; Sergeant Dean Aitken, twenty, Vernal, Utah; Chief Warrant Officer Tommy L. Kearsley, twenty-two, Buhl, Idaho; First Lieutenant Larry Franklin Mattingly, twenty-seven, of Indianapolis, Indiana; and Rodney Alan Taylor, eighteen, of Seadrift, Texas. All but Mattingly were single. Ahlberg, Aitken, and Kearsley were Mormons. Taylor, a month plus a day away from his nineteenth birthday, was the youngest American to die in Vietnam on May 4.

The AH-1 Cobra held a crew of two: Warrant Officer Dean Louis Bonneau, twenty, of Oshkosh, Wisconsin, and Captain Douglas Nelson Winfrey, twenty-five, of Smyrna, Georgia. Bonneau was married.

As with the larger war, the American dead on May 4, 1970, were mostly white, mostly single, mostly volunteers, and mostly just out of their teens or still in them. Thirteen of the twenty-four were age twenty or younger. But like all the other dead in that nearly endless and devastating war, these fatalities were more than names, more than data points in some statistical overview. They were sons, brothers, husbands, fathers, lovers, hooch mates, best buddies in the annealing heat and terror of war. They had stories. They left memories behind, and they are remembered still, if only as an empty space in lives long ago forced to go on without them.

Doc Rimmer, the army medic who died trying to save his platoon leader, left behind a son. An online photo shows the little boy, windblown and dressed in his Sunday best, as he helps raise the first flag flown on the pole dedicated in his father's honor in front of the Morris, Illinois, firehouse.

A *Life* magazine reporter captured the moment when the mother of Armando Cervera Luna, who died along with Doc Rimmer that day in Quang Tin, first found his name at Panel 11W, Line 96, of the newly dedicated Vietnam War Memorial on the National Mall in Washington, DC: "As she wept, she kept rubbing his name with her forefinger—as if trying to read it. As if it were Braille."

"I will always miss you and wish I had had the chance to get to know you as we grew old together," Patty Nickolaus wrote to her brother, Tom Ahlberg, in an April 2002 post on the virtual wall maintained by the Vietnam Veterans Memorial. Joyce Aitken-Morrison posted much the same about her uncle, Dean Aitken, killed with Ahlberg in the helicopter wreck over Thua Thien.

In a blog entry about the midair collision, Richard Edwards remembered barging in on a small group of officers gathered around their commanding officer as they digested the news that Douglas Winfrey had been killed when the Huey flare-ship dropped down on his Cobra like some avenging, blazing angel. "Around him were many teary eyed Officers. This was something an enlisted man was not supposed to see and our CO knew it. So he yelled, 'Get him out of here.'"

The time, Edwards writes, was eleven forty-five p.m. Half a world away, in Northeast Ohio, the shootings at Kent State University were twenty minutes old. Four students lay dead, nine wounded. Protestors and National Guardsmen were still regrouping on the campus Commons, with the possibility of far worse to come.

1

"We Have to Say 'F---' Everywhere"

Just about everyone remembers that first weekend in May 1970 as blessed by beautiful weather. For most of April, temperatures had been below average for Northeast Ohio. In the last week, though, the trend turned sharply, and on Thursday, April 30, the thermometer soared to 84 degrees Fahrenheit, only 5 degrees below the high for the entire year. There would be one more frost day—May 7, when temperatures plunged to 27 degrees—but spring had unofficially arrived.

The twenty-one thousand students at Kent State University were on a quarterly system. Midterm exams lay ahead, but a sense of release was in the air, as it always is on northern campuses when the drudgery of winter finally departs. The weekend lay ahead. Sap was rising. That was part of the mixture that would come to a boil near midnight outside a strip of off-campus bars along North Water Street in downtown Kent: sheer youthful exuberance, the joy of being alive with summer ahead.

Vietnam was another, more volatile part of the mixture. The night before, in a nationally televised address to the nation, President Richard Nixon had announced that the war there, which appeared to be winding down, was being expanded instead into Cambodia, to interdict enemy supply lines and attack its base camps.

Seated at his nearly empty desk in the Oval Office—with a vacant in-out box to his right and a multiline black phone nearby on his left—the president read from a stack of typed sheets as he laid out in elaborate detail the argument for carrying the war next door into Cambodia. The North Vietnamese had repeatedly violated Cambodia's neutrality. Enemy military sanctuaries—"major base camps, training sites, logistics facilities, weapons and ammunition factories, airstrips, and prisoner-of-war compounds"—could be found all along the border between Cambodia and South Vietnam.

Ten days earlier in another address to the nation, Nixon had announced that an additional 150,000 Americans would soon be withdrawn from South Vietnam. Now, in light of stepped-up enemy activity along the Cambodian border, he and his advisers, military and civilian, had concluded that the planned withdrawal would "constitute an unacceptable risk" to the 400,000 Americans who would remain on duty in Vietnam, as well as to the South Vietnamese themselves.

Five times during his talk, the president rose from his desk and, looking like a stiff-limbed geography teacher, made his way to a large map of the war theater set up on an easel off to his right. The North Vietnamese base camps along the border glowed in red. One, dubbed the "Parrot's Beak," pointed directly to Saigon and from not far away. It was, the president said, closer to the South Vietnamese capital "than Baltimore is to Washington."

America, the president said, "will be patient in working for peace; we will be conciliatory at the conference table, but we will not be humiliated. We will not be defeated. We will not allow American men by the thousands to be killed by an enemy from privileged sanctuaries."

Half a minute later, in his twenty-two-minute speech, Nixon paused, mopped perspiration from his upper lip, briefly closed his eyes in what looked like pain or prayer, and then turned to what he knew would be the inevitable antiwar blowback from his address:

My fellow Americans, we live in an age of anarchy, both abroad and at home. We see mindless attacks on all the great institutions which have been created by free civilizations in the last 500 years. Even here in the United States, great universities are being systematically destroyed. Small nations all over the world find themselves under attack from within and from without.

If, when the chips are down, the world's most powerful nation, the United States of America, acts like a pitiful, helpless giant, the forces of totalitarianism and anarchy will threaten free nations and free institutions throughout the world.

The president had promised during his 1968 campaign to bring American troops home from Vietnam, and "they *are* coming home," he vowed. He had promised to end the war and win a just peace, and "I shall keep" both promises. He was taking this action, Nixon assured his nationwide audience, with no regard to the political consequences. He would rather be a one-term president who had done what he believed was right than a two-term president "at the cost of seeing America become a second-rate power."*

As for the war protestors, the president struck a conciliatory note just before closing: "I realize that in this war there are honest and deep differences in this country about whether we should have become involved, that there are differences as to how the war should have been conducted. But the decision I announce tonight transcends those differences."

By the next day, though—with the reaction mounting—the olive branch had been withdrawn. The antiwar protesters, Nixon said on a brief outing to the Pentagon, were "bums blowing up campuses."

---

*Three years to the hour later, by then in his second term, Nixon would sit at the same desk and deliver his first national address on the Watergate break-in. The last American troops had left Vietnam thirty-two days earlier.

At Kent State, the "bums blowing up campuses" dug a hole instead, at least initially. At noon on Friday, May 1, a small cadre largely composed of graduate history students and calling itself WHORE buried a copy of the US Constitution at the north end of the university Commons, beside the Victory Bell, a onetime railroad fixture commonly used to celebrate football wins.* The New University Conference— faculty members, mostly young, and graduate students—cosponsored the interment, meant to suggest the "murder" of constitutional principles inherent in sending US troops into Cambodia without a declaration of war or even consultation with Congress.

If the symbolism was heavy, attendance was not, and enthusiasm was at best wayward. Rob Fox, then a student senator, heard rumors about the event and walked by on his way to class. "There were maybe 500–600 students just milling around, talking. . . . Not too much was going on, quite honestly. You know, they talked, somebody buried the Constitution at the corner of the Bell there. . . . Really, nothing happened."

A second rally at three that afternoon, sponsored by Black United Students (BUS), attracted a slightly smaller crowd—around four hundred—and ended as the earlier one had—peacefully—after about forty-five minutes.

Kent State president Robert White would later say that his wife's account of Nixon's Cambodia speech the previous night, which he hadn't seen, had left him with a "sinking feeling," but buoyed by the calm of the two afternoon rallies, he decided to honor a long-standing commitment to visit his sister-in-law in Mason City, Iowa, and attend the Sunday annual meeting in Iowa City of the American College Testing Program, where he served as the unsalaried chairman of the board of trustees. By the time he returned to Kent Sunday

---

*WHORE was short for World Historians Opposed to Racism and Exploitation; the late '60s was a time of expansive acronyms.

morning, he would be a president in name only: the university no longer controlled its own campus.

Later, after Neil Young's "four dead in Ohio" anthem, after the nine wounded and the national shock and the bitter editorial recriminations in all directions, it would be common to ask: Why Kent State? This wasn't Berkeley or Columbia or even Ohio State, about three hours southwest, where students and police had been in running battles for more than two weeks when Kent State finally erupted so spectacularly.

Kent State was commonly described as a working-class university and a local one: 80 percent of the students were from Ohio, many from surrounding counties and close-in cities like Cleveland and Akron. Admission standards were modest. By law, Kent State had to accept any graduate of an accredited Ohio high school. Someone had nicknamed the school "Suitcase U" because so many students headed home for the weekend. After-school jobs were common to help meet tuition. One popular work option as the Vietnam War heated up was the National Guard, a sure paycheck and a refuge from the Selective Service draft.

Many Kent students assumed that a kind of firewall—part demographics, part tradition, part "otherness"—exempted their school from the front lines of the war against the war. Richard Karl Watkins, an undergraduate in 1970, recalled talking only a few weeks earlier about the Ohio State unrest with one of the cafeteria workers as he stood in line at an on-campus eatery. "I remember one of us saying we were glad we were in Kent because that [kind of thing] wouldn't happen here. We're not like Ohio State. . . . In retrospect, it seems absurd. Seemed very real when we were talking about it."

In fact, Kent State had a robust history of political unrest that had flown under the radar of national attention, precisely because the school was so regional. By the mid-1960s, antiwar activism was a staple of campus life, sometimes with a dramatic flair. Timothy App recalled the homecoming parade his freshman year, 1966: "All the organizations on campus built floats. The parade went right down Main Street. One float was an old, burned-out car. The members were walking in silence beside it, with gas masks on and dressed in military paraphernalia. The townspeople hated it."

J. R. Hipple—then a seventh grader, the son of a Kent State romance language professor—remembered hearing Muhammad Ali speak on campus in 1967, shortly after "the Greatest" had been stripped of his world heavyweight boxing title for refusing induction into the US Army, in part based on his religious beliefs (Ali had converted to the Nation of Islam two years earlier and changed his name from Cassius Clay) and in part because of his opposition to the American presence in Vietnam.

Not all the action, though, was rhetoric or symbolic gestures. In the fall of 1968, BUS, the black student organization, and Students for a Democratic Society (SDS) staged a five-hour sit-in to protest the presence of police recruiters from Oakland, California. The school had a well-regarded law-enforcement program, but for many younger African Americans, Oakland had become the Devil Force. Seven months earlier, on April 7, 1968, Bobby Hutton, age seventeen and already the national treasurer of the Black Panther Party, had been killed in a shootout with Oakland police that also wounded Eldridge Cleaver, the party's minister of information and soon to be one of the FBI's most wanted persons.

Planned disciplinary action against the protestors was put on hold when 250 black students walked off campus, demanding full amnesty. Two days later, the administration granted them their wish. The university sweetened the package later that winter with a new Institute of African-American Affairs.

A spring 1969 protest organized by SDS was less gentle, in both tactics and outcome. On April 8, some fifty white students, led by SDS, attempted to enter the main administration building, with the intent of posting four demands on an office door: abolition of the campus ROTC program and of the university's degree program in law enforcement, removal of a campus-based state crime lab, and the closing of the Liquid Crystal Institute, a university research facility backed, in part, by the US Department of Defense. (Because they are extremely sensitive to minute temperature changes, liquid crystals are a key element in both night-vision goggles and very early cancer detection, among other uses.)

The broader intent, consistent with SDS strategy nationwide, was to provoke a confrontation with officials, and that was achieved. Campus police were waiting when the student contingent arrived, entrance was refused, and scuffling broke out—more or less on cue—during which several officers were hit. With that, the university revoked the charter of the local SDS chapter and suspended several students, but the show was not over. Eight days later, at what was meant to be a private disciplinary hearing for two students involved in the April 8 fracas, a second, larger brawl broke out—this time between a hundred or so supporters of the suspended students and twice as many student counterdemonstrators, mostly varsity athletes and fraternity men. By the time the dust settled on this one, the Ohio State Highway Patrol had been called in and fifty-eight people arrested.

That fall, a local Portage County jury found four SDS leaders guilty of assault and battery arising from the April protests. The four also pled guilty to charges of inciting to riot. Each of the Kent State 4, as they became known locally, was sentenced to six months in the Portage County jail.

Until its charter was revoked in the spring of 1969, the Kent State SDS chapter also served as a draw for national leaders of the organization. Mark Rudd, who commanded banner headlines as an SDS leader at New York's Columbia University, spoke to the Kent State faithful in October 1968. The next month, Rennie Davis addressed a regional SDS conference hosted by the Kent State contingent. By then, Davis was well on his way to becoming an iconic movement figure, one of the Chicago Eight activists who would eventually be prosecuted for inciting a riot at the August 1968 Democratic Presidential Convention in the Windy City.*

Even without an official SDS chapter on campus, the spirit of the times continued to sweep through the Kent State campus. A curfew for women disappeared. The sexes were allowed to mingle in dormitory rooms. The school became one of the first in the country, maybe the very first, to offer a course on the Beatles—before the 1970 breakup, before "Let It Be," back when Lucy was still in the sky with diamonds. Eighteen-year-olds were already of legal age in Ohio to drink what was known as "three-two beer," half the 6.4 percent alcohol content of standard beer. Now the thin beer went on sale at the student union. Then, on April 10, 1970, Jerry Rubin showed up on campus to speak at yet another campus rally.

A cofounder in 1967 of the Youth International Party—YIP, hence Yippies—Rubin had a deep history in political activism, but the Yippies themselves remain hard to categorize almost half a century later. The group's flag featured a cannabis leaf over a red star, both superimposed on a black backdrop: dope, Marxism, revolution, all rolled into one. Its manifesto, cowritten by Rubin and Abbie Hoffman in the run-up to the 1968 national election, extended an invitation broadly to "all you rebels, youth spirits, rock minstrels, bomb throwers, bank robbers, peacock freaks, toe worshippers, poets, street folk, liberated women, professors and body snatchers" and called on them all to "parade in the thousands to the places where the votes are counted and let the murderous racists feel our power. Force the National Guard to protect every polling place in the country."

But as the language above suggests, Rubin and the Yippies were also the ongoing street theater of Movement politics, more interested in selling the idea of revolution than in achieving specific goals. Post–Kent State, for example, the thought of the National Guard protect-

---

*The Eight got pared to the Chicago Seven when Black Panther Bobby Seale's courtroom histrionics finally forced Judge Julius Hoffman to separate his trial from the others'.

ing every polling place in the country would become chilling at best. Whatever he was, revolutionary or ideological entrepreneur or likely something of both, on April 10, 1970, at Kent State, Rubin held little back, according to an unnamed administrator who attended the rally, took notes on the sly, and delivered them to President White's office that afternoon at 3:47 p.m., about two hours after the event ended. Among the Rubin quotations the spy jotted down:

"Kent State is a super prison."

"The first part of the Yippie program is to kill your parents. They are the first oppressors."

"We have to free the children who are imprisoned in the suburbs."

"We have to say 'f---' everywhere. What's everybody thinking out there? (Shouted back: F---!)"

"We're going to build a new society within American society, composed of long-hairs, women and blacks."

"The working class is becoming yippieized and black pantherized."

As Rubin talked, the administration spy noted, money was being collected from the crowd to help free the Kent State 4, still doing time in the "maximum-security" (Rubin's words) Portage County jail.

Press reports of Rubin's appearance tended to downplay both the crowd size—the spy put attendance at "1500–2000 strictly a guess"—and its enthusiasm, but the very presence at a university-sanctioned event of a nationally famous radical leader urging students to kill their parents fed the unease that many Kent townspeople were beginning to feel about their outsized university neighbor. They didn't think their children needed liberation from the prisons of their communities. A new society composed of longhairs, women, and blacks was not on their bucket lists. Nor had they signed on to an America where everyone said "Fuck!" everywhere, all the time. Witness the inability of the administration spy to even spell the word out, but as the spy's reticence suggests, it wasn't just the nuance-challenged locals who took the theatric Rubin more literally than perhaps he took himself. Jerry Lewis, then a young sociology professor at Kent State, took his sociology class to hear the Rubin talk. "The next time we

met, I said 'kill your parents' was a metaphor for socialization, right?'
They said, 'No, he meant kill your parents!'"

Less than two weeks after Jerry Rubin's talk, Bill Arthrell celebrated his twenty-first birthday by handing out flyers on campus announcing plans to napalm a dog the next day, in front of the student
union. Arthrell had flunked out of Kent State a year earlier—largely
because, he said, he had been so heavily involved in SDS activity.
He'd returned in the spring of 1970, but his interest in political action clearly hadn't disappeared, and the dog stunt read like something
straight out of the Yippie playbook: take a horror of the war—the
broad use of napalm—and reduce it to street theater that the media
couldn't ignore.

The street-theater part worked. As many as four hundred students,
by Arthrell's estimate, showed up for what turned out to be not a rit-
ual canine sacrifice but a teach-in session on napalm, its development
near the end of World War II, and its applications in the Vietnam
War. By then, though, the larger Kent community was fully tuning in
to what was happening on campus, and it was in no mood for irony,
if it ever had been.

"There was never any napalm, or never any dog," Arthrell recalled
a quarter century later, "and yet, the newspapers reported—at least
one of them—that they took the dog out of my hands. And this is
how vivid people's imaginations are: the county prosecutor was there,
Ron Kane; the Animal Protective League; the Sheriff's deputies."

Also in the crowd was Glenn Frank, a popular geology professor
and later to be one of the bona fide heroes of the May 4 shootings.
According to Jerry Lewis, Frank, too, had taken Arthrell literally: the
dog, he believed, existed and was soon to be a goner.

Real or not, the "napalmed dog" was still on locals' minds on April
29, when the Kent State 4, whom Rubin had been soliciting funds
for only nineteen days earlier, were finally released from county jail.
The next night came Nixon's Cambodia speech, fresh meat for an
antiwar movement that had been ebbing as the war slowed down. In
retrospect, a number of students talk about a sense of foreboding that

seemed to creep across the campus along with the warming weather, like the eerie calm just before the leading edge of a hurricane arrives.

Chuck Ayers, who would go on to national renown as the illustrator of the comic strip *Crankshaft*, recalled a water fight that Monday as the warm spell spilled over Northeast Ohio. "It was big, and it spread across the campus. . . . I don't think there had ever been a water fight on campus where there was actual physical damage to buildings, other than some water damage. But there were broken windows, there were things pulled down from buildings, and I remember thinking: This is kind of strange.

"There was a tension in almost everything people did at that time," Ayers went on. "Things in the war were just building up; the antiwar feelings were getting stronger and stronger. So even a Friday night down in the bars . . . had a tension about it."

————

The community of Kent felt the tension, too, although from a different perspective. For many residents, the university had grown in what seemed a few short years from the polite, sometimes rambunctious boy next door into a hulking, snarling teenage neighbor from hell. In fact, plenty of locals in 1970 remembered a time when there was *no* university on the edge of what had been born as a mill town along the Cayuhoga River.*

The college, originally Kent Normal School, didn't open for its first full academic year until September 1913, tasked with educating teachers for the public schools of Northeast Ohio. Even as late as 1940, by which time it had attained university status, Kent State enrolled fewer than 3,000 students, a total chopped to 777 in 1943, as would-be educators marched off to war.

———

*From its founding in the late eighteenth century to the end of the Civil War, Kent was known as Franklin Mills.

The Servicemen's Readjustment Act of 1944—commonly known as the GI Bill of Rights—changed Kent State's fortunes as it changed the fortunes of American higher education in general. Flush with tuition benefits and glad to have survived the war, returning veterans enrolled in colleges and universities in record numbers. At Kent State, the GI Bill would swell enrollment cumulatively by ten thousand students, the underpinnings of a growth boom that was still very much in evidence a quarter century later, by which time the campus population was closing in on the population of Kent itself (roughly thirty thousand residents) and the university dominated the local economy. But the vast benefits of a rapidly growing university had brought vast cultural changes as well—radical speakers, the Kent State 4, Bill Arthrell's napalmed-dog stunt—that left many locals feeling they were caught in the crosshairs of current events.

"The town hated the students, and the town hated the faculty," recalled Lew Fried, who joined the English faculty in the fall of 1969 and would remain at Kent State for the rest of his career. "This was a very conservative, right-wing-to-reactionary town. I was told that after the shootings, when students were being forced to leave campus, the majority of the town, which had grown fat on student-generated income, refused to sell them food, refused to sell them gas."

On May 11, a week after the shootings, Ruth Cope Mulvihill, a Kent resident, wrote to the national council of Delta Gamma sorority, in part to answer the question of why such a horrible thing had happened on such a seemingly unlikely campus.*

Spring 1968 "saw a big change here," she wrote. "We were invaded by a group of students very different from the usual Kent student—not just freakish clothes, but a dirty looking bunch of hoodlum-looking ones who apparently seldom attended classes but were ever-present in passing out literature and often obscene literature. One of the most common slogans found on handbills and painted on walls was that

---

*Mulvihill had been a Delta Gamma at Northwestern University. The sorority had a Kent State chapter.

Kent was to be the next Columbia or Berkeley. We had apparently been chosen as a target school for this area—an idea which subsequent events would verify."

Mulvihill asked herself the same question that many other locals were pondering: Why pick on Kent? Her answer ranged over many subjects: "far-out" faculty members, a poorly funded local police force, campus police who were "often very inept at dealing with students, since many of them are students themselves," the presence of ready targets like the ROTC program and the Liquid Crystals Institute, and the school's location.

"We are near large urban centers from which it is possible to draw outside help for agitation and into which it is possible to make a rapid disappearance. We are also near many other campuses, from which radical students can easily come and to which others go when desirable to stir other places." The fact that the university had also been the first in the country "to make use of the legal injunction as a means of making charges stick for trespass, violation of school rules, disturbing university functions, etc."—specifically in the case of the Kent State 4—had made the school "an even more certain prime target for trouble."

Federal law enforcement officials, long on the lookout for President Nixon's "bums blowing up campuses," had also ramped up local anxiety, according to the daughter of a Kent police officer. "My father told me a year to two years before violence broke out . . . that the FBI had come into the city of Kent, met with the Kent Police Department and the University Police Department to inform them that there was a groundswell of radical activity going on. And they knew that some of the universities would be targeted. They weren't sure which ones, but Kent State was a strong possibility because of the size of it. . . . It was just very vulnerable."

———

Friday night, May 1, all these disparate forces—high spirits, the first springlike weather, Vietnam, Nixon's Cambodia speech, campus radicalism, Jerry Rubin's exhortations, local anxiety, the fear that Kent (the town and university) had somehow been targeted by national forces, the mounting expectation of worse, a decade of growing generational divide, and ever-greater town-gown tensions surrounding campuses nationwide—came together in downtown Kent.

Carol Mirman was a senior fine arts major at the time: "Some people think that it was only just the Vietnam War that was the impetus. I believe that some of what happened on Friday night happened because it had been a very hard winter—it had really been a long, cold, dark winter—and that weekend was the first weekend of real spring that year. Consequently, people were down in the bars, down on Water Street, and out on the streets, and just in kind of one of those youthful, hormonal party places, and I was there with a girlfriend. We decided we were going downtown to find her a boyfriend—she'd been lonely too long."

The bars, Mirman remembered, were hot and crowded. Eventually, she and her friend went back out on the street. "There were a lot of people gathered around, including bikers and the political people. . . . Somebody brought a barrel and started to put things in there, and they lit a fire in the barrel. And more and more people gathered, and some started talking about the war, and people were drinking, and what I do remember is that people started to block off the street."

At that point, she said, things began to get scarier. "I remember distinctly an elderly couple trapped in their car. The light had turned, and they were stopped in the traffic, and they were surrounded by students. And students started to rock the car, and they were scared. . . . I think people were just kind of feeling their oats basically. I didn't understand it as being a political sort of an issue. Some people did mention Vietnam, and we were aware that Cambodia had been bombed and that things had begun down in Ohio State. But from my perspective, it was drinking beer, looking for guys. I mean that was what it was about. Then it went from there."

———

According to various law-enforcement accounts, events that night in downtown Kent began to heat up around eleven p.m. when the crowd outside the six bars clustered together on North Water Street started jeering at the two local police cars on patrol. Soon after, a motorcycle gang that called itself the Chosen Few began entertaining the crowd with bike tricks. A little before eleven thirty, someone threw a beer bottle at one of the squad cars, and the city police, which had only ten officers total on duty at the time, opted to cease patrolling and wait for reinforcements.

Facing no resistance, the crowd, by now swelled to about five hundred, began blocking the street and quizzing motorists on their opinions about expanding the war into Cambodia. One driver, rather than stop, sped up to escape, barely missing several pedestrians and further enflaming the crowd. The barrel fire was roaring by then, and an assault on downtown businesses was soon under way. Shoe and jewelry shops and a hardware store all had their front windows busted out. Someone used a fertilizer spreader taken from the hardware store to smash the window of a bank. And so it went through the immediate area: forty-seven windows in fifteen different businesses and offices broken, and two police officers injured by thrown objects.

As would happen sixty hours later on the Kent State Commons, the crowd became almost self-replicating. Diane Gallagher was behind the counter at Big Daddy's, a pizza parlor on Water Street, when a friend came bursting through the door with an almost irresistible message: "The revolution is here. . . . We're taking over Main Street. We're taking over the campus." Who can keep working when the revolution has arrived?

At about the same time, J. R. Hipple and a bunch of his high school friends called into another pizza parlor, the Deck, to place an order. "They said, 'You can get your pizza, but it will take a couple hours because of the riots.' So naturally, we jumped in two cars and headed downtown."

In the age of cell phones, Instagram, and flash mobs, thousands of students, the curious, the offended, and more might have descended on downtown Kent that night. By twelve thirty that night, though, local officials had seen enough. With the trashing still under way and the street crowd swelling, Kent mayor LeRoy Satrom declared a state of emergency and ordered all bars in the city closed. The subsequent forced exodus onto Water Street added yet another element to the increasingly volatile and growing mob. Finally, at one a.m., a thirty-person joint force of Kent police and Portage County deputies began using tear gas to drive the crowd out of the downtown area, up East Main Street, and onto the Kent State campus.

By two a.m., the job was largely done, and an uncertain peace settled over town and campus. A total of fifteen people, all with Ohio addresses, would be arrested for various acts during the melee and handcuffed. Most were driven to jail by Mayor Satrom himself, who ended up behind the wheel of a police cruiser that night.

———

To most Kent residents, the Friday night riot was all the proof needed that radicals—both from the university and from outside—had targeted their city. Merchants had been calling the police department in a steady stream for several days, complaining of "seedy-looking characters" disgorging from out-of-state vans covered with "psychedelic paintings." Now the dam, it seemed, had burst. Mayor Satrom originally estimated the damage from the broken windows at $50,000, a figure he later reduced to $15,000 and which the Chamber of Commerce eventually knocked down to $10,000, but the dollar figure was less the issue than the fact that their businesses had gone unprotected once the trashing started in earnest. The next night would find many of those same merchants inside their stores, armed with shotguns, deer rifles, and whatever other weapons they could lay their hands on, prepared for a showdown.

Even after the shootings three days later, residents were still complaining about the media's "seemingly deliberate omission of developments prior to this time which helped 'pull the trigger,'" as one local woman whose son was attending the university put it in a letter to Mayor Satrom.

"Nothing is being reported as to previous incidents leading up to this terrifying episode. . . . Nothing is told about residents fearing for their property and even their lives. Nothing is being reported about the damaging and defacing of public buildings, smashing of windows, obscene words 'gracing' walls, windows, streets. Nothing is said about merchants being robbed blind."

Students, not surprisingly, tended to see events differently. Many had paid covers at the bars, expecting to hear live music. In a college town on a Friday night in 1970, much like today, headliners were likely to just be coming on stage at twelve thirty a.m., when the state of emergency was declared and the bars ordered closed.

Others were there to drink beer and watch sports on TV. They were just settling into Game 4 of one of the legendary NBA championship series of all time—the New York Knicks versus Los Angeles Lakers, playing that night on the West Coast—when the bars were shut down and patrons tossed out into the street.*

As for the out-of-towners, Kent State students weren't the only ones feeling frisky in that first burst of spring, and the Kent bars had a natural drawing power that had nothing to do with radicalism. The club owners along North Water Street basically had been issued, along with their liquor licenses, permits to print money. A number of surrounding jurisdictions were still dry, relics of Prohibition. Neither Cleveland nor Akron, the nearest big cities, was particularly known as a "youthful, hormonal party place"—unlike, say, a bar strip with a twenty-one-thousand-student university next door. One student,

---

*Both teams were packed with future Hall of Famers: Elgin Baylor, Wilt Chamberlain, and Jerry West for the Lakers; Bill Bradley, Dave DeBusschere, Walt Frazier, and Willis Reed for the Knicks. Two nights earlier, the Knicks had won in overtime, 111–08. The Lakers took this one, also in overtime, by a 121–115 score. By the time the Knicks bounced back three nights later, on May 4, Kent State was the lead story in newspapers nationwide and on all three TV networks. On May 8, when New York took the NBA title in Madison Square Garden, inspired by its hobbled center, Willis Reed, the university was deserted.

perhaps carried away with the subject, described Kent as a kind of "Lauderdale" North. What's more, the fact that the Water Street bars could serve three-two beer to eighteen-year-olds meant, in practical terms, that anyone tall enough to get his or her money on the bar was likely to end up with a beer in hand. Better still, from the bar owners' point of view, patrons had to order twice as much three-two beer as six-four beer to end up with the same buzz.

Even the motorcycle gangs—which in 1970 still evoked memories of Marlon Brando's 1954 cult classic *The Wild One*, not to mention *Easy Rider*, Peter Fonda and Dennis Hopper's 1969 tribute to drugs, violence, rock and roll, and nihilism—were at least partially explicable in terms of electoral politics, not radical ones. Ronald Sterlekar, a senior graphics major in 1970, remembers inviting motorcycle gangs from Youngstown and Cleveland to Kent State that weekend to take part in a satirical political campaign for one T. P. Waterhouse for campus president.

"That weekend we were to have a motorcycle parade for him through campus with 100 choppers," Sterlekar told an interviewer in 2007. "On Friday night, May 1st, we were going from bar to bar, and everybody knew T. P. He had this costume on, dressed like Captain America, with a cape. And we had motorcycle colors on, and we were going from bar to bar because we were getting free beer. And the crowd would cheer, 'T. P. Waterhouse for President!' All of a sudden the bar got shut down . . . and we went out into the street, and what we saw immediately were two of the motorcycle gangs that we had called in beating on each other."

Outside political agitation would be a constant theme in the days and weeks and even years ahead. Rabble-rousing radicals from afar fit the story line already formed in the local imagination. Eventually, after the killings, outside agitation would offer a kind of exoneration for the university, the National Guard, and ultimately (as we will see) President Nixon, but according to many of those closest to the action, the real problem was that the university barely knew the radicals within its own ranks.

"The most important fact that I took away from the shootings was the importance of knowing your community," said Richard Bredemeier, who would spend nearly three decades as a Kent State administrator. "I thought as director of student activities, I had a lot of contact with students, and I did, but there were more than twenty thousand of them. . . . When I looked at the surveillance pictures afterwards, I was sure I would find that we had been invaded by all kinds of SDS and Weathermen, but that wasn't the case. These were our own students; we just didn't know who they were."

How many outside agitators had played a key role in the events leading up to and including the May 4 shootings? "I wouldn't argue with zero," Bredemeier said.

Efforts to blame the Friday night unrest on the newly released Kent State 4 proved equally fruitless. One of the four was positively identified on a downtown street earlier that evening—as might be expected of someone freed after half a year in jail—but no positive connection was ever made between any of the four and the events that transpired on the first four days of May 1970.

"It was almost like if you said 'outside agitators' often enough, people would believe that there were agent provocateurs in every dorm, ready to cause havoc," Lafayette Tolliver remembered.

Besides, as Peter Jedick suggests, the immediate catalyst of most of the mayhem that followed on Friday night might have been neither a Weatherman nor an SDS provocateur, but instead an inebriated 250-pound former high school wrestler from Cleveland who had been tossed out of the bars at twelve thirty a.m. along with everyone else.

"He said he actually started the riot Friday night," Jedick recalled. "He said he broke the first window. He came out. He was drunk, saw all the cops, and he threw something through a window, and it went on from there. That was his claim to fame. . . . Try to blame that on the outside agitators, but he was just a drunken [kid] from Cleveland."

In its September 1970 report on Kent State, the Nixon-appointed Presidential Commission on Campus Unrest, commonly known as the Scranton Commission,* summarized the events of the night of May 1 at Kent State University as follows:

"There were disorderly incidents; authorities could not or did not respond in time to apprehend those responsible or to stop the incidents in their early stages; the disorder grew; the police action, when it came, involved bystanders as well as participants; and, finally, the students drew together in the conviction that they were being arbitrarily harassed." That pattern, the authors of the report wrote, "was to recur throughout the weekend."

At 12:47 a.m. on Saturday morning, seventeen minutes after he had declared a state of emergency and less than two hours after the confrontation had begun in earnest, Mayor Satrom telephoned the office of Ohio governor James A. Rhodes in Columbus and reported to Rhodes's administrative assistant, John McElroy, that SDS students were rampaging through Kent and had taken over a portion of the city. "SDS students," a supposition at best, unsupported by evidence then or later, clearly added urgency to the call. A few minutes later, McElroy phoned Sylvester T. Del Corso, the adjutant general of the Ohio National Guard, to relay Satrom's news. Major General Del Corso then directed a National Guard liaison officer stationed in Akron to travel to nearby Kent to weigh the situation.

What had begun as a civilian confrontation was already on its way to a military solution.

---

*The commission was chaired by former Pennsylvania governor William Scranton.

2

Burn, Baby—Burn

More than half a decade after the August 10, 1964, Gulf of Tonkin Resolution gave a semi-official veneer to the Vietnam War, the idea of attacking, trashing, burning, or otherwise laying waste to campus ROTC buildings was hardly novel. During 1969–1970 alone, 197 ROTC buildings came under assault at universities big and small, left-leaning and largely conservative, all across the nation. ROTC headquarters at the University of Delaware; University of California, Berkeley; and the University of Washington were all firebombed or attacked with explosives and/or incendiaries. At SUNY Buffalo, protestors broke into the Air Force ROTC building, burned files, and destroyed office equipment. At the University of Kentucky, an ROTC building was burned to the ground. Efforts to do the same at the University of Virginia and the University of Georgia—iconic Old South schools—failed, but not for lack of effort. At Georgia, protestors tried twice.

As the most ready symbol of militarization available on most college campuses, ROTC programs were obvious targets for the antiwar movement. The programs were typically housed in buildings thrown up in a hurry during World War II, when the ROTC programs collectively contributed some hundred thousand officers to the war effort.

The buildings were often logistically easy to assault as well, constructed on the periphery of campuses or on isolated bits of land where entry would be less noticeable and flames not so likely to spread to other structures.

The Army ROTC building at Kent State was no exception. A two-story frame structure dating back to World War II, it sat on the northwest edge of the Commons, more or less opposite across a long grassy stretch from the Victory Bell, where students frequently gathered. Nor had the building gone unmarked by antiwar protestors. On Friday, while WHORE and the New University Conference were burying the Constitution beside the Victory Bell, a sign hung from a nearby tree. Visible to one and all, it asked, "Why is the ROTC building still standing?" By the end of Saturday, May 2, it wasn't.

Even without the destructive euphoria of the night before or the hand-painted sign on the Commons asking why the ROTC building was still standing, it didn't take much of an ear to the ground on the Kent State campus to realize that the structure might not survive the weekend. ROTC members were routinely harassed. Junior Walt Wagner remembered that one of his friends was afraid to wear his uniform on campus. For all practical purposes, the building that housed the ROTC program had a "BURN ME!" sign painted over its door.

Chuck Ayers and his wife both felt cold chills on Thursday evening as they walked by the ROTC building after Nixon's Cambodia speech—on the warmest day of the year to date in Northeast Ohio. Vita Semeraro, a supervisor in the registrar's office, said that she had been warned on Friday by the girlfriend of a student radical leader to stay away from campus the next day.

On Saturday morning forty ROTC cadets had gone off to a rifle range for practice. When they returned mid-afternoon, still in uniform, they were met by a small group of student hecklers, one of whom reportedly told an ROTC officer, "You'd better watch your building. It would make a pretty fire."

That last quote sounds a little Shakespearean, but at roughly the same time, Kent police chief Roy Thompson was telling Mayor Satrom that a usually reliable campus informant had passed on word that the ROTC building, the Kent US Army recruiting station, and the local post office had all been targeted for destruction that night—news that Thompson said he had also passed on to the university police. At the same rough time, several local merchants were reporting that what they presumed to be Kent State students had threatened to damage or burn their businesses if they didn't display antiwar slogans in their front windows.

Not only were Kent State students restless; they also woke up Saturday morning to a shrunken world. That morning, Mayor Satrom had laid down the terms of the civil emergency facing Kent: no sale of liquor and beer, of firearms, or of gasoline unless pumped directly into a vehicle tank until further notice, along with a citywide eight p.m. to six a.m. curfew, and a campus curfew set at one a.m.

On campus, preparations were multipronged. Early that morning, vice president for student affairs Robert Matson and other university officials set in process a court order that would enjoin anyone from "breaking any windows, defacing any buildings with paint, starting any fires on campus, and damaging and destroying any property." The injunction included the name of one student who had been hauled in Friday night for breaking a window in the ROTC building, plus five hundred "John Doe's." It did not, however, include a ban on rallies.

The university also activated its emergency-operations and rumor-control centers. The latter, according to faculty member Jerry Lewis, who helped staff the phones, was mostly a misinformation center. "Mainly, we answered calls from townspeople, and we had no information whatsoever because the senior administration wasn't talking to us at all. . . . Basically, we spread rumors rather than curtail them."

Teachers were also recruited to serve as faculty marshals, under the leadership of geology professor Glenn Frank. To mark them as such, Frank went to Clarkson's, the local "superstore," bought a robin-egg's-blue bedsheet, and tore it into strips for armbands. But what the blue-armbanded marshals were to "marshal" remained largely a mystery in the absence of explicit instructions from on high. Most finally decided that they would limit their role to counseling students and reporting breaking events to the emergency-operations center, rather than physically intervening with protestors.

Vice President Matson and others also finalized plans for entertaining and occupying students who otherwise, precurfew, might have spent the evening hours back in the Kent bars. Bands had been laid on to play at dorm dances; movies would be shown. As a final nod to the inmates, cafeteria hours were being extended.

Carolyn Mallon Fair, who had graduated the previous year and was now assistant manager of the Lake-Olson Dining Hall, was working those extended hours later on Saturday evening when what she described as "twenty Black Panthers" came into her cafeteria. "They walked toward me and said, 'Don't be alarmed. We just want to be inside with a witness because they are going to set fire to the ROTC building.' They got cookies and sat all around me at the surrounding tables. I looked outside to see a red-orange reflection in the glass grow and engulf the night. At this point dozens of students flooded the dining hall and sat in silence. It had begun."

————

"It," the conflagration that would consume the ROTC building, had in fact been a long process notable for the almost complete absence of any serious attempt on the part of administrators or campus police to intervene. Apparently, the one thing campus officials hadn't planned for was the possibility that the rumors that had been building for days might actually come to life.

Kay Jankowski left her dorm at about eight that night, drawn by word that a group gathering would be happening on the Commons. "We were warned not to go, but a friend who lived next door, Jackie Florough, and I decided to . . . see what was happening."

At first, the purpose of the get-together was unclear, other than some antiwar sentiments being shouted from the vicinity of the Victory Bell. Soon the core group was heading off to the large Tri-Towers dorm complex to pick up more people. When they returned, about 8:20, the mystery was over.

"They had gathered around the ROTC building and were beginning to mill around and throw stones at the building. . . . They broke the windows and threw flares inside. We saw members of the administration come out and stand by the ROTC building to watch."

Jankowski remembered in particular one university official: tall, with a long, thin face and very prominent nose. "There was one man on either side of him, and at least one policeman—KSU policeman—on either side." None of them, she said, made any attempt to intervene, even when a faculty marshal warned them that the building was going to ignite soon. "They just continued to stand and watch the mob."

Not until marshal Glenn Frank appealed to the officials did they finally act. He "came running up very fast, out of breath, and cried that they were burning the building. The building was on fire and would someone please call the police. At this point the officials turned around and walked back into the Administration Building, presumably to ask for help."

Within minutes, Jankowski remembered, Kent Fire Department trucks came racing up to the building, laying down hoses. Fire fighters tried to pull the hoses to the back of the building, away from the Commons and the crowd, but the forward edge of the mob dragged the hoses back into open ground and attacked them with various instruments, including an ice pick and what everyone recalls as a two-foot-long machete. "It took them about five to ten minutes before [the hoses] could actually begin to spill water."

Still without help from the campus police, who were housed only a few hundred yards away, and with rocks flying from some in the crowd, the firefighters finally gave up and left, fearful for their equipment and their own well-being. At that point, according to Jankowski, a hard core of five to fifteen people, mostly male, was leading the assault on the building, backed up by maybe a hundred cheering supporters and, behind them, the larger, mostly curious crowd.

Jankowski recalled seeing twelve policemen "dressed in black with gas masks" walking down the street in the general proximity of the mob scene, but they walked around the ROTC building and were soon out of sight. Meanwhile, rioters were reaching through the smashed windows to rip down curtains and throw them on flares burning inside the rooms. Others were struggling to pull siding off the exterior walls to add to the burn pile. Two men, she said, were throwing additional flares into the building, from opposite sides. Still no obvious law enforcement figures were present, although several members of the immediate mob did grab a photographer's camera and rip the film out, suspecting him of being a police plant.

"At this point, Jackie and I saw a policeman, one lone policeman, sneaking up along the side of the building, the south side. He proceeded around to the front where one boy was hitting the building with a board. The boy grabbed some papers and threw them on the flares, and everyone cheered as they saw small flames shoot up."

Just then, she said, the lone policeman fired tear gas into the mob, and the crowd scattered. By the time Jankowski and Florough were able to again get a good look at the ROTC building, one side was in flames, and smoke was beginning to pour out of the upper windows on the opposite side. Eventually, the crackle of the flames would be punctuated with small explosions as the fire reached ammunition stores—an eerie precursor to the rat-a-tat-tat of two days later.

"We were amazed," Kay Jankowski said, "that no one had done anything to stop them previous to the one tear gassing."

So were plenty of others. Even decades later, variations of the word "amazed" keep appearing in their accounts.

Student senator Rob Fox had a similar experience. "I noticed one student walked up to the old ROTC building and broke out the glass, took his lighter, started lighting the curtains. Then I saw a couple others break some more glass, and the amazing thing I noticed was that there were police officers at the top of the hill down there by the old Student Union. They were just sitting there, watching. Then the little flames started going. . . . That is a puzzle to this day: why the police sat up there on top of that hill?"

Arthur Koushel, a sophomore, had been in the crowd as well. He remembers walking by the ROTC building the next day and thinking, "Either they have the worst fire department in the world or they let the building burn down just to say, 'Do you see what these kids, students, did?'—because I was amazed at how it was totally destroyed."

Gerald Casale, cofounder of the enduring New Wave band Devo and then an undergraduate art major, had much the same thought, in more specific terms: "I stayed away from that. . . . I thought it played right into the hands of the administration and all the people who wanted to delegitimatize any student protest over the expansion of the war. It was destruction of property, a criminal act . . . a set-up, and of course the students played right into the hands of anyone who wanted to detract from the validity of the movement. It wasn't really activists who did that. It was just thugs."

Lafayette Tolliver agreed: "It was almost as if [the administrators] intentionally turned their heads so they could then say, see, we've got to stop this kind of thing from happening."

Others see a much less sinister inattention. The building was a World War II–era throw-together, never meant to be a permanent addition to the campus, yet it occupied prime ground, coveted by multiple academic departments. "The space that was left was more valuable than when the building was there," according to Ray Bye, a Kent State graduate student and assistant to President Robert White in the spring of 1970. "Nobody was going to take a stand on that."

Like actions, though, inactions have consequences. In a 1990 interview, Timothy DeFrange, a senior education major at the time of the shootings and later a teacher, speculated about "the people, the administrators, that stood there and watched the building burn, that just sort of stood there quietly without really saying much." Maybe, DeFrange said, they saw they had no real control over the situation. "Maybe they feared for their own safety if they were to try to stop a mob that was out of control. I don't blame them, but . . . I deal with kids, and kids, if these adults say nothing, they take it for approval. They take it for permission."

By nine thirty that evening, the ROTC building was beyond rescue. By then, too, what many in Kent were thinking of as the cavalry was riding into town, just (they hoped) in the nick of time and at the very moment when, as Timothy DeFrange suggests above, the students on campus were beginning to feel that the light had turned an approving green.

———

That same night, Rosann Rissland, a young mother, was home alone on South Water Street while her husband, a Kent State student, was off folding and stuffing the *Cleveland Plain Dealer* newspapers he would deliver around town on Sunday morning. The red glow of the ROTC building, now engulfed in flames, was terrifying to her. "People thought—I thought—that they were going to burn the town down."

An anonymous Ohio National Guardsman, also a student at Kent State, had the same thought as he approached the city on Interstate 76, coming from the southwest out of Akron. "We had the top down on the Jeep. We had the top down on all the trucks—canvas tops. You could see the fire, the glow of the fire on 76 as we approached Kent, and my first thought was, my God, the whole town is burning, the whole campus. It was literally an orange glow in the sky."

In a 2007 interview, Ronald Snyder, then a captain with Company C of the 145th Infantry of the Ohio National Guard, described the fire in terms of the March 2003 "shock and awe" aerial bombardment that launched the second Iraq War. The sky over Kent, he said, "was glowing very bright. It was kind of like something you would see when they showed pictures of Baghdad after the bombing although there was no noise, you understand. It was just a bright red glow. . . . You could tell it was from a huge fire."

Having alerted the National Guard with his middle-of-the-night call to Governor Rhodes's office, LeRoy Satrom, the mayor of Kent, spent much of Saturday trying to find a workaround to the Guard's actual presence. Friday night's rampage had taxed Kent's own police force and Portage County resources almost to the breaking point. Curfew or not, another, larger outburst of student discontent was likely to overwhelm the public safety infrastructure. Kent's residents were scared. Local merchants were preparing to protect their businesses; some were undoubtedly itching for the opportunity to do so.

Satrom was convinced he needed more manpower, but where to find it? Not only had the university's thirty-person police force been a no-show Friday night; Chester Williams, the school's director of Safety and Public Services, insisted that his force was needed on campus and would not venture into the city no matter the circumstances. Efforts to recruit a seventy-five-person force of Portage County "auxiliary deputies"—sworn in for this occasion only—had proved difficult. All parties including the university wanted the highway patrol to get involved, but its brief was limited to state roads and to property either owned or leased by the state. That included the Kent State campus, but the patrol took the stand that it could enter the campus only for arrests, not for crowd control.

Meanwhile, Lieutenant Charles Barnette, the National Guard liaison who had arrived in Kent within hours of Satrom's call to Rhodes's office, had set a five p.m. deadline for requesting the Guard's help. Roughly nine hundred troops would be needed to secure the situation, both on campus and in Kent itself, but for a combined university-city population of roughly fifty thousand, nine hundred troops posed large logistical challenges.*

The Guard units to be sent were bivouacked only ten miles away, in Akron, where they had been dealing with a contentious Teamsters Union strike, but there would be new encampments to set up—at a local elementary school, in one instance; in the Kent State gym, in another. Heavy equipment had to be loaded and moved. Troop transports needed to be readied. Major General Sylvester Del Corso, the Ohio National Guard top commander, and Brigadier General Robert Canterbury, who would handle mission planning on the ground, had to travel greater distances to get to Kent. If a formal request for assistance was delayed beyond five o'clock, Guardsmen wouldn't have time to prepare for assisting with crowd control and other necessities that night.

Satrom was meeting with Barnette; Kent State safety director Williams; Williams's boss, Richard Dunn, the university's vice president for financial affairs; and others as the deadline approached. At five sharp, the two principals, Satrom and Barnette, vacated the room to formally request the National Guard's presence. Williams and Dunn both left the meeting at that point, under the impression that the Guard's purview was limited to Kent city only, not the campus, but Barnette's terms of engagement—or surrender, depending on perspective—had been clear: the Ohio National Guard would recognize no distinction between city and campus, town and gown. As of the moment its assistance was approved by the governor, the Guard was in charge everywhere.

Perhaps to reinforce the fact that there was a new sheriff in town, the Guard hit the ground running.

———

*Proportionally, fitting nine hundred Guardsmen into the combined Kent community in 1970 would be the same as fitting, say, ninety thousand troops into a metropolitan area of five million.

Denny Benedict, a freshman in 1970, was in his dorm, watching the James Bond movie *Thunderball*—one of the diversions meant to entertain students on Saturday evening—when he learned that his campus had basically been turned upside down while Sean Connery was trying to hunt down two NATO A-bombs stolen by SPECTRE and protected by beautiful women with large breasts.

"Right in the middle of the movie, they stopped the projector, and one of the dorm directors gets up and says, 'The ROTC building is on fire. The National Guard's taken over the campus. Nobody leaves the dorm!'—which is, like, where did this come from? Of course, I've got to see what's going on."

Benedict headed up to his room and grabbed a jacket, only to find the dorm entrances blocked when he got back to ground level. So he went to a first-floor laundry room and jumped out the window. The ROTC fire, he said, was already dying down when he got there, but he picked up a rumor that something was going to happen on Front Campus, as the main entrance along East Main Street was known.

"So I go, well, I better go down there and see what's going on. It was pretty well blocked, so I started going through the town. . . . Every corner there was a cop or National Guardsman. I was trying to go through people's yards, and I just couldn't make it. I thought, okay, I'll go back to the dorm, and I'm walking back up by where the Business School is, and I just hear this rumbling noise. And here's this tank-like vehicle with treads. Two National Guardsman are on top with guns, and the guy with the machine gun [says], 'You need to get back to your dorm.'

"I went, 'Yeah, right.' So I took off back to the dorm."

The original Guard entrance on to the Kent State campus was a two-pronged affair. One contingent was dispatched to the burning ROTC building. Now that protection was on hand, the Kent fire department had decided to return to the blaze. After watching the building being attacked and originally set afire without intervening, campus police also agreed to assist in protecting the firefighters. Given that a demonstrable crime had been committed on campus—arson of a federal building, to be exact—the highway patrol was also willing to join the party but in a supporting role only. The National Guard was in charge, and in any event, everyone was too late. Not only was the ROTC building beyond saving when the fire department arrived the second time, a nearby small building—a shed used to store archery equipment—had also gone up in flames. By then, too, the crowd was moving on. The action now was on Front Campus, where Denny Benedict had been trying to go. That's where the other Guard contingent had been sent: to stop students from marching downtown in violation of Kent's eight p.m. curfew.

An Ohio National Guardsman and Kent State student who was interviewed in 2000 on the condition his name not be used was among those in this second contingent:

"We got the order to line up shoulder to shoulder and form a straight line somewhat behind the old Student Center and the ROTC building. We stood there about ten minutes and . . . I couldn't figure out what was the big deal. It was dark. A helicopter came over, shone a light on the hill where the Architecture building was, and there were several thousand kids up there. They were very quietly massed there, and they started moving and shouting, 'Here we come!' And they did."

A lot of thoughts, the Guardsman said, ran through his mind at that moment. "If we're told to lock and load, are we going to fire? Are we gonna protect our lives? Are we going to run?"

The several thousand protestors, the Guardsman remembered, stopped about a hundred yards in front of the Guard line, then started around the Student Center, headed to the front of the campus, where the major confrontation would take place. His contingent of Guardsmen was soon there as well.

"This is the point where we got hit with rocks, human feces in plastic bags—uh, we were given the finger, we were yelled at. Things came flying out of the air. It was weird. It was dark, but things were flying out of the air. We laid some tear gas down."

They were laying more tear gas down, he said, when his group was approached by three or four people holding a white flag. "They said they wanted to talk to us . . . and the captain says, 'Easy, easy, don't do anything. Maybe we can calm this crowd down.' Maybe they were leaders. They were waving a white flag. They got about 25 feet away from us, and they unloaded with a barrage of rocks."

Still more tear gas followed, some of it in powdered form, dropped from helicopters so the blades could help spread it.

"We were actually told that we were going to stop the crowd from going downtown. I knew some of the businessmen in town, and believe me, to this day I think it's just as well because they were better armed than we were, and had those students gone downtown—and I think the authorities knew this—there were people sitting on rooftops on buildings. Had those people moved on downtown to trash it again, there would have been gunfire; it was that simple. . . . It was like saving someone from themselves, I guess."

The tear gas, he said, quickly dispersed the curious students and those who were there for the party. A hard core, though, remained. "It's at that point that I saw the students again let go with the rocks, and men standing there waving their genitals at us and women shouting obscenities. I was no virgin—I was used to a lot of things, but not on my campus. And I looked at this and I said, 'This gives me a whole different point of view on what's happening here.'"

———

The Guardsmen, it turned out, had been rushed into the fray with full battle equipment but with only minimal briefing. In one potentially explosive moment Saturday night, a group of faculty marshals wearing those homemade blue armbands encountered a Guard unit newly arrived on campus.

"We were told point-blank that the National Guard knew who we were and what we were," remembered one of the marshals, Steven

Sharoff. "The Guard told us to stop. We kept saying, 'We're faculty marshals. We're faculty marshals.' And they went down on one knee and pointed their rifles at us."

At just about the same time, Art Krummel, a National Guard sergeant, was helping patrol a roadblock preventing cars from coming into Kent in violation of the eight p.m. curfew when he noticed a driver arguing with one of his fellow Guardsman.

"I heard a man yelling out of his car window to get out of his way; he was going through the roadblock. And the National Guardsman who was blocking him by standing in front of his car said, 'No, you aren't, sir. You have to turn your car around.'"

Eventually, Krummel said, the driver, who turned out to be a drunk Kent State professor, began edging his car forward, bumping the Guardsman, who staggered back a couple steps each time.

"I realized that this could be a very, very unhappy outcome at least and very dangerous. I then unclicked the safety on my M1, which was loaded. And one thing we're trained pretty well on in the National Guard—and in the Army where we were trained on active duty—was to never click the safety off your weapon until you were ready to use it. And I was fully ready to use it. I can remember still the feeling on my finger of clicking that safety."

It was at that moment, Krummel recalled, that a police car pulled up and took charge of the situation.

"That was then settled peacefully. There were no more incidents that night. But in my mind, that very incident could have changed the history of the world. If it had come to the point where I had to shoot the man, where he had run over my friend, the campus would have been closed then. There would have been no shootings on May 4th. Very likely the events in Vietnam would have unfolded differently—although May 4th was only one of several events that were instrumental in changing the course of Vietnam. I feel like that event could have avoided at least four additional deaths, among other things."

But Krummel didn't shoot the drunk professor, the drunk professor didn't run over his friend, the campus wasn't closed, the National Guard didn't go away, no one seemed to glom on to the fact that there were live rounds in the M1s the Guardsmen were carrying, and history continued to march forward to its grim conclusion.

3

Night of the Helicopters

University president Robert White had been monitoring the deteriorating situation by phone, from his sister-in-law's house in Mason City, Iowa. By Saturday afternoon, it was clear he was needed at the mother ship. The Kent State airplane picked him up Sunday morning for the seven-hundred-mile flight home.

Ohio governor Jim Rhodes, who had ordered the National Guard to Kent, was on his way there as well. Saturday night, while the ROTC building was under siege, Rhodes and Robert Taft Jr., his opponent in the Republican primary for the US Senate seat being vacated by Stephen Young, had held their fourth and final debate in Cleveland, forty miles to the north. Sunday morning, Rhodes, too, was flying into Kent. His staff had scheduled a ten a.m. press conference at the city firehouse.

The many students who had vacated Suitcase U over the weekend were also returning, much-needed ballast for a ship that had been pitching back and forth for two days in rough seas. Monday was a class day. Midterms were coming. Time to get back to the business of educating young minds—exactly what many of those young minds were hoping for.

Although their campus had been wracked by violence the night before, university administrators, too, generally, regarded the situation as reparable.

"Sunday morning, I went in at nine, and that's when the conversation started," recalled Ray Bye, a graduate student assistant to President White, "three or four senior administrators talking about what had happened, including Ron Roskens [White's executive vice president] and Ron Beer [executive assistant to the president]. There were discussions beginning about coordinating with the governor's office and with the Guard. . . . At that point there still was a sense of the administration being in control of the campus, but I guarantee that if you had sat down with the Guard leaders, they had no concept of the administration being in control."

As for the Guardsmen themselves, after a long night of confrontations, they had some welcome space Sunday to find their footing. The Guard had been asked in a very brief time frame to adjust to an entirely different mission. In Akron, its role had been to protect non-union truckers from assaults by striking Teamsters—physical attacks, pot shots from highway overpasses, tough going all the way. Jimmy Hoffa had been in jail since March 1967, but he was still president of the International Brotherhood of Teamsters, and the union reflected his combative personality. But Guardsmen knew where they stood with union members. Whatever they thought of the National Guard as a fighting force, many of the striking truckers had served on active duty. They respected the uniform.

One Guardsman recalled waiting in front of an Akron bar to protect a convoy that was soon to roll by. "When the trucks were approaching, probably 75 to 80 men came out [of the bar] carrying guns and sticks," he recalled. "There were about 20 of us, obviously outnumbered. We were armed; we had bullets. Our sergeant said, 'We're here to protect the truck drivers,' and the one man who was obviously the leader . . . turned to his group and said, 'Men, we have no battle with these National Guardsmen. They're here doing a job; let's go back inside.' And they did."

The few hours the Guard had spent patrolling in and around Kent State the night before had convinced them they were now dealing with a whole different sort of opposition. "Disperse" meant "scatter and reassemble." Guardsmen, not third-party scab truckers, were the object of the crowd's anger. White flags were ruses. Not only was everyone saying "Fuck!" all the time; they were giving Guardsmen the finger and even (among a few male demonstrators) waving their genitals. As the same Guardsman put it, "I found the striking truck drivers to be much more civilized than the students on campus."

Adjusting would take some time, and just when it was needed most, time seemed to magically appear. At noon a state of emergency was declared for the campus. All gatherings, even peaceful ones, were now banned.

———

However much Friday night's rampage in downtown Kent might be credited to youthful exuberance and drunken excess—let loose in part by the summery weather and Nixon's Cambodia speech—Saturday's burning of the ROTC building left many with the feeling of a premeditated attack. As the Scranton Commission noted, "Railroad flares, a machete, and ice picks are not customarily carried to peaceful rallies." A nonstudent from Canton, Ohio, furnished the FBI with a signed statement that he had handed a gasoline-soaked rag to an unknown person who placed it in the ROTC building and ignited it—what appears to have been the finishing touch of the conflagration. Thomas Miller, a former KSU student who went by the nickname Aquinas, said that he had been present at the assault on the building as well—"right in there with the top guys who started the fire," according to one anonymous source. (Miller would gain a measure of fame two days later, on May 4, for dragging his black banner through the blood of Jeff Miller, no relation.)

Who might have planned the ROTC building attack, though, is a harder question. The remnants of Students for a Democratic Society were the obvious choice for many observers. Even though the local chapter had been disbanded the previous year, many of its former members were still students and active in the antiwar movement, but on Saturday night the most identifiable campus SDS leaders—people like Ken Hammond and his then-wife Marilyn Davis—were more than two hundred miles northeast of Kent, in Buffalo, New York, attending a meeting of the Revolutionary Youth Movement.

"We had been downtown in Kent Friday night, then left early the next morning for Buffalo," Hammond said. "We got a call Saturday night: 'Oh, my God, they're burning down the ROTC building!' At the time, we were in a workshop titled What Is To Be Done?—we'd taken the title from a Lenin quote—having an abstract conversation about how do you carry forth political education, blah-de-blah. Meanwhile people are going crazy back in Kent."

Rather than prima facie evidence of advanced planning, as the Scranton Report suggested, the machetes used in several instances to attack the fire hoses might well have been compulsory equipment for Brinsley Tyrrell's sculpture class. "I had required my students to have a machete because we were carving these big plaster sculptures, and a machete is the best tool for it. I phoned several people—university lawyers and the like—and said, 'If you're detaining people with a machete and they're signed up for my sculpture class, they're required to have one.'"

Similar claims of protest advanced planning and "professionalism" extended to the running battles later that night between Guardsmen and demonstrators intent on marching downtown in violation of Kent's eight p.m. curfew. The anonymous Guardsman-student cited earlier remembered a cadre of older men and women who would corral and push groups of students, fifty to one hundred strong, toward Guard units.

"They would bring the crowds to us. . . . They were in front of the crowd. Then, they quickly dispersed, went around behind the crowd, locked hands—this was a group of ten or fifteen people—and pushed the crowd into us. . . . These were not traditional student-age student people. These were older—28, 30, that age group."

Albert Van Kirk, a Vietnam War vet who began at Kent State in 1969, said in a 2009 interview that he had developed a working relationship with several intelligence agencies monitoring events that weekend. "What was clear to me was that this was very well planned, very well financed, and very well executed. By one FBI count, there were 120 license plates in Kent the night the ROTC burned that had no business being there."

Allegations of outside agitators would not disappear in the days ahead, or in the months and years to follow. Nor would the FBI stop counting license plates or anything else it could obsess on and try to quantify. But as Sunday, May 3, moved along, Cambodia, the Vietnam War, the ROTC generally, Marxism, capitalism, the military-industrial complex, free love, dope, and just about every other subject that could attract significant outside participation slid progressively to the back burner, and the specific Guard units detailed to Kent State and their presence on its campus moved steadily to the fore. This was not all to the good.

———

In their Saturday night senatorial campaign debate, Bob Taft Jr., then a congressman, and Governor Rhodes had traded predictable potshots over the earlier rioting at Ohio State and now at Kent State. Taft was coddling rioters, Rhodes said. Taft countered that Ohio, under Rhodes, lacked adequate plans to handle campus disorders. "What is wrong with the wonderful world of Ohio when you have to send troops into a campus amid a pall of tear gas?" Taft asked, implying that court injunctions such as Kent State had sought and obtained on multiple occasions were the more appropriate response. Rhodes's answer: "Getting a court injunction is all well and good, except they are usually ignored. By the time you obtain one, buildings could be destroyed."*

---

*The account of the debate in the May 3 *Akron Beacon Journal* ran on page 7. The banner headline on page 1 read: "KSU Rioters Put Torch to ROTC Building."

In an earlier debate, Rhodes had sought to draw a sharp class distinction between himself and his opponent, accusing Taft of being a "playboy." Rhodes was from a rough-and-tumble background—his father, a mine superintendent, died when he was nine. (Cleveland Democratic mayor Carl Stokes would later write in his memoir that Rhodes resembled "a football player turned mortician.") Taft by contrast was the son of a long-time Ohio senator and national Republican powerbroker and the grandson of William Howard Taft, the twenty-seventh president of the United States and, later, the tenth chief justice of the Supreme Court. In this debate, Taft struck back, noting that he had received a telegram from *Playboy* magazine publisher Hugh Hefner that read, in part, "I never even heard of you." That nonendorsement might have been the highlight of the evening, but Gene Jordan, who covered the event for the *Columbus Dispatch*, declared the debate a draw.

At his Sunday morning press conference in Kent, with the primary vote two days away and trailing in the polls, Jim Rhodes was taking no prisoners. It wasn't just colleges and universities that were at risk now. Kent was proof that the towns neighboring and in some cases surrounding institutions of higher education were on the front lines as well.

"We have seen here at the City of Kent especially probably the most vicious form of campus-oriented violence ever perpetrated by dissident groups in the State of Ohio," Rhodes began. "Most of the dissident groups have operated within the campus. This has moved over [to] where they have threatened and intimidated merchants and people of this community."

Had it not been for the fortunate proximity of seven hundred National Guardsmen stationed in nearby Akron to deal with the Teamsters' strike, "there would have been fourteen or fifteen other burnouts" in Kent on Saturday night, Rhodes said a few minutes later—"and I'm talking about buildings," a conflagration that would have destroyed most of downtown Kent.

"These people just move from one campus to the other and terrorize a community," Rhodes said of the protest leaders, before opening up the press conference to questioning. "They're worse than the Brown Shirts and the Communist elements and also the Night Riders and Vigilantes. They're the worst type of people that we harbor in America, and I want to say that they're not going to take over a campus, and the campus now is going to be part of the County and the State of Ohio. There is no sanctuary for these people to burn buildings down of private citizens, of businesses in the community, then run into a sanctuary. It's over with in Ohio."

Early in the press conference, Rhodes had laid down his marker: "We are going to eradicate the problem. We are not going to treat the symptoms." Later in the gathering, a highway patrol colonel put a finer face on the governor's stand: "We have men that are well trained. They're not trained to receive bricks. They won't take it. Any hoodlum with a gun will be handled the same as any other hoodlum. The next phase that we have encountered elsewhere is where they start sniping. They can expect us to return fire."

Near the end of the press conference, after Chief Thompson of the Kent Police Department had vowed even stricter enforcement of the eight p.m. citywide curfew, National Guard Major General Del Corso added his own punctuation mark: "I'll be right behind with the National Guard to give our full support, anything that is necessary—like the Ohio law says, use any force that is necessary even to the point of shooting. We don't want to get into that, but the law says that we can if necessary."

———

Governor Rhodes and Kent State president Robert White did meet briefly at the local airport around noon—Rhodes departing, White arriving—but rather than clear up lines of authority, their exchange seems to have muddied the waters still further. White would later say that Rhodes told him: "Bob, you have 400 of the worst riffraff in this state from all the campuses. They are trying to close you down. Don't give in. Keep open." But how White or any other university official was to keep open—or close—a campus that the National Guard now claimed full control over was anyone's guess.

Nor was there any enduring clarity about exactly what the Guard was or was not allowing on the campus where they now served in effect as military governor. Rhodes at his press conference had talked vaguely about seeking an injunction "equivalent to a state of emergency," but the Scranton Commission investigators could find no evidence such an injunction had ever been obtained or even sought, and no university official seemed to have the slightest idea what the "state of emergency" might entail—until, that is, the executive assistant to a university vice president talked to a Guard officer and came away with the impression that "state of emergency" in this usage meant "no gatherings or rallies at all," even peaceful ones. Soon that message—secondhand or third-hand or whatever level of authority it represented—was being papered over the campus in twelve thousand freshly printed leaflets.

As vague as all that was, though, and as far removed from actual vested authority, any attempt to put a finer face on the Guard's purview was likely to end up almost in low farce. Dick Bredemeier recalled being at a Sunday meeting when one faculty member asked the Guard liaison exactly what a "gathering" was. "He says, 'I don't know.' So he runs back to find out and returns with 'three.' [The professor] then says, 'If two kids are talking to each other and I walk up to them, does that make it a 'gathering'? And the guy just shakes his head."

———

In any immediate sense, of course, who was in charge of what and to what extent—let alone precisely what a crowd might be—were pressing issues only if the campus returned to crisis mode, and for at least part of Sunday, May 3, that seemed an unlikely outcome. The burned-out ROTC building had become an instant tourist attraction despite or maybe because of the Guardsmen who stood at the site, rifles at the ready, in the manner of the Beefeaters who guard Buckingham Palace and no more threatening as long as one assumed their M1s were and would remain unloaded. And for the most part that was the assumption campus-wide throughout the weekend.

At an earlier meeting to organize the faculty marshals, Jerry Lewis had been asked whether he thought the Guard's rifles were loaded. "I said I didn't think they were. . . . When I was on active duty [in the army], I guarded a huge, multimillion-dollar facility, Fort Leonard Wood, with an unloaded rifle. They didn't trust us with live ammunition."

Sunday afternoon, still believing the M1s weren't live, he brought his young children to have a look at the ROTC ruins. Doing so, he would say in a 2010 interview, was his greatest regret of the entire four-day drama at Kent State. "I now know in retrospect that I exposed them to Guardsmen with loaded weapons. I feel terrible about that and still do, obviously. I'm talking about it 40 years later, and it still bothers me."

Jim Sprance, a junior in 1970, recalled specifically raising the issue of guns and live ammunition with a cluster of Guardsmen near Rockwell Hall, the old Library. "There were a bunch of them down there. I do remember talking to one of those guys who was there in line with a bunch of other ones. We asked them a question about bullets. 'Do you guys really have bullets in those guns?'" His answer, according to Sprance: "No, they did not issue us anything today."

Many students—this would be true up until the moment live ammunition was fired the next day, and in some cases for a few minutes beyond—recall an almost carnival atmosphere to Sunday morning and afternoon. It was another beautiful late-spring moment. Many of the Guardsmen were close in age to the average student or students themselves. Joining the Guard meant walking-around money, maybe tuition, an end-run around Vietnam.

Diane Yale-Peabody, a sophomore in 1970, remembered posing for photos with some of the Guards. "My fiancé took the picture. We thought the whole thing was just a big joke."

"Anywhere you went, you saw the Guardsmen talking to the students, and they seemed friendly. Everything was kind of jovial," recalled Ellen Mann, an area resident and at the time a student in the lab high school located on the Kent State campus. The next day she would be standing by Joe Lewis when an M1 cartridge ripped through his leg.

Ray Bye felt the same as he briefly toured the campus on Sunday. "I remember how relaxed things seemed. The students were in a very nonconfrontational mood. Students in shorts and short skirts were walking around, picking dandelions and putting them in the rifle barrels. I naively assumed it was all over."

Meanwhile, at his press conference, Jim Rhodes was vowing to eradicate the disease of student unrest, not merely treat the symptoms.

———

Long before that Sunday night collapsed into yet another show of force and defiance, rift lines were already heavily on display, both between Guards and students and among the Guardsmen themselves.

Jim Vacarella, a junior that spring, was roaming the campus with a small group when they came upon a Guard half-track parked on top of the school seal. "We went over and said, 'You know, we're not even allowed to step on the seal. . . . That tradition was still there when I was here. And I told the guy, 'You know, you have to move off the seal.'

"We felt cocky and powerful, and we were going to end this war, etc., etc. And we were met by Major Jones. I'll never forget. Major Jones put a pistol right to my face . . . and he said, 'I want your name.' I gave him a fake name, and he said, 'Thank you,' and he left.

(Major Harry Jones was battalion staff officer of the 145th Infantry.)

"We had heard all that Sunday that they were collecting names of all the long-hairs on campus, and they were just going to throw everybody out on Monday, and that would be the end of riots. And that's something they should've done 'cause that would've ended it! They didn't."

A few days earlier, Ralph Spielman and a friend had gone to see *Zabriskie Point*, Michelangelo Antonioni's dark cinematic take on the American counterculture, campus protests, and police confrontations. Now he looked out the university library window just in time to see a Guardsman, a "ranking officer" he remembered, using his baton to whack a student on the head.

John Panagos, then a new professor in Kent State's speech and hearing program, recalled talking with one of the young Guardsmen that Sunday afternoon. "He was very nonchalant and said that he didn't really want to be here—it didn't mean a lot to him—he just had to come here because it was his job. But he pointed over to an older man—a smaller, ruggedly built older man who had a sidearm on his belt—and he said, 'With that guy over there, now he really means business around here. He really gets into this.' And with the tone of it, I always thought that he meant that this man was very focused as to quelling whatever eventuality might take place on campus."

Panagos would later identify the older Guardsman as the shooter holding a pistol in his left hand in the searing photo of the famous volley, standing bent slightly in front and to the side of the kneeling skirmish line that fired on students the next day: Sergeant Myron "Mike" Pryor, of Troop G. Sandy Scheuer, one of four students killed in the thirteen-second onslaught, had attended Panagos's speech and hearing class that morning.

Allison Krause, another of the four dead, had a similar Guard encounter that afternoon, according to her boyfriend, Barry Levine. The two had taken a walk to the Front Campus, hoping to talk with some Guardsmen. One particular soldier caught their eye, not only for his pleasant smile but for the lilac blossoming in his rifle barrel. "He said he did not want to be guarding the campus," Levine wrote, "but when asked why he didn't leave, he looked at the ground and shyly said he couldn't."

Before long, though, an officer came along and berated the soldier at close quarters until he pulled the flower out of his rifle barrel. "That's better," Levine recalled the officer saying. "Now straighten up and start acting like a soldier and forget all this peace stuff."

Even for those soldiers inclined to identify with the Kent State students and share the "peace-stuff" sentiments of many of them, harsh living conditions were beginning to take a toll. During their duty in Akron, the Guardsmen had slept as best they could in various armories and in the back of trucks. Now many of them were bivouacked in the undersized gym of Wall Elementary School.

"At best," one Guardsman remembered, "they were horrible conditions because the lights were on, and we constantly had troops coming and going. We got little if any sleep. You just couldn't sleep in that situation. We were on the floor. Not that as infantry we weren't used to that . . . [but], understand, we were civilians thrown into a no-sleep situation."

The schoolyard, too, left little room for maneuvering the jeeps, troop transports, and heavier equipment the Guard traveled with. Two decades after the shootings, Scott Swan, who was seven years old at the time and living near the school, would say that his most profound memories of May 4 were "the tanks on my playground and the soldiers sleeping in the gymnasium. And the one thing in particular about the tanks was that they bumped into our jungle gym and made it crooked."

———

The students who left Kent State on Friday to spend the weekend at home returned Sunday to a campus utterly transformed. "When I got back Sunday late afternoon, I thought I was in a war zone in Vietnam," Joseph Sima recalled. "Helicopters that were three times anything I had ever seen, armored cars, Jeeps, machine guns, mini-tanks, soldiers everywhere. It was just unbelievable. And they were patrolling even up and down the residential streets."

Eldon Fender, a freshman education major, had much the same experience. "Frankly, you felt like you made a wrong turn off [Interstate] 76 going into Kent because of all the armed vehicles, military hardware, military vehicles on campus. You almost felt like you drove into Fort Knox . . . a highly protected federal property or something of that nature. The atmosphere on campus certainly was very tense and very different than the way I left it."

William Derry Heasley, a Kent State student and Vietnam War veteran, remembered cresting one of the highest hills in Portage County as he was returning to campus that evening and seeing Kent laid out below him. "It was like coming out on *War of the Worlds*. . . . There were lights flashing all over town. You know, police, other emergency vehicles flashing in several different parts of the town, helicopters crisscrossing over the town with spotlights. It was astonishing to us. And then we came down to the city limits and encountered Checkpoint Charlie, and yes, we knew something was up. I don't think at that point I knew that I was then in a militarily occupied town, that martial law had been declared."

Returning students who lived off campus had the additional challenge of beating a citywide curfew that was being strictly enforced by the Guard. Janice Marie (Gierman) Wascko and a friend were nearing the deadline when they were dropped off several blocks from their house:

"We were trying to make it to our house by curfew, and as we rounded our corner, people from our house were sitting on the front lawn, going 'Run! Run faster! They're patrolling it. They're not kidding.' I remember us running down the street, and my friend had a hundred donuts in her backpack, and they started rolling out of her backpack and rolling down the street. We made it to our house just as a Jeep came by with guys in uniform. . . . It was really bizarre—never saw that before—and [our housemates] said, 'Wait'll you see the university!'"

———

"Looking back, people kept saying it was such a surprise anything like that had happened," Murvin Perry, then head of the journalism school, said of the shootings. "Actually I, at the time, said, 'Why are you surprised?' The kind of conduct that everyone was engaging in was bound to fire into violence."

On Saturday night, Perry had walked over to campus from his house after the ROTC building had gone up in flames. As the Guard was clearing students away toward a steep hill, he saw a female student giving one particular Guardsman holy hell. "She was slapping at his face. She spit on him, and he was pushing her back with his rifle until she got to the edge of that hill. Of course, as steep as it was, it caused her to stumble, and she had to turn around to get herself down the hill." When she did that, Perry remembered, the Guardsman kicked her hard in the rear end with his GI boot.

Faculty wife Lillian Tyrrell was walking across campus that weekend when she overheard an officer telling a small group of Guardsmen serving under him: "'We're going to teach these goddamned hippies a lesson. We're not going to allow them to push us around.' I mean, these were things he was saying to young soldiers who had guns in their hands. I think the officers were totally out of control."

For its part, the university not only had surrendered all meaningful authority but also lacked the institutional capacity to respond to the events that swirled around it. John Panagos recalled an "executive meeting" of the speech and hearing department that was held a few days before the shootings. "I wasn't there, but someone told me, and I think it was accurate, that there was a bomb threat in the building, and the chair of the department actually called for a vote on whether they should evacuate or not, which always seemed kind of typical of the mentality of the university administration. . . . They were fumbling around to find some institutional way of responding to something of a magnitude that was far beyond their sense of things."

Simultaneously, too, the campus had been transformed in less than twenty-four hours into some middle ground between an academic institution and an occupied territory. For Panagos, seeing the "soldiers in military uniform with rifles, blowing whistles to all of us who might be trespassing or doing the wrong thing," was an object lesson in "how quickly that [military] presence can be focused and concentrated, even on a domestic dispute such as the kind we had here." It seemed to happen so "instantaneously," he said.

Meanwhile communication between all parties—military, institutional, police, civic authorities, and students—which had been increasingly miserable as the campus underwent its metamorphosis, managed to take a turn for the even worse.

By eight forty-five p.m. on Sunday, the crowd gathered on the Commons, near the Victory Bell, had grown large enough that representatives of the highway patrol and campus police recommended to the National Guard that the one a.m. campus curfew be abandoned and a new, immediate curfew imposed. Thus, at a little before nine, Major Jones read the Ohio Riot Act to the crowd and gave them five minutes to clear out. When they didn't disperse, police fired tear gas into the crowd, but without the intended result.

One part of the student crowd took off for President White's on-campus house, where they were again met with tear gas and driven away. A second group headed for Prentice Gate, the main entrance to the campus, where a sizable crowd sat down in one of Kent's main intersections while leaders insisted that White and Mayor Satrom meet with them about a list of demands that seems in retrospect both predictable and entirely off the wall: abolition of the now building-less ROTC, of course; lifting of the curfew that had just been shortened by more than four hours; full amnesty for all those arrested the night before; lower tuition; and from way out in left field, granting any demands made by BUS, the Black United Students, "whatever they be."

Two university vice presidents on duty at the administration building rejected the idea of White participating in any such gathering on the grounds that (a) the National Guard was running the show and (b) negotiating in the streets was pointless in any event. Mayor Satrom agreed to attend and even set out for the campus but never arrived on the scene.

At Prentice Gate, an unidentified young man who had been given access to the police public-address system announced to the crowd that the mayor was coming and efforts were still under way to contact President White. He went on to say that if students would move out of the street, the Guardsman would move off campus. Both withdrew slightly, but at eleven p.m. police learned that neither White nor Satrom would be attending and once more read the Ohio Riot Act to the protestors. The Guard colonel in charge of the contingent at the gate then announced that the campus curfew, which had yo-yoed during the night from one a.m. to nine p.m. and back toward midnight again was now set for eleven p.m., and in effect immediately. And with that the battle was joined once more.

The scene at Prentice Gate, Denny Benedict remembered, had been "peaceful, just not a lot going on. One of the student leaders came back and said, 'The mayor is coming.' Everybody was happy. He'd agreed to meet with us and take our demands and stuff. Next thing you know, the National Guard are putting on their helmets, putting on their gas masks, fixing their bayonets. So basically they lied to us. They start cleaning the area. There's one or two helicopters just above the treetops, and it was just chaos.

"They had bullhorns, trying to tell us who knows what—you couldn't understand them because they were so loud. The Guards come, and the kids are scattering . . . and basically they chased us all the way back to our dorms. [The helicopters] were shooting tear gas at us."

The helicopters, he said, "just flew over all night long. They were just out there all night. Tear gas smells in the air. Just didn't make any sense."

Thirty years later, Rob Fox still remembered May 3 as "the night of the helicopters. . . . This was the most frightening thing I can remember—with these helicopters, with their searchlights. I felt like I was in Vietnam." Helicopters, he said, were buzzing Tri-Towers, the large dorm complex, shouting from their speakers. "In fact, the Guards marched right up to the Tri-Towers windows and had some kids pressed against the windows. . . . There was screaming, pandemonium taking place."

Jim Vacarella recalled standing on the sidewalk near Prentice Gate shortly after the Riot Act was read for the second time that night and the eleven p.m. curfew imposed. "I heard this [stomping sound]. And it was boots—hundreds of Guardsmen in a flying 'V.' And they came right in, charged right into the crowd without any warning whatsoever. . . . It became Guardsmen against students. All we had were rocks and maybe plates from the dining hall and so on. But it was a real fight all night long. The rest of that night we were really pissed, and word went around the whole campus that school's going to close tomorrow. We are going to close this school."

Later in the interview, Vacarella returned to the subject of closing Kent State down: "We didn't know how. We didn't know when. But we knew that it couldn't go on like this. It was getting increasingly violent. . . . So Monday started with that feeling."

Many Guardsmen, too, were reaching a kind of breaking point as Sunday night slipped into Monday. "We had [gas] masks on. We were anonymous. We had taken our name tags off our jackets," one Guardsman remembered of the running battles that brought Sunday to an end. "I don't recall who the fellow was down from me, but I recall him putting a bayonet to a man's nose and saying, 'I know your face, but you don't know mine. If I ever see you again, this is going to go up in your head.' I think the man urinated himself right there on the spot. He had nowhere to go, nowhere to run. He was up against the wall with his hands up, and I don't recall ever seeing him again. . . . I'm not saying we were right or we were wrong, but you have to realize the situation that you get into emotionally."

The same, of course, can be said of the students. Henry Mankowski spent part of Sunday night zigzagging across the campus with a friend, "hiding in the shadows of buildings because helicopters were swooping and there were searchlight all over the grounds." As that was going on, another of his friends was bayoneted in his back. "The Guardsman didn't give him a chance—told him to get up and then he didn't get a chance to move fast enough, and the Guardsman lunged and stabbed him right in the back. He ended up in Robinson Memorial [Hospital]." Alan Frank told a similar story—another friend bayoneted by a Guardsman because he wasn't fast enough.

John Cleary, who would be shot in the chest the next day, described Sunday night in almost Catch-22 terms. "We had problems in Stopher Hall because the wind brought the tear gas into the dorm, so we had to leave the building. As we went out the front of the building, [the Guard] ordered us back inside. We were trying to explain to them that we can't go back in the building because of the tear gas, and they said, 'We don't care; you're not allowed to be out here.'" Damned if they did—damned if they didn't.

Ellis Berns, a nineteen-year-old undergraduate at Kent State in 1970, had gone home to nearby Akron over the weekend. He returned Sunday afternoon, in time for this latest bout of drama. "My protest became more and more adamant about getting the National Guard off of the university more than anything because I felt passionate that, as students, we had the right to protest. These were like hallowed grounds. This is where freedom of speech means something. . . .

"That's how strongly I felt about the National Guard and why they shouldn't be on campus because this is an institution of higher learning. I remember just before I left Akron, I said to my parents, 'I'm going to lay down my life on this'—because I believed. I don't know, I was still a kid."

Like a lot of other "kids" at Kent State, though, Ellis Berns would grow up fast in the day just ahead.

4

Danse Macabre

If there was one thing wholly predictable about Monday, May 4, 1970, on the campus of Kent State University in Northeast Ohio, it was that students would attempt to hold a protest rally. The time was known: noon. So was the place: the southeast end of the Commons, beginning at the Victory Bell. News of the rally had been circulating around campus by word of mouth since early morning. The time and place had been posted on school bulletin boards and scribbled in chalk on classroom blackboards.

By Monday morning, there could be no question to whom the protest would be directed: not Richard Nixon, not Cambodia, not Vietnam, but the National Guardsmen present on the campus—the very ones who, without a radical change of course, would be called on to contain or disperse the gathering. Guard helicopters had been flying overhead all night long, searchlights blazing, a pointed reminder of who was in charge of Kent State.

The previous three days had amounted to "an exchange of symbolic gestures," according to Joe Lewis, soon to be wounded. By Monday, though, "Vietnam had receded. Cambodia had receded. It was clear that the issue was the Guard's occupation of the Kent State campus."

Because the university remained open and classes would be meeting, certain logistical problems were in play as well. The Commons was a central crossing point. Students and faculty passing by or through the Commons as they moved from class to class or headed to lunch at the student union would inevitably be pulled into the protest web. Some would find it an impediment to be gotten through or around. Others would be drawn to the rally like moths to a flame. Still others would simply be swept up in the momentum of events.

The Kent State Commons is often described as an amphitheater, but it's more in the shape of a baseball field with—on the morning of May 4, 1970—the ruins of the ROTC building at roughly home plate and the Victory Bell, where the students would be gathering at noon, over five hundred feet away in deep center field. Two-thirds of the way down the short right-field line, the hills begin to gently slope up, a natural grandstand. By centerfield, the hills are steeper. At the end of the long left-field line the hills are steepest. Like a huge scoreboard, Taylor Hall and its terrace dominate the landscape at the top of the hill behind deepest center field. Amphitheater or baseball stadium, the Commons provides excellent sightlines from multiple elevated angles. Not only would students not directly involved in the protest have an unimpeded view of whatever was taking place in the Commons itself; any conflict there was likely to feel much like a Roman gladiatorial contest.

Another new certainty: It didn't require a PhD in psychology to predict that prohibitions against peaceful assembly would be ignored; that efforts to disperse those already gathered would be resisted by many, particularly the hard core of protestors; and that increasingly forceful behavior on the part of students and Guardsmen was all but certain to ensue. Look at Saturday night. Look at Sunday night. Monday would have been anomalous, had it not repeated the pattern of the previous two days. Instead, it was like the third X in the row of an especially dangerous tic-tac-toe game.

All of which makes it all the more astonishing that everyone involved in oversight in any significant way did not convene until ten a.m. that Monday to discuss how to handle what was all but a surefire confrontation.

Part of the problem was proximity and fatigue: General Canterbury, mission chief for the Guard, had been away for much of Sunday. He returned late in the evening and went straight into a midnight meeting in the Tactical Operations Center, in space claimed in the administration building, where it was determined "that groups of people, peaceful or otherwise, were to be prohibited on the campus," according to Lieutenant Colonel Charles Fassinger, one of the attendees. Canterbury was still awake at two a.m., when he called President White to ask if he and some members of his senior staff could attend the next morning's gathering.

The larger problems, though, were definitional, managerial, and hierarchical, complicated in every instance by miserable intelligence gathering. Those summoned to the meeting by General Canterbury included White and Vice President Robert Matson, Mayor Satrom and City Safety Director Paul Hershey, State Highway Patrol Major Donald Manley, and Ohio National Guard legal officer Major William Shimp—high-rankers from all the relevant authorities. But not one of them still knew for sure what curfew the campus was operating under or whether any rally of any size would be legal under the terms of Governor Rhodes's state of emergency (had the state of emergency even existed), the Guard's own campus-imposed rules (such as for crowd size), or what might be thought of as normal university customs and procedures had this been a normal time and the school administration still in charge of its own procedures.

Worse still, the fast-approaching noon rally seems to have been the last thing on everyone's mind. According to Robert White, only late in the meeting, which adjourned around 11:20, did Bob Matson report "that he had just been informed from the campus that there were rumors that there was to be a rally." Rumors? *Life* magazine had contacted student photographer Howard Ruffner hours earlier with a request to cover the event. Nonetheless, Robert Canterbury would also say later that Matson's report was the first time he learned of the upcoming rally.

In the many investigations that were to follow, this meeting, too, evolved into a he-said dustup. Canterbury would testify that White had said allowing the rally "would be highly dangerous." White's reaction: "From past history, all know that my response would have been affirmative to a rally." The highest legal ground the Scranton Commission could discern seems to be Vice President Matson's contribution that all present had "more or less assumed" the state of emergency declared by Rhodes the previous day had prohibited any and all gatherings, but as we've seen, that assumption traced back to a passing conversation between a lesser university official and a lesser Guard officer—one assumption, in effect, piled on another.

Nonetheless, Canterbury, according to Matson, told the group "the rally would not be allowed unless he heard strong objections to its prohibition." Hearing none, he closed the matter and set about enforcing what he understood the unanimous consensus of the meeting to be. Canterbury had attended in civilian clothes so as not to attract undue attention. With no time to change into uniform after the meeting adjourned, he would end up leading the Guard force in a business shirt and tie, another piece of dissonance for a campus that would soon be drowning in it.

———

That Monday morning found Kent State a place strangely divided against itself: part university, part military installation; a school where students were encouraged to gather in classrooms but prohibited from doing so on the campus Commons. Professors preached caution, or encouraged opposition to authority, or in some cases even tried to lead it. Top administrators fretted over what was to come—

President White had called a seven a.m. meeting of his cabinet and an eight o'clock one with the executive committee of the faculty senate. Then, shortly after the conclusion of General Canterbury's prolonged ten a.m. meeting, White and his brain trust left campus for a pre-scheduled, off-campus luncheon meeting. By then, the only certainty seemed to be that thousands of Kent State students would be swept up—by intent, circumstance, or proximity—in a noon rally that the National Guard clearly had no intent of allowing.

"Guards were there in front of the buildings, on the street," Joseph Sima, then a junior, remembered of school that morning. "They had bayonets on their rifles. . . . I had a class in Bowman Hall, and I had a Guardsman right outside the door. And it was like that in many of the classes."

Laura Dressler, also a junior in May 1970, had a similar experience. "I got up and went to class like I normally would. . . . In classes that morning all the professors seemed to have the same little script, and they told us not to participate in any assemblies and just pretty much to behave ourselves and not assemble and not take part in any rallies. There were a lot of armored personnel carriers, and men with rifles all over the campus.

"I was prepared to do what they told me to do because I see people with guns and I see what look like army tanks all over campus, I'm going to listen."

Brinsley Tyrrell arrived at his off-campus, in-town sculpture studio that morning to find armed Guardsmen on the roof and at the door. "The whole thing was surreal," he recalled. "I guess they were protecting my students from my students."

Barclay McMillen was among the teachers advising caution. A Kent State alumnus, class of 1953, McMillen served as a legal adviser to President White and a lecturer in the political science department as well as maintaining his own law practice in Washington, DC. He devoted the entirety of his nine a.m. American government class to the activities of that weekend and to the coming noon rally.

The demonstrations Friday, Saturday, and Sunday nights, he said, were planned operations. (He'd witnessed parts of all of them.) Students were being used as "dupes" by "anarchists" who were taking advantage of their antiwar sentiments to "simply destroy the system through violence." Of Saturday night, he said, "I have never seen so many unfamiliar faces in my life . . . and I've taught, I think, 20 percent of the student body."

As for the upcoming rally, "The Governor has assumed legal control of this university [and] has prohibited all forms of outdoor demonstrations or rallies, peaceful or otherwise. . . . We're under martial law on this campus. . . . This is the state of reality which we are in today, and we shall be in that until such time as this campus returns to something normal."

As for students who might be tempted by simple curiosity to join the rally, "When your head is busted or when you are arrested or when you're tear-gassed, you have only yourself to blame. If you have an IQ over 20, you now know the name of the game on this campus, and that is: Stay Away."

The entire class was audio-recorded by the campus radio station, WKSU, and broadcast in its entirety beginning at eleven a.m. The broadcast ended almost exactly at the moment when General Canterbury began deploying his National Guard troops from their position on the grounds of the burned-out ROTC building.

Diane Yale-Peabody's class on the modern short story met at 11:55, just as McMillen's rebroadcast class was ending and five minutes before the protest was to begin. "When I got there, the professor said he knew there was a rally going on, so anyone who wanted to leave class that day and go to the rally, he would not mark them down as being absent. Anybody who wanted to sit in class and talk about what was going on—he was willing to do that, too. Or if the people who stayed in class would rather talk about the story we were studying at that time, we would do that. So we all agreed we were there to learn about this course, so we talked about the story."

At the same time, Jim Vacarella and as many as fifty other students, by his account, were crammed into his dorm room, preparing for the rally by doing joints. "That was very interesting," he said in a 2000 interview, "getting a downer drug and then going out there to fight an upper war. It was just pretty weird. . . . That morning, I had a feeling that something was really wrong."

Freshman Dean Kahler, who had turned twenty on May 1, took a far more measured approached to the day's possibilities: "We'd all heard that there was going to be some kind of a rally at noon, and being a farm boy, I didn't have time to go to civil rights marches or antiwar rallies. So I was curious. There was a second thing, too: if I could lend my voice to stopping the expansion of the war . . . I was hoping something like that would come out of it."

Kahler decided not to go to classes Monday, but he did call all his professors that morning to tell them he wouldn't be there and to find out what assignments he would be missing. "My zoology professor basically told me to relax and try not to get too close to the Guard and not do anything stupid, so I listened to him." Kahler would be in the crowd but well away from the action when he got shot in the spine.

———

The tear gas had begun flying by the time Robert Pescatore finished lunch in the cafeteria at Prentice Hall and started out for his next class.

"The street was just filled with all kinds of people. I remember one girl. . . . She had bandoliers on her, or across her, like the Mexicans did from the movies. And there were some bullets in those bandoliers. Now how many, I don't know. But I remember that. And I remember her saying, 'Let's get those pigs and throw them off campus.' There may be some swearing in there, but that's basically what she said, and she said it like right in front of me, like right directly to me.

And I'm thinking, I don't want to do this. I just want to get to my class. That's what I'm paying for."

By the time Lowell Zurbuch and a fellow professor were crossing the Commons to the faculty dining area at the student union, the National Guard and students seemed to be chasing one another across the open field, almost as if they were involved in a massive game of Capture the Flag.

"So here was a young Guardsman standing there with a rifle and fixed bayonet," Zurbuch remembered, "and my friend walked up to him and said . . . 'Hey, shoot one of them for me, will ya?' And the Guardsman says, 'Yes, sir, I will.' Well, they were both smiling and laughing as this was happening, and then moments later, it occurred."

That exchange sounds horrible in retrospect, but in recounting the events of that midday, like so much of the previous weekend, witnesses frequently mention the relaxed atmosphere in the twenty minutes or so before the shooting began, how much like a beach party the campus seemed.

John Snediker was making sales calls in and around Kent that noontime. "Minutes before the tragedy occurred," he remembered, "I had driven west by the campus and smiled as I saw a co-ed sitting on the lap of a Guardsman near the main entrance. My immediate thought: Well, at least the young people seem to be getting along pretty well."

Suzanne Irvin left her journalism class at 11:50, walked over to Lilac Lane "to see how far along the lilacs were in budding out," and was just reaching the Commons when "a long line of Guardsmen suddenly appeared . . . in front of the ruins of what had been an old wooden shack used by the ROTC."

"A few Guardsmen were riding around in a jeep before us, shouting through a bullhorn, which oddly distorted the voices," she remembered. "We were told to disperse immediately, that this was an unlawful assembly, and that we were under martial law. I was 21 years old and had never even heard of martial law. . . . There was some laughter, as I recall. Then the Guard began to fire tear-gas canisters toward the group of students who were near the old Victory Bell, by Taylor Hall. The young guys threw the tear-gas canisters back at the Guardsmen."

Peter Jedick ran into a woman he knew just as events were building up momentum on the Commons. "She had this bandana around her face, for the tear gas. She said, 'Come on. Join us. This is fun.' I said, 'No, I think I'll just watch.' That was one of the best decisions I ever made in my life."

William Derry Heasley was in the midst of a similar scene—students and Guardsmen throwing smoking tear-gas canisters back and forth. "It looked . . . funny and ridiculous. It seemed like students and soldiers alike were at a loss for what happens next."

J. R. Hipple's sister, a freshman, was walking near the Commons, texts and notebooks in hand, on her way from class to her job at the bookstore, when she was tear-gassed and eventually taken by ambulance to the student health center.

Among those throwing the tear-gas canisters back at the Guard as the next twenty minutes unfolded was Jeffrey Miller, a junior from Plainview, New York, who had transferred from Michigan State University only a few months earlier. Miller would be killed at exactly 12:24 p.m.

———

In an on-campus interview on the twentieth anniversary of the shootings, a Kent State alum who had been on Guard duty that weekend speculated on all those in attendance who were saying to themselves, *"I wish you could have seen our minds and have been standing in front of those weapons when the puff of smoke came and the M1's came whizzing by.* I would say to them, *I wish you could have put yourself in the mindset of the man pulling the trigger.* For whatever reason, enough's enough."

Cause and effect, action and reaction, cumulative insult, pure fatigue, sheer chance—they would all factor into the time directly ahead. They couldn't help but do so. Events, though, were moving far too quickly for anyone to read anyone else's mind.

General Canterbury reached the Guard staging area next to the burned-out ROTC building by 11:40 that morning. Across the Commons, a crowd of perhaps five hundred was gathered around the Victory Bell. At age fifty-five, with twenty-three years of military service including leading Guard forces in such racially charged hotspots as the Hough section of Cleveland, Canterbury would later tell the Scranton Commission that he felt the crowd at that point did not represent a significant threat.

However, five minutes later, at 11:45, Canterbury's deputy, Lieutenant Colonel Charles Fassinger, ordered the Guard troops to form up: roughly a hundred men, divided into Companies A and C of the First Battalion, 145th Infantry Regiment, with thirty-five to fifty men in each unit, and Troop G of the Second Squadron, 107th Armored Cavalry Regiment (eighteen Guardsmen). At the same time, Guardsmen were told to "lock and load" weapons. Those who had not previously fitted their M1s with eight-round magazines now did so, moving one round of .30-caliber ball ammunition into the firing chamber. To discharge their weapons, they needed only to slip off the safety and squeeze the trigger.

Simultaneously, Kent State policeman Harold Rice, who had been hit in the groin with a rock Saturday night, was standing near the ROTC ruins, using a bullhorn to order the crowd gathered by the Victory Bell, almost two football fields away, to disperse. When that proved futile, Rice, a driver, and two Guardsmen with rifles at the ready set out across the Commons in a jeep and again ordered the students to disperse—the distorted voice that Suzanne Irvin mentioned, talking about martial law, a concept she didn't understand, and reading an Ohio Riot Act that almost no one in the crowd could possibly hear. It's doubtful, however, that better audio equipment would have made much of a difference. As with other similar orders during the long weekend, this one was met by a predictable stream of curses, antiwar chants, and raised middle fingers, plus a small volley of stones and rocks.

"Reading the Riot Act to students," Dean Kahler said, "was like waving a red cape at a bull."

When an effort to drive into the crowd to apprehend a student Rice believed to be one of the instigators of the weekend riots was similarly rebuffed, the jeep returned to the ROTC site, and at 11:58 a.m. Canterbury ordered the ninety-six men and seven officers under his command to form a skirmish line, shoulder to shoulder, with bayonets fixed.

Again on orders from Canterbury, as many as ten Guard grenadiers used M-79 grenade launchers to fire two volleys of tear-gas canisters at the crowd, which now numbered an estimated eight hundred people on the Commons and another thousand or more watching the spectacle from the surrounding hillsides. And at twelve noon sharp, the Guardsmen moved out.

The *danse macabre* had begun.

———

"Somebody decided to clear the area," Denny Benedict remembered. "If they would have just let it go on, it would have just been a protest, petered out, and that would have been the end of it. . . . But they fixed the bayonets, put the gas masks on, started coming up the hill. There were maybe 40 people really protesting, the hard-core protesters. Most everybody were onlookers because it was at noon, right in the center of campus, change of classes. You might see pictures of hundreds or thousands of kids, but really it was maybe 40 or 50 hardcore people involved in that."

"These were not 2,000 people hell-bent on anything," William Derry Heasley said in a 1990 interview. "These were people who wished they had some answers, and there were a few who were hellbent on something . . . 30 people at the most who did this, and they gave the finger and they shouted obscenities across the Commons, but right behind them were all these people going: Why are they doing this? What's this about?"

General Canterbury's job, though, was to clear the Commons and disperse the crowd, and to that end, he made no distinctions between hard-core protestors, the curious, the inquiring, faculty members heading to lunch, slow walkers, dawdlers, lilac watchers, or any other subset of the two thousand or so people who were now in violation of the Ohio Riot Act, as he saw it.

With Company A on Canterbury's right flank, Company C on his left, and Troop G in the center, the Guardsmen marched across the Commons, clearing the crowd around the Victory Bell and pushing it up and over what is still known as Blanket Hill (for its sunbathing and romantic associations), through the natural chokepoint between the southern end of Taylor Hall and the northern tip of Johnson Hall, and then down the other side of the hill into the parking lots below. Canterbury's hope, he would later say, was to reach the crest of Blanket Hill, declare his mission accomplished, and return to the ROTC ruins at the far end of the Commons. But there were problems from the beginning.

His grenadiers did a spotty job at best of aiming and delivering the tear-gas canisters, but the elements were working against them, too. Not only had some students turned the canisters into seething beach balls; a fourteen-mile-an-hour breeze compromised the immediate effectiveness of the tear gas while disbursing it far and wide, across the Commons and around the spectators on the surrounding hillsides.

The crowd also hadn't fled in lockstep from the Guard advance. When one group broke to the north end of Taylor Hall, Canterbury sent Company C in pursuit. Thus, when he arrived at the top of Blanket Hill, it was with a depleted main force.

What General Canterbury saw from the crest wasn't cheering either: milling students below him, many in the Prentice Hall parking lot, forced together by the Guard's advance, now more united and angry, and—since they were publicly gathered—still in violation of the Ohio Riot Act. Rather than retrace his steps to the ROTC site, Canterbury ordered the Guardsmen forward another eighty yards, down the backside of Blanket Hill and onto a practice football field. The general, though, had marched his men into a strategically weak position, what amounted almost to a cul de sac with a hundred yards of fencing on one side. Worse, perhaps, a construction site sat nearby, with more rocks, pieces of lumber, and other debris for an increasingly aggressive crowd.

Mounting abuse followed. At one point, a dozen or so soldiers went down on one knee with M1s aimed at the protesters in the parking lot just to the north—a clear warning as well as a presaging of the same formation Guardsmen would reassume with lethal results not many minutes later. Randy Gardner recalled the soldiers moving their sights occasionally, as if they were targeting specific protestors. Henry Mankowski remembered asking a fellow student standing with him nearby in the parking lot if they were the ones being targeted. One of the best-known photos of the event shows kneeling Guardsmen on the practice field zeroing in on Alan Canfora, waving a large banner and soon to be shot through the wrist.

The intent clearly was intimidation, in some cases at a personal level, but as with so much else about the Guard's actions that day, this one had an opposite effect for many of those in the crowd. "People were saying . . . 'They don't have live ammunition in their weapons. It's just to scare us. Don't worry about it,'" Rob Fox recalled.

According to the Scranton Commission report, an officer on the practice field might have fired a single shot from his .45 pistol at a forty-five-degree angle over the heads of the rock throwers, but if that happened, it, too, had little if any deterrent effect.

Finally, after ten minutes on the practice field, General Canterbury ordered Guardsmen to return to the top of Blanket Hill. Tear gas, he mistakenly thought, was exhausted. In fact, one grenadier still had four canisters to fire, but the gas, in any event, had proved largely ineffective. The strategic foibles of Canterbury's position had become obvious, too. The only viable exit for the roughly fifty Guardsmen on the practice field was to retrace their steps back up Blanket Hill—in short, a retreat.

"My purpose," Canterbury would later testify, "was to make it clear beyond any doubt to the mob that our posture was now defensive and that we were clearly returning to the Commons, thus reducing the possibility of injury either to soldiers or students."

The "mob," as he referred to it, found a different takeaway. "They were going back up the hill towards Taylor Hall, and everyone was happy," Denny Benedict remembered. "We won! You lost! You're retreating, going back to where you came from!"

———

Jerry Casale once described the Guardsmen in those moments before disaster struck as looking "like scared little boys." Many were indeed young men, some barely more than boys, and they were scared with cause. The FBI would later collect all the debris left on or anywhere near Blanket Hill—175 pounds of bricks, rocks, chunks of ripped-out lumber with nails still in it. Along with such hard-impact improvised weapons, Guardsmen had also been pelted with bags full of shit, human or otherwise, and urine, almost certainly human in origin.

Questions would rage for years—they still do in some circles—about just how much of this incoming debris the Guards were dealing with as they started up the back side of Blanket Hill, where it was coming from, and how effective the assault was.

Carol Mirman was among those in on the chase. "I did throw some rocks . . . [but] I quit. I couldn't hit a darned thing. It didn't make any sense to me to throw a rock if you couldn't hit something. These guys were really far away, and I couldn't throw for beans anyway. It was more an angry statement for me. I never really wanted to hurt anybody, but I was mad at all this. . . .

"I did see one rock hit a Guardsman, and I say this because there were reports that came out in the press that fire hydrants had been thrown. Guardsmen had been bleeding, and there are lots of lies afterwards, but I was right there—right in the middle of it—*nada*, did not happen. The one rock I saw bounced off a Guardsman's helmet, and we're talking like a long way away."

Randy Gardner, who would be shot in the foot more that four decades later in the Arizona assault on Congresswoman Gabby Giffords, was among those following the Guard up the hill: "I didn't see any [Guardsmen] getting hurt or anything like that. There were a few stragglers maybe who were closer to the Guard . . . just three or four people, something like that. Most of the people were keeping their distance."

Rob Fox said much the same in a 2000 interview: "If you listen to the media or listen to what some people have said, they make it sound like the sun was blotted out by stones. It was not. First of all, this campus is mostly grass like it is now. . . . I did see a few kids throwing stones, but it was from a great distance. Nor did I see any students get closer than 50 to 75 yards.

"You hear people saying, 'Oh, they were about to be overrun; they were fearing for their lives.' There was nobody even close to them. There were students parting [in front of them]," said one of the most prominent activists that day. "I mean, if I was the most active one, and I was down the hill, then what was there to really be afraid of?"

Ronald Sterlekar was equally unimpressed by the barrage—"just a few kids on the perimeter" hurling rocks that were "bouncing yards in front" of the Guardsmen—and the broader threat. "There were just people wandering with their books through the parking lot," he remembered, "and I said, This is silliness. I'm going back to my dorm." Like just about everything else, though, "silliness" is relative.

In the same way rumors had swept through the city of Kent— protestors were plotting to spike the town water supply with LSD; they were planning to blow up the old mill that was the city's historical centerpiece—so rumors had swept through Guard units: protestors had access to their own cache of semiautomatic rifles; snipers were in place, waiting for their moment to strike. One student photographer working behind his tripod on the roof of Johnson Hall had temporarily raised fears of just such a sniper. Multiple Guardsmen would later say that they had heard one gunshot. No hard evidence supports that, but this was not an environment for the clearest possible thinking.

The Guardsmen were also tired. Because of duty rotations and limited numbers, none had slept more than three hours the night before. Company C had gone off duty at two a.m. Monday morning, only to be ordered at five thirty a.m. to return to duty, patrolling the streets of Kent. Company A had been on duty all night. At six a.m., it was relieved by Troop G, but because the company had to move its bivouac area, no one had much of a chance to lie down before nine a.m., and at eleven thirty in the morning, members were aroused to deal with the upcoming noon rally. Troop G looked to have won the sleep lottery: members went off duty at six p.m. Sunday, but they were called back to duty around midnight after the situation at Prentice Gate fell into ruin, and then roused again between four and four thirty a.m. to relieve Company A.

Poor decision making had already imperiled the Guard on the football practice field, sleep deprivation was in play, and confusion in interpreting and following orders would come next—any element of which might have tripped a wire—but Guardsmen were also carrying live ammunition, and their rifles were locked and loaded.

"When you pick all of those ingredients," said Art Krummel, who was among the Guardsmen that day, "what other kind of cake are you going to end up with? I mean, to take young, tired, poorly trained people, hand them bullets, say, 'You're going to oppose these other angry young people who are going to be throwing rocks, and you're going to be . . . put in dangerous situations,' and then expect that no one's going to get shot, that's kind of a pretty unrealistic expectation."

The jubilant protestors, now emboldened by retreat, also had to be dealt with. "There was taunting and jeering at the Guards, calling for them to get off campus," Naomi Goelman Etzkin remembered. The going, she said, was particularly hard for the group that had knelt on the practice field and raised their rifles at the crowd. "They were separated from the rest of the Guardsmen. This time they really had been surrounded by students." Denny Benedict remembered the same group glaring back at the protestors as they marched up the hill.

Some Guardsmen would later say that protestors had come almost within range of their bayonets during the retreat up Blanket Hill. Photo and film evidence is incomplete, but it suggests that the most active, front edge of the protestors—twenty to fifty people—never surged closer than about twenty yards from the Guardsmen, and then only episodically, with the bulk of the crowd no closer than seventy yards. And if the thrown objects hadn't exactly blotted out the sun, they were nonetheless real incoming. Lieutenant Colonel Charles Fassinger said he was hit six times by stones. One blow on his shoulder made him stumble.

Only a few minutes earlier, near the base of the hill, Michael Erwin thought the Guardsmen were ready to "start whacking us over the head and hauling us to jail." Jerry Casale expected the same thing as he watched fresh troops move out of the gymnasium, where the Guard had set up headquarters after originally taking over the board of trustees' meeting room. "It was the classic Battle of the Bulge strategy, where they would seal off any escape route through the parking lot and trap us by the journalism building. That was the game—they were going to arrest everybody, put us on buses, and haul us off to the county jail in Ravenna."

Instead, as the unit that had earlier threatened protestors reached a campus landmark known as the Pagoda—a square bench shaded by a concrete umbrella—the Guardsmen turned back toward the parking lot, went down on one knee or crouched, and raised their M1s to their shoulders.

By then, Chuck Ayers, who had been photographing the demonstration for the campus newspaper, had returned with his film to the

Kent Stater office, convinced as most were that events would be dying down as the Guard crossed over Blanket Hill and returned to the ROTC site.

"I got down to the first floor, went into the *Stater* office. I saw Karen [his girlfriend] and her roommate. I remember saying, 'I think it's all over. What did you guys see?' . . . And just about that time it was like this *bang*, like the doors, and there was screaming and yelling, and I thought, What's going on? And this surge of people just came through the hallways, past the *Stater* office. I remember going to the doors, and the first words I heard were, 'They just killed four kids.' I don't know how this person determined this in seconds. They must have seen four people down. They were yelling, 'They're shooting! They're killing people!' . . .

"There was one guy who I recall was a freshman, who had been somewhere and saw most of the shootings. [He] came into the *Stater* office crying, had a puppy with him, and he crawled under a desk and just sat there and cried."

Tears, shock, rage, disbelief—on and around Blanket Hill they would soon become commonplaces, the shared experience of the early afternoon.

5

Blood Like a River

The M1 Garand battle rifle was patented in 1934 by John Garand, born in Canada and raised from the age of eleven in the United States. The Garand (pronounced to rhyme with "errand") is a heavy rifle—nine pounds—with provisions for fixing a bayonet with a ten-inch blade at the front end, an echo of the trench warfare of earlier times. It fires a .30–06, 150-grain, full-metal-jacket round, a long, skinny bullet designed to travel great distances and arrive with maximum impact.

Muzzle energy at the barrel is 2,500 foot-pounds. At 200 yards, the force of impact is still over 2,000 foot-pounds, enough to penetrate a steel helmet, transit through a skull, and come out the helmet's other side. Line up three human beings in a row at 250 yards—two and a half football fields—and the .30–06 round will go through all three so long as it doesn't get diverted by a major bone. It will go through two to three car bodies as well, unless it encounters something like an engine, and even then, it is likely to crack the cast-iron block. (In a frictionless environment, the force of a projectile generating 2,000 foot-pounds would be enough to shift a solid, 500-pound object four feet on impact.)

In part because it generates so much muzzle energy, the Garand is also highly accurate. An expert marksman should be able to hit a man-size target four hundred yards away almost 75 percent of the time. At that distance, an M1 bullet loses only twenty-four inches of elevation. Aim between the eyes, and you'll hit your target in the heart. Accuracy fades further out, but the Garand is still lethal to a thousand yards, more than half a mile away.

At the start of World War II, the M1 Garand was considered the most advanced battle rifle in the world, mostly because of its eight-shot magazine. By 1970, just about the only people still using the Garand were National Guardsmen. The M14 had long supplanted the M1 as the standard infantry rifle, and now it was being replaced in Vietnam by the M16.

When Ohio National Guardsmen formed a skirmish line at the Pagoda on the back side of Blanket Hill and leveled their rifles at the protestors in front of them, all but one was a Garand. (One Guardsman carried a shotgun, instead. Two officers were armed with .45-caliber pistols, originally designed to stop charging Moro tribesmen in the Philippines, or so the story goes.)

When the Guardsmen began firing at 12:24 p.m. on May 4, 1970—sixty-seven shots in thirteen seconds—all but six rounds were the Garand's long, skinny .30–06 bullets, leaving muzzles with 2,500 foot-pounds of energy, lethal more than half a mile away.

———

Of the twenty-eight rounds from Guard weapons known to impact objects or people, four went into the ground at distances from 25 to 40 yards out from the skirmish line. A fifth embedded itself in a brick wall over 150 yards away. Another four rounds struck automobiles in the Prentice Hall parking lot, where many of the protestors were gathered. The closest automobile hit was 98 yards from the line; the farthest, struck twice, was 145 yards away. Three bullets hit trees.

One entered 11 feet from the ground and 31 yards away from the skirmish line. Another tree was hit twice, at 44 inches from the ground and again at 7 feet, 50 yards out. This is probably the tree one student remembered ducking behind when the firing began. When he stood up again, he said a bullet had traveled completely through the trunk at about chest high.

Dorm resident adviser Bart Bixenstine, the oldest son of faculty members Anita and Edwin Bixenstine, was standing behind a metal sculpture about 30 yards from the skirmish line when a .30–06 round penetrated one of the metal pieces, passed through, and kept on going.

Steven Grudzinski was waiting with several others for an elevator on the sixth floor of his dorm, Leebrick Hall, more than a third of a mile from the skirmish line, when a bullet smashed through a window above his head. "Being from New York and not firing many guns in my lifetime," he said, "I didn't realize you could fire a gun that far." The bullet embedded itself in the far wall of the elevator waiting area.

Yet another bullet passed through a second-floor window at Prentice Hall, 175 yards away.

———

Of the wounded that day, Donald McKenzie was the most distant from the skirmish line: almost 250 yards, struck in the back of his neck on the left side. At that distance, the .30–06 round would have reached McKenzie in about a third of a second. The bullet missed his spinal column by an inch, shattered part of his jawbone, and exited through his left cheek.* Robert Stamps, 165 yards out, was hit by a ricochet in the buttocks; James Russell, 125–130 yards away, in the

---

*In his postexamination report, the physician who treated McKenzie wrote that he had been shot "during the fracas" at Kent State University.

back and the hand by pellets from the shotgun; Doug Wrentmore, 110 yards out, in the right knee.

Alan Canfora, prominent in the demonstrations all weekend long and carrying a black flag when the Guard turned, was shot in the right wrist from 75 yards away. Like Donald McKenzie, Canfora was running away from the line of fire when he was hit. John Cleary was 37 yards out, advancing the film in a disposable camera he had borrowed from his roommate, when he was shot in the left upper chest, close by his heart. It was like "getting hit by a sledgehammer," Cleary remembered. He would spend the next three days in the intensive care unit at Robinson Memorial Hospital. Thomas Grace, still closer at 20 yards out, was wounded in the left ankle.

Joe Lewis was also 20 yards away, giving the finger, when he was shot twice, in the right abdomen and lower left leg. When the Guards formed their skirmish line and began pointing rifles at him, Lewis said, "I took it to be a threatening gesture, and so being eighteen and foolish, I gestured back to them by raising the middle finger of my right hand." Lewis would later say that there was no one between him and the skirmish line.

Guard sergeant Larry Shafer fired the round that passed through Lewis's abdomen. He said that while he could clearly see Lewis's right hand and its extended finger, the left one was out of view, behind his back, holding who knows what. Shafer said he had been hit on his forearm by half a brick as the Guard retreated up the hill toward the Pagoda.

Ellen Mann, then attending high school on the KSU campus, was standing a few feet from Lewis when he was hit. "I saw he was giving them the finger. The next thing I know . . . he screams, 'Oh, my God, they shot me!' And he falls to the ground. . . . A couple of other guys came up, and we took his pants down because there was a lot of blood. So we unzipped his jeans, pulled it down, and there was a hole blown out of him."

Dean Kahler was about 100 yards away, lying prone on the ground, when he was shot in the left side of the small of his back. The bullet lodged in his spine, where it remains to this day. Kahler has been without the use of his legs ever since.

———————

"Something had to happen at the top of that hill to create a situation where we could retreat safely," Guardsmen Rudy Morris told an interviewer thirty years later. But why that something was gunfire remains a mystery to this day.

Guardsmen in the aftermath talked about a surge that brought the crowd perilously close to their position. Joe Lewis and Thomas Grace, as we've seen, were only twenty yards away from the skirmish line when they were shot—maybe a 2.5-second sprint for the collegiate football running stars who try out at the annual National Football League scouting combine. In an age of suicide bombers, twenty yards is within the kill zone. But this was 1970, these were college students, and photographic and/or film evidence of a potentially deadly surge in the Guard's direction has never been found.

Other Guardsmen said they thought their position was taking incoming fire—one shot, perhaps several. Albert Van Kirk, active in the KSU student veterans association, happened to be crossing campus at the time. He said that he distinctly heard a shot coming from a direction other than the Pagoda, but again, evidence is lacking, and the acoustics of gunfire echoing off surrounding buildings can be confusing at best. An exhaustive 1970 study by the *Akron Beacon Journal* of recovered projectiles, angles of fire, the elevation of Guardsmen and of the students and other objects hit concluded that every shot that could be analyzed had originated at the skirmish line and nowhere else.

Student Terry Strubbe audiotaped the entire confrontation from his dormitory room window in Johnson Hall only to have his audio evidence disappear in the hands of the FBI. However, a copy of the tape reemerged in 2007, thanks to the investigative zeal of Alan Canfora, who has identified the words "right here," "point," and "fire" amid the general static and clatter of the recording. Stuart Allen and Tom Owen, audio engineers and forensics specialists hired by the *Cleveland Plain Dealer* in 2010 to examine the tape, determined that the decipherable language captured by the Strubbe tape consisted of three phrases: "All right, prepare to fire," "Get down," and "Guard fire." The key point, according to Canfora, is that in both versions "the last word was 'fire' . . . and the word 'fire' is cut off by the beginning of the gunfire."

Rudy Morris, one of the retreating Guardsmen, also heard the word "fire" before the shooting began but couldn't place the word in any meaningful context.

"It could have been from a student," he said in a 1975 deposition. "It could have been from a teacher. . . . There was so much noise out there, it could have come from anyone. . . . It could have been from a Guardsman who may have been saying, 'Don't fire,' 'Cease fire,' 'Watch your fire,' 'Place your fire.' It could have been from anyone in any given sentence."

Under the pressure of the moment, other Guardsmen might have heard the same word and taken it as a simple imperative: squeeze the trigger. Moments like this are always bathed in confusion. But even with highly sophisticated technology, the tape remains muddled at best.

What's more, not everyone who was within eyesight or ear range of the Pagoda that early afternoon believes that the command to fire—if one was given—was oral. Jerry Casale remembered seeing Robert Canterbury make a gesture with his hand just before the fusillade began. "The gesture," he said, "looked like an order, and they all in unison faced down the hill and shot." Others are convinced the critical gesture was made by Sergeant Myron Pryor—an up-and-down shift of his .45 pistol that launched the barrage.

Canfora had expected, at the least, that the Strubbe tape would give the US Department of Justice cause to reopen the investigation of the shootings. Instead, in 2012, the Justice Department determined that the tape was "unintelligible with no consensus."

According to audio engineers Allen and Owen, the Strubbe tape also contains seventy seconds prior to the possible "fire" command, four popping sounds that appear to come from a .38-caliber pistol such as that carried by Terry Norman, a law-enforcement plant who had spent the weekend posing as a news photographer. Norman did turn over a .38-caliber pistol to campus police immediately after the shootings, but according to Harold Rice, who received the gun from Norman, it had not been fired. For his part, Alan Canfora is convinced the popping sounds came from doors slamming in the wind-blown dormitory where Strubbe made the recording. "I lived in Johnson Hall the year before. Each room had a large oak door with a metal frame. Anytime the wind would blow, there were doors slamming all over that dorm."*

Whatever the cause or causes, the volley was only seconds old when officers began pounding Guardsmen on their helmets with fists and batons, yelling "Cease fire! Cease fire!" General Canterbury, thirty-five yards past the Pagoda, with a gas mask pushed up on top of his head, rushed to join them as soon as the shooting began. That quick action on all their parts undoubtedly saved lives. The sheer logistics of the moment saved lives, too. The Pagoda, where the Guard formed its skirmish line, is a tight space then occupied by many armed men. If the Guardsmen hadn't been hemmed in so close together that many couldn't get off a shot without endangering their comrades-in-arms, the body count would have been significantly higher.

"Several of us were lowering our weapons into the firing position, but our own men were in front of us," one Guardsman recalled twenty years later. "I can't speak for anyone else in the Guard, but knowing that there was firing going on, I would have more than

---

*As we'll see in Chapter 10, the Terry Norman story is steeped in controversy on all sides, but given that the four shots in question, even if they did occur, preceded the fusillade from the Pagoda by more than a full minute, they are unlikely to have been mistaken for sniper fire that would provoke an instant response.

likely emptied my weapon . . . at anything that was there, because obviously the crowd was advancing."

In a tangled way, the antiquated M1s themselves were a saving grace, too. Each of the eight shots in the magazines had to be squeezed off individually—one reason twenty-eight Guardsmen managed to get off only sixty-seven shots in thirteen seconds. The M1 rounds were also steel-jacketed, meant to go through targets unless they struck a heavy impediment such as a bone. The M16 battle rifles then in use in Vietnam are fully automatic, magazines hold nearly four times as many rounds, and the rounds themselves are more lethal. Once an M16's "tumbling" projectile enters a body, it seeks out bone pathways to assure maximum damage. Clean exit wounds are commonplace with M1 rounds; with an M16, they are rare. Thirteen seconds of M16 fire could have mowed a literal swath through the crowd at Kent State. But the demand for the newer rifle in Vietnam was so great that Guard units had to make do with what was left behind—a supply-chain shortfall that might have saved dozens of lives that day.

All that is speculation, though. What we know for certain is the outcome of the barrage, and it does not easily conform to the story line that the Guard was protecting itself from imminent danger. Instead, there seems to have been a strange mix of intentionality, horrific judgment (on multiple sides), terrible luck, preventability, and inevitability. The times, the war, the '60s, a growing generational divide, the Age of Aquarius, and the Age of Hate all collided at Kent State University at 12:24 p.m. on May 4, 1970, and four flesh-and-blood human beings—sons and daughters, brothers and sisters—did not survive the wreckage.

————

Jeffrey Miller—twenty-one years old, five-foot-six, approximately 150 pounds, wearing "a dark maroon colored western style shirt with a white design on the front shoulders and sleeves, a wide brown leather belt, blue denim bell bottom pants and dirty white tennis shoes with white soles" (this from the coroner's report)—was ninety-five yards from the skirmish line the Guardsmen formed before firing, the closest of the students to die.

Miller had been active in the protests throughout the long weekend—tossing tear-gas canisters back at Guardsmen, darting back and forth, shouting the usual slogans: "One, two, three, four, / We don't want your fucking war." He was shot through the mouth, with the bullet exiting the "right posterior neck and occipital area." "The gross aspect," the coroner wrote, "is a horrifying one."

Freshman Eldon Fender was watching Miller when he was hit: "He threw a rock, was shot the minute he threw it, the second he threw it, and he stumbled probably a good fifty feet into the road and fell." Those who saw Miller once he came to rest on the service road almost invariably describe a "river of blood." It must have seemed exactly that way.

In the single most iconic photo of the Kent State shootings, Mary Ann Vecchio, a fourteen-year-old Florida runaway, kneels on the pavement, her arms raised in the air in protest, horror, maybe supplication. The photo ran the next morning three columns wide at the top of the front page of the *New York Times*, where Jeff Miller's father worked in the composing room as a linotype operator.*

John Filo, the student photographer who took the photo, was heading toward Miller when Vecchio "came running up to the body and knelt down to feel a pulse or see what she could do. . . . I moved around to get more of her because she was starting to shake and sob." Filo was still focusing and positioning himself when "she let out with this scream, and then I proceeded to take the picture," he testified in 1975.

---

*Looking at the Vecchio photo, I'm always reminded of Edvard Munch's famous painting *The Scream*. Both are silent images that nonetheless shriek in pain.

Carol Mirman had taken cover behind a yellow Volkswagen in the Prentice Hall parking lot when the shooting began. When the volley stopped and she reemerged, Miller was lying on the pavement near her.

"I'd never seen blood like that," she recalled. "I'd never seen anything like it. It was a complete shock. I wanted to touch him. I remember wanting to hold him, but I was afraid of the blood. I did touch, I did touch and hold his hand 'cause I didn't want him to feel alone. . . . His life was running down the sidewalk—running, just kept flowing. And there was nothing to be done."

Mirman went to look for a friend. When she returned, Mary Ann Vecchio was by Miller's side: "I put my arms around her shoulder. . . . She felt like a block of ice. She was frozen, she was stone. She couldn't move."

Four years earlier, as a high school student in New York State, Jeff Miller had written a poem now on display at Kent State's May 4 Visitors Center. "The War Without a Purpose marches on relentlessly," the third stanza goes, "not stopping to mourn for its dead, / content to wait for its end."

———

Like Jeff Miller, Allison Krause had been active in the protest that early afternoon and all through the long weekend. FBI analysis claims to have found fragments of projectiles in both their pockets, in Krause's case the pockets of a "light tan army type field jacket without any patches on the breast or arms." Krause was tall, striking looking in a very late '60s, early '70s way. She stood out in a crowd. People wanted to take her picture—one reason there is a such a rich photographic record of her from her one year at Kent State: helping hold a banner at the front of an antiwar parade, standing by a blushing Guardsman with a lilac in his M1 battle rifle barrel.

The bullet that struck Krause penetrated "the entire thickness of her upper left arm," exited into her left underarm, then reentered "the body in the mid-axillary line at the 8th, 9th, and 10th ribs with severe fragmentation of the bullet and ribs." Fragments of the .30–06 shell then went on to penetrate her lungs, vertebrae column, inferior vena cava (the large vessel that carries deoxygenated blood from the lower body back to the heart), and virtually all her viscera. Allison Krause, too, was dead on arrival at Robinson Memorial Hospital.

In the spring of 1969, then a senior at John F. Kennedy High School in Silver Spring, Maryland, Krause had written a cousin's friend who was attending Kent State's prestigious Honors College. By then, Krause had been admitted to the Honors College, but she was having doubts:

"I'm extremely afraid that I'll be classified as a 'brain,' 'egghead,' no fun, studious girl," she wrote. "I'm lucky enough to get good grades but believe me that isn't my only concern. I want to have a good time at school too. Are the kids in the Honor's College alienated from everyone else? I also heard that at some colleges honors students had their own dorms so that the 'atmosphere would be more conducive to learning' (as the saying goes). Please tell me that it isn't like that at Kent!" Later in the letter, Krause asks her cousin's friend about social life at Kent. "Are fraternities and sororities big on campus? Tell me all about it from a student's point of view. I've already heard from the administration's view."

———

William Schroeder, age nineteen, the third fatality, appears to have dropped in on the protests between classes, the way a tourist might stop to view a street show. Two crowd photos show him with books and a notebook cradled in his arm and a look on his face that seems to say, "What's this all about?"

Schroeder had been an Eagle Scout at age thirteen, a varsity basketball player in high school, and captain of his cross country team. He'd started college at the Colorado School of Mines on an Army ROTC scholarship, one of nine hundred high school seniors nationally so recognized. After a year, Schroeder gave up his scholarship and transferred to Kent State to study psychology. Six feet, about 180 pounds, brown hair and blue eyes, firmly built, Schroeder had played on the freshman basketball team that year, back when colleges had such things. At the time of his death, he ranked second in his class in the Army ROTC, whose headquarters had been burned to the ground two nights earlier.

Schroeder was walking away from the crowd when he was shot—the bullet entered his back and exited his front, fracturing ribs 3 through 7 along the way and destroying his thorax. Henry Mankowski was in the Prentice Hall parking lot, hearing bullets "whizzing past my head," when he saw Bill Schroeder get hit.

"The impact of the bullet just picked him up off the ground and thrust him backwards, arms and legs," Mankowski said in a 2010 interview. "I mean, it's burnt into my mind and my memory. . . . I was in total disbelief of what I had witnessed and what had happened. I went over to Schroeder, and by the time I got there, there was a group of people around him. Someone was calling to stand back, to give him room to breathe. [There was] a big bloodstain on his chest, and he was having a hard time breathing."

Unlike Jeff Miller and Allison Krause, Bill Schroeder was still alive when ambulances arrived on the scene. He died either en route to Robinson Memorial Hospital or moments after he got there.

———

Sandra Lee Scheuer hadn't attended the protest rally at all. She was 130 yards away from the Guard's skirmish line, walking between classes, when the volley began. Ellis Berns, who was walking with her, grabbed her in that split second and dove with her to the ground. "I remember I had my arm around her, and she was laying on her stomach face down. I remember calling out to her, 'Sandy, it's over. Let's go. Let's go.' I remember calling out to her, and there was no response. And then I looked. And then I realized that . . . she was hit."

The "hit" was in her neck. The bullet had penetrated Scheuer's jugular vein.

"I remember trying to administer first aid," Berns said. "I remember trying to reach in, to try to stop the bleeding, into her neck. . . . There was just blood all over, and she was totally unconscious."

Like Jeff Miller, Sandy Scheuer "bled out" before any help could arrive, or most likely beyond help of any kind. Unlike Miller, though, or Krause and perhaps Schroeder too, Sandy Scheuer appears not to have had a political bone in her body. She was by all accounts an extremely nice, extremely funny, extremely traditional young woman, even to the clothes she was wearing when she died: "Red long sleeved blouse with four (4) buttons in front," according to the coroner. "The buttons started at the neck and did not go all the way down in front, a wide green, red, and white beaded belt, bell bottom denim pants and closed toe sandals with a buckle across the top."

The Scheuers arrived at Robinson Memorial Hospital from their home in Youngstown, Ohio, forty miles way, at four thirty p.m. that afternoon to identify Sandy's body, according to the local *Record-Courier* newspaper:

"Mr. Scheuer sobbed on the shoulder of a priest. Mrs. Scheuer collapsed into a wheelchair that was provided by the hospital.

"'Dear God, Dear God. She's our daughter,' the father murmured to the priest."

Martin Scheuer would later tell a reporter: "My daughter was a special person who was not involved in any of the demonstrations, yet in the press, she was called a communist. I left Germany to guarantee that my daughters could live in a country with freedom. It doesn't make sense. The pain will always be there."

"Two of the students were killed because of commitment," then Dean of Student Activities Dick Bredemeier would later say. "One was killed because he was nosy, and one because she chose the wrong route to class."

Off campus, the shootings were heralded by the wail of ambulance sirens. Timothy DeFrange, a last-quarter senior education major at Kent State, had just finished his student-teaching day at Field High School in nearby Brimfield when he heard, erroneously, that several National Guardsmen had been shot at the university. DeFrange's brother Mark had been killed in Vietnam the previous year, nineteen days into his first tour of duty. His father, Nick, was dying of complications from pancreatitis in the Intensive Care Unit at Robinson Memorial Hospital. All weekend, DeFrange had been using a critical-patient pass to get through martial-law checkpoints in Kent on his way to the hospital in Ravenna. The shootings, he knew, were going to make the trip even harder.

"As I drove through Kent, I raced to the hospital, hurrying as fast as I could and flashing my critical-patient pass to the guards. . . . When I got there, my mom was already downstairs, and she said, 'He's gone.' And I said, "Well, how did it happen? How did he die?'

"She says, 'You just won't believe. . . . I was upstairs, and all of a sudden there was all this noise and commotion. And then all these young people were wheeled into the ICU, from the shootings. And the doctors and nurses were just crying. And one doctor went over, and he held an x-ray up, and he was holding it, showing it to another doctor, and he said, 'Look where this bullet is lodged. This bullet is lodged in this boy's spine. He's never going to walk again. In all my years in medicine, this is the most senseless thing I've ever seen.'"

———

On campus, the immediate aftermath of the shootings was what might be expected from any unforeseen disaster: disbelief, shock, horror—the gamut of emotions, on all sides.

Many of those out of line of sight of the kneeling Guardsmen assumed the *pop pop pop* they were hearing was a prank. Jim Sprance recalled turning to a friend and saying, "Who were the assholes who just shot off those damn firecrackers?" Even though he could see and hear the Guard line firing, Michael Erwin at first assumed they were blanks. "I was convinced of that until the last second or two of the firing. I saw dust kick up just in front of me to one side—blanks don't do that."

Ralph Spielman also thought the Guardsmen were firing blanks until he looked around the Prentice Hall parking lot after the fusillade and saw that baseball coach Dick Paskert's car had been hit by gunfire: "He had a gold [Oldsmobile] Toronado, a coupe, with the one big window and then a smaller triangular-shaped window behind it. And I remember seeing a bullet hole in one of the triangular windows, and it went straight through to the other."*

Ronald Sterlekar remembered everyone around him hitting the ground when the volley started. "Everybody got up laughing because, of course, there wouldn't be live ammunition. And all of a sudden there was screaming from just the other side of the hilltop. And a fellow graphics students came up, and all of a sudden someone was leaning on my shoulder with both hands. . . . He starts laughing, and I said, 'What's wrong?' And there's kind of a small surge at first of people running by. And he said, 'Ron, I've been hit.' 'What are you talking about?' He said, 'Look.' And I looked down, and he showed me his thigh, and there was blood coming from his thigh, not much, it was like a trickle. And then the surge of people kind of almost knocked us over."

William Derry Heasley, who had served in the navy in Vietnam, recalled seeing three men running toward him just after the shooting. "One . . . was saying, 'Oh, he'll be all right!' The other one [said], 'Are you crazy? Half his head was blown away!' At which point I realized, uh-oh, something had happened here. And I walked back up over the hill, over underneath the Pagoda, and as I rose up over the hill and my point of view encompassed the parking lot, I saw people lying

---

*Among the players Paskert coached during his ten years at Kent State was Thurman Munson, the New York Yankees perennial all-star catcher who was killed in 1979 while practicing takeoffs and landings at the Akron-Canton Regional Airport.

about, and I went to the nearest person. It was Jeffrey Miller, and I saw a large pool of blood, large enough that I knew it was too late. . . . Then I walked away, over to a tree, and sat down and started to cry."

Jeff Miller was also the first person Chuck Ayers saw when he raced out of the *Stater* office to see what all the wailing was about:

"Somebody had turned him over, and there were several people kneeling around him, and there was already this river of blood rolling down. I mean it must have been 12 to 15 feet long at that time. . . . I just remember looking at how utterly limp he was, and they had pulled his shirt up, and how absolutely hollow his stomach looked. Everything had just collapsed on this guy, and I kept saying to myself, No, he's not dead, he's not dead, until I heard an ambulance come up over the hill and started picking up people, and the gurneys went right past him. I thought, Oh, my God, he's dead because they didn't stop to pick him up."

As he wandered through the parking lot after watching Bill Schroeder get shot in the chest, Henry Mankowski first came across the body of Allison Krause—the two had been part of a group of maybe six students who had gone sledding on the front campus that winter. By the time he got to Jeff Miller's corpse, one demonstrator was holding high a black flag dipped in Miller's blood. "He was jumping up and down in the blood. I had to move because by that time the blood had started to coagulate, and instead of splashing, pieces of blood were flying. . . . I just didn't want to get hit by blood."

"After the immediate shots were fired, there was chaos," Arthur Koushel recalled. "There were people lying all over the place. . . . I never really saw a dead person before that day. I never saw people massively bleeding. Some people would just look at people and pass out. So you weren't sure who was actually shot and who had just fainted."

As horrible as the scene was, relief was also part of the mixture, too, as it always is. Diane Yale-Peabody, who sat out the protest in her class on the modern short story, was looking out her dormitory window afterward when she spotted her fiancé running down the sidewalk: "When I saw him, I ran down the steps out to him, and when he saw me, he fell down on the grass and started crying because he thought that I had been out there and that I might have gotten hurt."

That feeling seems to have been common: huge sorrow for those shot, huge relief for those spared. How could it not have been so? "May 4 is like Passover for me," Janice Marie Wascko told an interviewer in 1990, "because everyone I loved survived."

Even today, going on half a century later, many of those on the back side of Blanket Hill or in the Prentice Hall parking lot when the Guards opened fire marvel that they were not among the wounded or dead. One of the most active protestors was standing slightly southwest of Jeff Miller and Alan Canfora, just far enough downhill from them that he dropped below the Guardsmen's line of sight, while Miller and Canfora filled the horizon above him. Otherwise, he said, his distinctive clothing would had made him an easy target to pick out: an army jacket worn by his brother, who was killed in Vietnam, a bright kerchief, and a brown hat his brother had taken off a dead Viet Cong soldier.

"Everything seemed bigger in 2010 when I went back and looked at the space," Jerry Casale said. "I just lucked out. The crowd I was with was maybe thirty yards away [from the skirmish line]. If the Guard had wanted to shoot into our crowd, they could have picked off anyone they wanted to."

———

Until the moment of the shooting, an implicit social contract had prevailed at Kent State. White, middle-class Americans could scream and shout at each other; they could give each other the finger and throw tear-gas canisters back and forth, and shout "Fuck!" as loud as they wanted to. They could even chase each other with bayonets and helicopters, throw bricks and cement and bags full of shit, but as bitter and divisive as the times were, they didn't shoot each other, and especially didn't shoot each other dead. The sixty-seven shots fired across thirteen seconds at 12:24 p.m. on May 4, 1970, changed that bargain, and Guardsmen seemed as surprised as students that whatever unspoken truce existed had fallen apart for good.*

"I remember the Guard . . . were as shocked as I was," Carol Mirman said. "I remember the looks on their faces. They didn't know what to do, and they didn't know what to say."

"Hundreds of people were falling on the ground, and I believed many were being hit," Guardsman Rudy Morris told an interviewer for the 2001 documentary *Kent State: The Day the War Came Home*. As he marched back to the staging area, Morris said, "We had no idea as to how many people had been hurt. Our fear was that it was awful."

In a February 1975 deposition, another Guardsman recalled one of his fellow soldiers who, after the shooting, "broke up and was on the ground."

Do you remember what he said "while he was broke up?" the lawyer asked.

"No, other than 'Oh, God.'"

Bill Barrett, then the university's alumni publications editor, was standing at the corner of Johnson Hall when the Guard came over the hill, heading back to its original staging area near the burned-out ruins of the ROTC building. "The closest Guardsman was . . . about five yards from me, maybe, and through their gas masks, you could just see the looks of horror on the faces of these guys coming down. . . . And I thought God, thank God, I'm not out there. Those guys are so scared anything else could happen."

Within minutes of the shootings, art teacher Brinsley Tyrrell came across a Vietnam veteran student dressing down the Guardsmen—a

---

*Black Americans had a different history. At Kent State, they avoided the weekend demonstrations like the plague.

"big, hulking guy, crew cut, screaming at the Guard, calling them toy soldiers, calling them a disgrace to their uniform." At about the same time, William Derry Heasley, also a veteran-student, watched an encounter between a Guardsman and "a very tall bear of a student—a bear, I mean, he was six foot, plump, carrying a briefcase, true egghead, with a beard and hair that was long enough to fall over his collar. . . . He approached the soldier as they were marching back [to the ROTC staging ground], saying 'Can I talk to you?'" The soldier, Heasley said, "turned around and rammed the butt of his gun into this guy's jaw, with force, and went on his way."

One of the Guardsmen who had been at the Pagoda but had not fired remembered the silence immediately after the shooting. "It got totally quiet. I heard air hissing out of a tire, that sound, the air hissing, and then there were some screams." He and the other Guardsmen who hadn't used their weapons were quickly ordered to about-face and form up, and then marched off the hill, down to a road near where some of the victims laid, heading by a somewhat circuitous route to the Guard staging area.

"We were a small group, thirty or forty," he remembered. "And . . . there was a group of students standing in the road, and I figured, 'Boy, here it comes.' And the sergeant said, 'Keep moving. Do not, I say, do *not* move your weapons again.' And like the Red Sea, they parted. We went through and went back down to the bivouac."

"Those Guardsmen came down, and they moved right past us," Jim Vacarella remembered. "We were within ten feet. I could have touched one of them. They walked right past us. . . . Everyone was frozen. . . . Then the ambulances started. That was the first noise anybody heard—the ambulances."

6

Once to Every Man and Nation

Half an hour after he had first marched his men out of the burned-out ROTC grounds, General Canterbury found himself back where he'd begun—with a quickly re-formed National Guard contingent, facing a crowd of students across the Commons—but the situation had changed dramatically. The noon crowd he had sought to disperse had had a radical core of maybe fifty students at most, supplemented by many hundreds of the curious, the mildly offended, students, and faculty members passing to classes or lunch and drawn into the spectacle forming before them. Whatever innocence had existed then, whatever naïveté had prevailed, was gone now. The earlier staccato of gunfire and now the wail of sirens had moved Kent State onto a different plane of existence, and everyone seemed to be making up the response as they went along.

"You have to remember, most of the crowd had remained on the Commons," said art teacher Brinsley Tyrrell. "They couldn't see what happened. They saw the aftermath instead. They saw the Guardsmen coming down the hill, terrified. . . . Incoherent people were coming down the hillside and starting to mix with the crowd, some weeping, some just furious."

"People who were not radical, who were not militant, became very militant in seconds," Arthur Koushel recalled. "I thought at one point the people were going to charge that military line and actually engage in hand-to-hand-type combat."

"You have to imagine what everybody felt," freshman Eldon Fender told an interviewer in 2007. "The National Guard had just shot and killed students. You have a feeling of anger because you feel like your campus had been invaded. You're being violated. And I'm sure all the students that congregated at that point felt the same way."

Almost four decades later, Fender still remembered vividly a Guard jeep "with a .50 caliber machine gun mounted on the back and clipped, ready to go."

"You felt like you were invincible," Rob Fox remembered, "because you were so angry [about] what happened."

Another protester who requested anonymity for his 2010 interview said: "I think the feeling was . . . they killed four of us. What the hell, might as well make it a couple hundred."

Of particular note was a group of perhaps twenty students, stripped to the waist, with large Xs now painted on their chests and backs and across their foreheads. Film footage shows them massed on the hill, across the commons from the Guard—a tight cluster for shooters, with kill spots highlighted. Rage all but pulsates out from them.

"They were going to go down and battle the Guardsmen, and whoever died was going to die," Jim Vacarella said. "Everybody was gone. It was Freakville! There wasn't any rational thought now."

Rational or not, angry, feeling invincible, whatever its collective state of mind, the crowd including onlookers numbered probably in the thousands and was still in violation of the Ohio Riot Act, as General Canterbury understood the act he had been seeking to enforce. To that end, he notified faculty marshals that students had fifteen minutes to disperse. At just about the same time, he sent word via his commanders that the Guardsmen were to defend themselves by all possible means.

"There was a point in time when General Canterbury came up, and I don't recall the exact words but pretty much it was to the effect that if we had a huge assault on our position, [we were] to fire," Ronald Snyder remembered. "I went down the line, checked every trooper's gun, made sure it was on safe because I didn't want any accidents to happen. . . . I just didn't want anything further to go on that wasn't necessary."

The math here gets truly appalling. If only the conveniently self-targeted students, stripped to the waist, had charged the Guard line, they would have been mowed down long before they reached the halfway point across the Commons. Gas masks were off. Sighting would have been easy and motivation strong. Had that first wave been followed by a second or third wave of students, sucked into the vortex of irrationality by the killing in front of them, the dead and wounded would, of course, had grown exponentially. The Guard had that .50-caliber machine gun, mounted and ready on a jeep. Even without new magazines for the Guardsmen who had emptied theirs on the other side of Blanket Hill, 70 or more M1s stood ready with 8 rounds to the magazines—560 of those long, skinny .30–06 projectiles leaving muzzles with 2,500 foot-pounds of energy, each one squeeze away from firing. Any students who survived that barrage were sure to be met by fixed bayonets as they descended on Guard lines.

Why none of that happened is largely the work of four people: Major Don Manley of the highway patrol, who against great resistance finally convinced General Canterbury to give faculty marshals additional time to talk students into dispersing, and three faculty marshals who were stationed near the Victory Bell when students began wandering back from the other side of Blanket Hill: graduate history student Steven Sharoff, psychology professor Sy Baron, and geology professor Glenn Frank.

"I was telling the students to sit down," Sharoff recalled, "when somebody came over to me from the National Guard and said, 'General Canterbury wants to speak to you,' and I said, 'Who's General Canterbury?' He said, 'He's the commander of the National Guard here,' so I went over and talked with him. He said basically you need to move these students out of here because this is an illegal gathering. And I said, 'You can't be serious. These students just watched their friends being killed.' He said, 'I am serious. You have to tell them they need to leave. They don't have a choice, and I don't have a choice either.' . . . I remember him saying to me very directly, 'These are my orders.' As an historian, it reminded me of Nazi Germany: These are my orders. This is what I have to do. So I went back and said, 'Everyone needs to sit down.' And that's when Glenn Frank said everything he said."

———

In a sea of longhairs, grungy fatigue jackets, and bell-bottoms, Glenn Frank stands out like an artifact of the distant past: flattop, white shirt, striped tie held in place with a clasp, clear-framed glasses, a square face atop a solid build. He had been born in 1928 in Mayfield Heights, Ohio; joined the US Marines at eighteen, just after the end of World War II; and more than twenty years later still looked like a Marine in mufti. By 1970, he had been a virtual lifer at Kent State. He had taken his undergraduate degree there in 1951, become an instructor in the geology department two years later, and rose through the ranks to full professor (in 1969) while earning his doctorate at Western Reserve University in nearby Cleveland.

Glenn Frank's hands-on introductory geology courses were highly popular with students. Locally, he was also well known for his community service. Fellow Franklin Township trustees liked to tell about the time Frank manned the bulldozer for a township road worker who had fallen ill and did the grading work himself. Love of his students, love of school, love of country, a sense of duty, a roll-up-your-sleeves approach to crisis—in all, it seems to have been exactly the package that was called for on the early afternoon of May 4, 1970, at Kent State University, but even then, it very nearly was not enough, and maybe too much for Glenn Frank himself.

In the collective memory of those present, Frank seems to have been almost everywhere: shuttling back and forth between the Guard and the students, pleading for more time on the one hand and more cooperation on the other. To calm the students, he and others began offering popsicles; they talked of bringing out lunch platters—whatever might work.

"I realize now this man was blithering to save our lives," Janice Marie Wascko said in 1990, "but at one point he said something about, 'Well, it's a beautiful day. Sit down in the sunshine; we'll get some sandwiches and things.' And I lost it. I just came unhinged, and I jumped up and started screaming, 'What is this, a fucking picnic?'"

That it wasn't a picnic, or anything like one, became obvious a few minutes later when the Guard began moving out toward the crowd of students. That's when Glenn Frank rose to the moment never forgotten by those who were there.

"I don't care whether you've never listened to anyone before in your life," he pleaded. "I am begging you right now. If you don't disperse right now, they are going to move in, and it can only be a slaughter."

As he spoke those words, film footage shows Guardsmen slipping into position behind the protestors. To their front now, a phalanx of Guardsmen, M1 at the ready; to their rear, a thinner row of armed Guardsmen, also armed with M1s and holding the high ground behind them. Frank seems to take in this new positioning as he talks.

"Would you please listen to me! Jesus Christ! I don't want to be a part of this!"

By then, anguish was in his voice, even tears. The tears are what finally awoke Diane Yale-Peabody to the gravity of what had taken place and what might lie ahead.

Frank, she said, was "one of the faculty marshals that really cared about the students, and he came along with a loudspeaker, crying and saying, 'Please, get off the hill. Please go back to your dorms. Please go back to your classes.' He said, 'People have been hurt, and we don't want anyone else hurt. Please go away.' And when I saw Glenn Frank crying, I knew that something awful had happened."

"We were really pissed," Jim Vacarella said, "but didn't know what to do with that anger. We didn't have anything, anywhere to put that anger. . . . Dr. Frank convinced us to get up and leave. There's no question that he did that. . . . He definitely saved our lives."

Among the lives Glenn Frank might well have saved on the early afternoon of May 4, 1970, was that of his own son, freshman Alan Frank. As with so many others who were on and around Blanket Hill that day, Alan Frank found himself completely swept up in the emotions of the moment; unlike many others, though, he washed in from a far shore. Frank was, by his own definition, a "jock," a freshman swimmer; he saw his job on May 4 as making sure the lefties and radicals didn't get out of hand.

"I was in the Student Center, just finishing up lunch," he recalled, "when—and this where my head was at the time—I said to a friend, 'Let's go beat up some hippies,' in a joking way. We went up on the hill and just watched. It was kind of like a circus. As the Guard came back up the hill from the practice field, we were walking maybe fifty, seventy-five feet in front of them, and I said to my friend, 'Shouldn't we be walking a little faster?' He said, 'Why, what are they going to do? Shoot?' And I thought, 'How could I even think of anything so stupid?' and within fifteen or twenty seconds, they pivoted, turned around, and started shooting."

Even then, Frank said, it still seemed a lark. He and his friend took off running and jumped through an open window into a dorm bathroom, sure that while the firing was real, the cartridges were blanks. They were still laughing over their scare when "this one kid came up, and he said, 'They killed them! They killed them!' And my reality [changed] immediately. I looked down into the parking lot, and I was just dumbfounded.

"It wasn't an angry group of students until they shot. The great majority of us were just watching, something to do on a sunny day. Afterwards, people got together who normally wouldn't have done so. We all sat down on the ground and basically said to the Guard, 'If you're going to shoot somebody else, shoot me.' I was in that crowd, and I wasn't going to listen to my dad either."

Eventually, though, the crowd did listen to Glenn Frank, convinced (many said) by his tears. Alan Frank remembered events slightly differently. "It wasn't until the very end when he got all this shit out that he started to cry. I thought someone had thrown a rock and he'd gotten hit because he stumbled and fell down."

Frank doubted his father could see him in the crowd, but once Glenn Frank fell, Alan was by his side. "I helped him get up. We walked over to the tennis courts together. I think he was still weeping. There were probably a thousand people who were ready to just stay there, and how many of those bullets would have gone through three or four people?"

None of this heroism, however, came without an apparent cost. In a March 1980 response to an Ohio eighth grader seeking background information for a middle-school social studies panel on the events of May 4, Glenn Frank wrote: "You ask that I relate my feelings and understanding of that weekend. I have trouble describing them. I felt the anger of the shop keepers who had their life's work partially destroyed by a mob who lashed out at a distant but 'decadent' government. I felt the horror of an escalating war in Vietnam and that my son might be called. I felt the frustration of the police in trying unsuccessfully to cope with the mob. . . . I felt the need to maintain a semblance of order in a chaotic situation. I felt the anguish and hopelessness of moving a group of 'students' who would not move after the shootings, and I broke down and wept when they did move." Earlier in the letter, he had explained: "I am sad that I was even remotely involved in this tragedy since my mental and physical well-being has certainly been affected."

In fact, Alan said, his father was pained afterwards on several fronts. A fellow faculty member had told him that his actions that afternoon had landed him on two assassination lists, one radical, the other conservative. "He didn't know what to do with that," Alan

Frank said, "but late one night a couple years later, this van pulled up in front of their house with its lights off. He saw them shining a light on the mailbox, and he thought, this is it."

The university, too, seemed to shift under Glenn Frank in the years after his May 4 heroism. A retirement contract, Alan said, was not fully honored. "He bled blue-and-gold for the university. He went to football games, to basketball games. I think that really helped kill him." Whatever the causes, whatever the reality, Glenn Frank died of kidney cancer in 1983, at age sixty-five, thirteen years after he had helped save so many lives. His wife died of the same cancer two years later.

In the stoic way of so many similar families, father and son never talked about those twenty minutes or so on the Commons when so much hung in the balance, but like his father, Alan Frank had trouble letting go of the moment, too.

"For the first ten years afterwards, I couldn't talk about it without crying. I'd be on vacation, and someone would ask me about it, and I'd start . . . but I just couldn't do it."

———

One immediate problem remained after Glenn Frank and others brokered a tenuous peace between Guard leaders and student protesters: students who had been ordered to disperse and at last seemed willing to do so were completely penned in.

"They wanted everybody to leave," Denny Benedict recalled, "but the troops had basically surrounded the Commons. . . . They didn't leave an exit. And [Glenn Frank] finally goes, 'There's no way out.' And they realized their mistake and opened up some areas. Then slowly, one by one, people started to leave. It was over. There was just nothing you could do."

Slightly more than an hour after the shootings, the Commons and the hills around it were finally clear, but the campus was anything but calm.

Bruce Dzeda spent Monday morning student teaching at Shaw High School in East Cleveland. That afternoon he was to attend an extended afternoon class for student teachers on the Kent campus. He was just leaving Cleveland when he heard on the radio that two students and two Guardsmen had been shot dead. By the time he arrived in Kent, after negotiating a number of hastily set up roadblocks, the radio was reporting that the shootings had taken place near Taylor Hall.

"So I parked my car, I don't remember where, and there were students everywhere. Students were walking around as if they were ducks that had been struck on the head by a board. They were just stunned. Nobody knew where to go. . . . I don't remember it being chaotic, but I remember [it] being very confused and very upsetting."

The drama, though, was far from over. The afternoon of May 4, Stephen Titchenal told an interviewer in 2010, "was actually almost more scary than the morning."

Part of the issue inevitably was simple shock. Students had died; blood had flowed freely, in plain view of hundreds. "You hear a distinctive wailing and screaming. You turn around and see people down, and it's the old heart, stomach, shit-in-the-pants," Jerry Casale remembered. "I felt like I was going to pass out. I was so undone, I couldn't stand up."

Rage shaped events as well, and not only back on the Commons. Ellis Berns, who had been lying on the ground with Sandy Scheuer when she bled out, had been walking around campus "almost in a state of shock," he said, when he encountered a cluster of Guardsmen with rifles at the ready. "There was a roadway into campus, into the whole area where the [Victory] Bell and Blanket Hill [are], and it was all completely blocked off. . . . The Guard was not letting anybody in, and they were pointing guns. I remember I ripped off this green fatigue jacket with Sandra's blood, and I threw it at this Guardsman. And I told him to go fuck himself. I was just livid. I didn't know what to do. I could have been killed right there if you think about it."

Paranoia—or maybe just reasonable caution—was in the air as well. The unthinkable had happened. Maybe it would happen again. In the *Kent Stater* newspaper office, Chuck Ayers and his fellow student journalists were preparing for the worst.

"I remember saying, 'If [the Guard] comes back up, people are going to run in the building. If somebody has done something or a Guardsman is angry enough, is chasing an individual—they've already killed people. What's to say they're not going to come in the building and start shooting?' And we started looking around, trying to decide what to do. But we're standing in the *Stater* office with floor-to-ceiling windows, and we said, 'This is not the place to be.' And the *Burr* office, which was then the yearbook, was right next door. So we walked into there, and I remember going into the darkroom, and I said, 'This is a good spot.' I laugh at it now, but I remember saying to people, 'If they shoot us here, they have to shoot through two cinderblock walls to get us.' That's where I was at that moment."

Janice Marie Wascko, who had earlier screamed "What is this, a fucking picnic?" at Glenn Frank, was walking with a friend near the Student Center, when she felt a sudden need to leave the campus as quickly as possible. "We had to get out of there," she said, "because for all we knew they were going to kill us all just to silence the witnesses." Even leaving the campus, though, was fraught with peril. "[We] were walking behind [some Guardsmen]. . . . I was so scared they would wheel around. I was so scared. I didn't want them to hear us. I was so afraid my shoe would creak or something."

That feeling was widespread. Jeanne Anderson was heading across campus to her apartment building when she saw a Guardsman with a gun. "And I really was afraid he'd shoot me. . . . It wasn't intellectual. It was just the fear that for no reason I could be dead, too."

As part of his initiation rites for one of Kent State's African American fraternities, Bill Forrester was supposed to be carrying a brick everywhere he went. That stricture at least had been lifted once the Guard took over the university, but Forrester was still sporting a required shaved head and a dog collar when the order came to clear the campus.

"I wasn't running," he recalled, "but I was walking really fast. I'm a black guy. I've got a bald head and a dog-collar around my neck. I'm thinking, if I run, someone's going to shoot me."

Ken Hammond and his then-wife Marilyn Davis had split up during the protest—part of a previous agreement not to imperil each other in dangerous situations. After the shootings, they found each other in short order and hotfooted it off campus before the university was even closed.

"We decided that the cops or the Guard might come back. I had just stood up on the Victory Bell and called for a strike. I was the only person who had spoken that day, so I thought, holy shit, they might be coming after me. . . . They'd shot these people. There was blood everywhere, screaming. I didn't think they were going to take me out and just shoot me down, but you get taken into custody in these kinds of circumstances, who knows what can happen? I just thought it would be best not to place myself into the hands of the state at that point."

Ellen Mann, the high school student who was beside Joe Lewis when he was shot, was recovering from surgery on her left leg, the result of childhood polio. "I was really limping bad," she recalled, "and I was just kind of dragging myself back up to the school. And the Guardsmen, the looks on their faces, they were smirking. They were kind of laughing. And I shouted at them, 'What are you laughing at? You just killed people!' And then another, I think he was an officer because he had the trappings of an officer on, he said, 'Just move along, ma'am.' So I looked at him, and I started moving along."

Jim Vacarella was wandering around the campus when "this big guy came out, big jock, and said, 'It should have been you, hippie! You should have died!' And I looked at this guy and the guy I was with, and I said, 'I can't take any more trauma today. I'm leaving. I'm going home.' . . . And we left."

Everyone—students and Guardsmen—was still on edge several hours later when *Life* reporter John Pekkanen and a photographer showed up in Kent, after scrambling from the magazine's Chicago bureau.

"We went into the campus, trying to get somewhere, and a National Guardsman was there," Pekkanen recalled. "He said, 'You can't go there.' I began to gently argue with him, and Christ Almighty, I thought he was going to shoot me. He didn't aim his rifle at me, but he held it, and he had a look in his eye that said, 'I'm not far away from doing something really bad.'"

The campus by then, Pekkanen said, "felt desolate."

———

The decision to shut down the university, by multiple authorities, only added to the postshooting confusion on the Kent State campus. Immediately after Robinson Memorial Hospital confirmed that four students had died, university president Robert White ordered the school closed but met resistance from several fronts, including members of his student affairs staff, who were still chasing down rumors of random gunfire and sniper shooting. Indeed, the *Record-Courier* newspaper of May 4 would carry a front-page report of a search "for a female sniper who is said to have started the shooting at Kent." There was also the matter of consistency: Guard jeeps had been telling students to get in their dormitories and stay there; closing the school and clearing out the dorms would have just the opposite effect. And there was the practical problem of clearing a campus of twenty-one thousand students living on the edge of a city under martial law, surrounded by other cities, towns, and villages that were themselves on edge about how far the violence would reach.

Albert Van Kirk, who had medic training in Vietnam and had administered first aid to some of his wounded fellow students, stopped on his way out of town at a gas station so he could wash the blood off his hands and arms. By the time he got home to Ravenna, seven miles from Kent, "guys were walking down the street with guns; guys were sitting on top of buildings with guns. [The students] were not going to come to Ravenna and burn it down."

Buses were requisitioned to carry students to transportation hubs in Cleveland, Akron, and elsewhere in Ohio, but for students who needed to make other plans, communication in that precellular time soon became entirely hit or miss. Switchboards were basically paralyzed with outgoing and incoming calls.

As had been the case the entire long weekend, who was in charge of closing the school was an open question. Several hours after President White shut down the campus, the Portage County Court of Common Pleas issued an injunction not only closing KSU but suspending its operations and banning all staff from entering the grounds. Enforcement once again was left to the Guard.

Robert White would later tell the Scranton Commission that "for a few hours there, the only reason I could come on campus was because the National Guard would permit it since they were in charge of the situation." Not until Friday, May 8, could the university get the injunction sufficiently modified even to hold an on-campus board meeting. The injunction itself wouldn't be lifted until June 19, just in time for summer school.

Meanwhile, students had to make do as best they could, with no knowledge of when they might be allowed back into their dorm rooms, no idea when or even if classes would resume, and no staff left on campus to provide basic services. Arthur Koushel and his roommates and several friends ended up taking over the kitchen at the Beall-McDowell dorm complex and cooking an early dinner for something like 1,200 people. "We were cooks, not cleaners," he explained. "We cooked for everybody, but we left it pretty messed up."

Kathy Bye's parents lived in Miami—Florida, not Ohio. Like a lot of students who couldn't easily get home, she had to make up a plan on the fly. "We got what clothes we thought we might need, but we had no idea how long we would be gone. I really just hung out with other people until I could get back to my room"—more than a month later, as things turned out.

For Naomi Goelman Etzkin's parents, roadblocks, checkpoints, and heavy traffic turned the forty-mile trip from Cleveland to Kent into a four-hour ordeal. In Streetsboro, seven miles north of Kent, shop owners were covering windows with large sheets of plywood as they drove through. Etzkin was the only resident left in her dorm, Olson Hall, when she wandered into the cafeteria, still open because Guardsmen were using it as a mess hall.

"I sat down at dinner," she remembered, "and a couple of them came and joined me. . . . The guys that I had dinner with were people my age who went into the National Guard so they didn't have to go to Vietnam, and they felt a deep sense of horror over what happened."

A new balance of power, though, had clearly been established—between protestors, the Guard, and local police—and students were on the short end of it. After his star turn as a cafeteria chef, Arthur Koushel was one block off Main Street, headed to Chicago with five friends, when his car ran out of gas. By then, the eight p.m. curfew had been moved up to five p.m.

"I saw two soldiers that I'd met the night before. . . . And I tried to talk them into taking their gas can and giving me gas to get out of town. But they would look forward as if I wasn't there. They just wouldn't move." Finally, he said, he went out into the middle of Main Street to try to flag down a police car. "They had their windows taped. They were riding five to a car, and they had shotguns sticking out of the windows. It was the first time I ever had a gun pointed at me directly. And he put that shotgun right in my face, and I took my hand and I actually pushed the gun away because I didn't want this guy to burp. . . . I explained to him that we were leaving town but that we had run out of gas. And his answer to me was, 'Find a fucking place to sleep, and get off the street.'"

Janice Marie Wascko was sitting with her roommates on the front lawn of their house in downtown Kent that evening when a patrolling police cruiser noticed antiwar slogans chalked on the sidewalk and a low retaining wall. The cruiser, she said, had no license plates. Badge numbers were taped over. "They had a sawed-off shotgun and pulled it on us. And they got out of the cruiser and stood there, pulled the guns on us, and said, 'Wipe it up, scum,' and made us get down on our hands and knees and wipe it off, the slogans off the wall and the sidewalk. [They were] saying, 'We should have killed you all,' and laughing at us. A short time later . . . they caught somebody down by what is Pufferbelly's [restaurant] now and beat the crap out of him against a wall."

Chuck Ayers had to flash his *Akron Beacon Journal* press pass to get through a Guard checkpoint on the way to his part-time job. "They have their helmets on," he remembered, "but they've pulled the gas masks down so they're hanging around their throats. And they've got a look on their face like they're angry and scared at the same time. I just didn't want to do anything to provoke them. . . . I drove through real slow."

Out on the road, on the short drive to Akron, he was listening to news reports about the shootings on the radio.

"They said, 'Okay, we'll be right back after some music, and we'll tell you some more about what's going on on the campus at Kent State.' And it was that song 'Everything Is Beautiful' by Ray Stevens. I'd just come off campus with everything that I had seen. I saw a dead student in the street. I saw other people being carted away into ambulances. I saw the blood and the gore, and I'm sitting in the car hearing this song: 'Everything is beautiful in its own way,' and I thought, God, what a joke."

7

"Oh, My God!
They've Killed the Guardsmen!"

More than the phones got scrambled on May 4. Facts went askew. Information went sliding down the wrong neural pathways. Something momentous had happened on the Kent State campus, but for what seemed a news-cycle eternity, even many people close to the action weren't sure exactly what it was—or they were certain of the wrong things.

A little after midday, Rosann Rissland, her almost two-year-old son, and maybe a dozen other children and mothers were in the backyard of her neighbor's house in Kent. Next door a roofer was listening to his radio as he worked. Suddenly, he shouted down to the crowd below, "Oh, my God! My God! They've killed the Guardsmen." By then, all the adults knew who "they" must be. "Everyone's being told to stay in their houses," the roofer went on. "No one's allowed to be on the street at all."

Rissland and her son went home as instructed, but she soon found herself worried about a friend two blocks away who was nine-months pregnant with twins. The phone lines were already hopeless. The woman wouldn't be able to dial 911 if she needed help, and her husband was on the journalism faculty at the school, Ground Zero of whatever had occurred.

"I was terrified," Rissland remembered. "I took my son by the hand, and we walked the two blocks to her house. . . . There weren't any police or any Guardsmen going up and down the streets in my area, but the fear was so great, and the sense that things had gotten so totally out of hand and that the students would come over the rise and attack."

Faculty wife Lillian Tyrrell was heading across campus hand in hand with her three-year-old son to look in on the protest demonstration on the Commons when she heard what sounded like a long string of firecrackers exploding. Instantly afterward, a student standing nearby told her, "I'm a Vietnam veteran, and that's *real* gunfire. Get the hell out of here!"

"I just ran with the rest of the crowd, got out of there, got a bus home," Tyrrell recalled. She and her son were walking up their street when one of her neighbors came toward her, screaming. "As she came by, I grabbed her, and I said, 'What's wrong?' And she said, 'I've got to get to [my children's] school. They're killing the Guardsmen!' And I—at that point, I didn't know who had died—and I just . . . dug my hand into her and said, 'Do be reasonable. Stop and think about this for a minute. I don't think any Guardsmen are killed. If anyone's killed, it's students.' . . . [But she just said] 'I've got to get up to the school to save my children from the students.'"

Not long after Tyrrell and her son got home, her daughter arrived from kindergarten. "She rushed in the door, and she was totally traumatized. She said, 'Mommy, is there a war?' And I said, 'No, darling, there is not a war. Come and talk to me about it.' And she said, 'Suddenly, we were all rushed into the buses and made to lie on the floor of the buses so that no one would hurt us. And the soldiers were shouting all the time, screaming 'Stay down! Stay down!'"

Mary Homer, then thirteen years old, was a student at Davey Junior High in Kent. "I remember being told that there were shootings on campus. And a fellow student started screaming as her mom and dad were on campus. School was closed immediately, and we were herded on buses. A very large man with a baseball bat came on board our bus to protect us. . . . I believe the general feeling of all our neighbors and relatives was that we were all in imminent danger."

Kent resident John Whyde, father of a small son and with a pregnant wife, was teaching at the Crestwood Schools in Mantua, fourteen miles northeast of Kent, when he heard that people had been killed at the university.

"We of course turned on the news and were listening to the local station, and found out that the city was supposedly sealed off, and I realized that I needed to get home to my family. I remember that I went to the principal and asked him for a note that would get me into the city if it were really sealed off. . . . They did inspect my car, looked in the backseat, and I did need to present the note to get back into the city. I had to promise that I wouldn't go near the university. I lived in the very west corner of Kent. I actually lived the first street inside of Kent from the road I was on. So I promised that I would go straight home and not go anywhere else. It was scary at the time—to have to have a note to get to your own house."

A daughter of a Kent police officer who had received several anonymous threats over the weekend was at her home, a dozen miles outside of Kent, when she first learned of the shootings.

"The first report that came over the radio was that police officers had been killed, and I immediately thought of my dad. I tried to call Kent, and all the lines were locked, and I couldn't get through to my husband. I couldn't get through to my parents. I had no idea if my dad had been one of the people who was killed. It was an extremely difficult time, and there was no place I could go, nothing I could do other than wait it out."

That afternoon, she said, her husband walked through the door with a rifle and ammunition. "We had never had a gun in the house before." Her father, who lived in Kent proper, slept for several days with a rifle across his stomach. It was "very hard to understand how this could be happening in the community that you grew up in, that you knew to be a peaceful and reasonable and a caring community—how people from the outside could come in and . . . corral so many people to destroy what you valued."

Meanwhile, too, the rumors that had been flying all weekend—a secret stash of semi-automatics hidden by students somewhere at Brady Lake, just outside town; the Kent water supply spiked with LSD—continued to multiply, now with the added urgency of the shootings and the quickly spreading assumption that the gunfire had flowed both ways or maybe only from the students toward the Guard and the police. Instead of coming over the rise, one such rumor had KSU student shock troops advancing on Clarkson's "superstore" on the south end of town via a series of underground tunnels.

"The radio kept talking about a Fifth Column of students going through the sewers to blow Clarkson's up," Brinsley Tyrrell remembered. "There weren't any sewers that went out there, but it shows how paranoid things had become that people broadcasted this stuff and believed it."

———

At the Brown Derby restaurant, where President Robert White and his top lieutenants were laying plans to resume normal operations at the university, word of the shootings arrived almost as a series of vagaries, at least as White described the session to the Scranton Commission.

"I was in a luncheon session with Messrs. Beer, Matson, Dunn, Roskens to discuss . . . ways in which we could move toward normal operations as quickly as possible . . . and I'd already resolved upon calling a faculty meeting that afternoon. As soon as this was over, I was going to visit the Vice President and Provost and work out the details of that faculty session when our luncheon was interrupted by the telephone message to Dr. Beer that there had been stories that there had been a shooting."

"There had been stories that there had been a shooting"—how elliptical can language get, especially when the events being described were so close at hand? A half mile—the rough distance from the campus to the restaurant—was still within the kill range of the M1 Garands that Guardsmen had been firing. But, in fact, the administration's eyes and ears on and near Blanket Hill were severely limited.

According to faculty member Jerry Lewis, the highest-ranking university official left on campus once the lunch party had departed was "the head of the conduct code, a fourth-level administrator." Meanwhile, the communications center created to deal with the ongoing crisis was in the hands of Ray Bye, the graduate student assistant to President White, and while Bye was in fitful contact with monitors near the action, he couldn't see a thing.

"The center was on the second floor of the main administration building," Bye recalled. "It was a windowless office that had a big conference table. . . . I think I was the only person there when the shooting began. I could hear on the walkie-talkie crackling conversation going back and forth between people, comments being made. I was taking notes as best I could, but I didn't have a window. All I had was this walkie-talkie that was being used infrequently, and you didn't know who was talking either, by the way.

"Then I hear this report coming in: 'Students have been shot! Students have been shot!' 'Several students have been shot on the hill or on the Commons.' I can hear all this screaming in the background, and so I picked up the phone and called the Brown Derby. I didn't ask for the president. I asked for Ron Beer, and I said, 'Ron, I just heard a report that several students have been shot. You need to get back to campus.'"

———

Even virtually on top of the action, with an unobstructed view, the story kept getting muddled, or heard in different ways. Laura Dressler was sitting in the student union, lunching with friends and looking out on the Commons and the Victory Bell, when she first learned that blood had been shed. "We were all just eating lunch and talking and visiting, and somebody rushed in and said, 'They've shot the pigs! They've shot the pigs! They've shot the pigs!' And it was so dramatic that everybody stood up and started running out of the room to see what had happened outside."

Bill Forrester was in the student union as well. "You could hear the commotion, the roar of the crowd. Then all of a sudden you could hear this *dat-dat-dat-dat*, this shooting, and I'm thinking, *What in the world is going on now? They've already burned down the ROTC building*. Then this hippie-like kid runs in and says, 'They're killing them! They're killing them!' And I'm going, 'What's wrong with you, you jackass?' And he goes, 'They're effing killing them!' And I said, 'Where?' And he said, 'On Blanket Hill.' I mean the guy was white as a sheet, his hair is all messed up, and he's doing all this screaming and carrying on. It was just pandemonium."

Jim Sprance had watched the Guard move out at noon from its staging area at the ROTC ruins. He had seen Guardsmen go up and over Blanket Hill, heard the shots fired (which he thought were fire-crackers), and watched the ambulances race toward the sound of those shots (at which point he realized the firecrackers were live am-munition). Eventually he learned from Guardsmen and his own peers that students had been shot, but he didn't learn that any students had been killed until hours later, when he was listening to his car radio on the way out of town.

Martha Dishman and a friend were late for the rally. As they walked over to join it, they met students running toward them, shouting, "Go back!" "Go back!" So they turned around and headed for their dorm instead—Metcalf Hall, the Honors College that included Allison Krause. "We went to the lounge, and on the radio—campus radio—they were announcing that a National Guardsman had been shot."

At one o'clock that afternoon, Mike Williams was at one of the epicenters of news gathering for that part of Ohio, working his part-time job at the *Akron Beacon Journal*, getting ready to pack up for his

Burned-out ruins of ROTC building, Sunday, May 3. (May 4 Collection)

Ohio Governor James Rhodes, at front, inspecting ROTC ruins. (© Howard Ruffner)

Students and National Guard gather.
(TOP: © HOWARD RUFFNER;
BOTTOM: MAY 4 COLLECTION)

Noon, Monday, May 4, eyeing the National Guard across the Commons. Jeffrey Miller is at center, in western shirt, with hands on hips. (© HOWARD RUFFNER)

Guardsmen with M1s and bayonets mounted. (May 4 Collection)

National Guardsmen begin advancing on students. Taylor Hall is in the background, at the top of Blanket Hill. (May 4 Collection)

Guardsmen kneeling and aiming on the practice field. Alan Canfora is in the foreground. (© Howard Ruffner)

Students heading toward the Prentice Hall parking lot before the shooting. (Chuck Ayers/May 4 Collection)

The firing begins. (© Howard Ruffner)

Close-up of shooters. Sergeant Myron Pryor is at front-center, with .45 pistol raised. Lieutenant Colonel Charles Fassinger is at rear, without a gas mask. (© Howard Ruffner)

Major Harry Jones,
at left, reacts to firing.
(© Howard Ruffner)

Mission commander
Brigadier General Robert
Canterbury at back right,
in civilian garb, responding
to the gunfire. (© Howard
Ruffner)

12:24 p.m., May 4. Students diving and running for cover in Prentice Hall parking lot. (May 4 Collection)

Fellow students with one of the wounded. (Ohio State Highway Patrol / May 4 Collection)

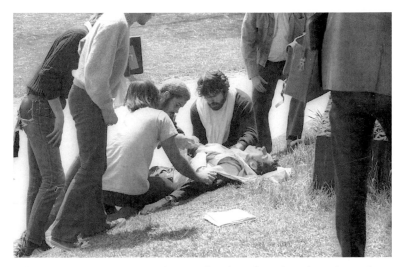

John Cleary, at center, was shot in the chest from less than 40 yards away. (© Howard Ruffner)

Guardsman after shooting, being treated for shock and hyperventilation. (MAY 4 COLLECTION)

Students assisting ambulance crews. (MAY 4 COLLECTION)

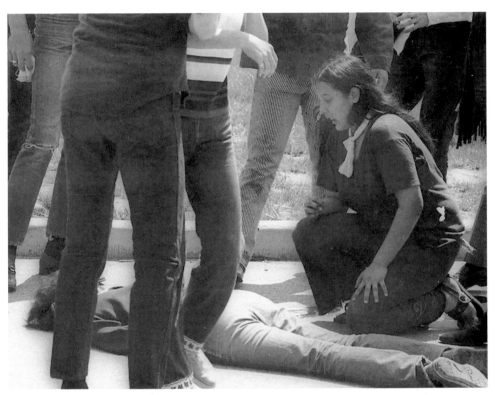

Mary Ann Vecchio kneels by Jeff Miller's body. (© Howard Ruffner)

A protestor jumping in Jeff Miller's blood. (May 4 Collection)

Faculty marshal Glenn Frank with students just after shootings as blood runs down the street behind him. (May 4 Collection)

Terry Norman, who had been photographing protestors for law-enforcement agencies, taking refuge behind National Guard lines.
(MAY 4 COLLECTION)

Students back on the Commons after the shootings. Glenn Frank, with flattop on the far side of the bullhorn, is widely credited with defusing student anger and saving perhaps countless lives. See Guardsmen massed on hill behind the students.
(© HOWARD RUFFNER)

The Kent State campus was closed hours after the shootings. It didn't reopen until mid-June. (May 4 Collection)

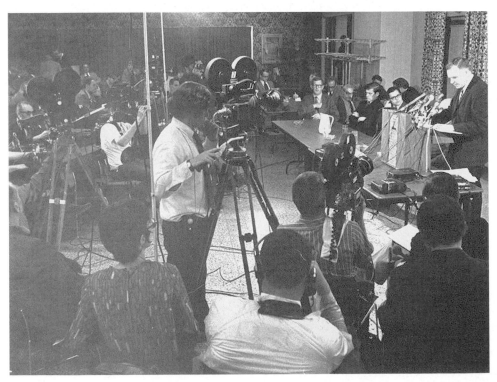

University president Robert White at his May 5 press conference. "I hear lunacy on one side, and frightening repression on the other," he told reporters. (May 4 Collection)

President Nixon meeting with protestors near the Lincoln Memorial, on the National Mall, early morning, May 9, 1970. (© Bettmann/CORBIS)

ALLISON B. KRAUSE

WILLIAM K. SCHROEDER

JEFFREY G. MILLER

SANDRA L. SCHEUER

The Dead. (May 4 Collection)

afternoon class at KSU, when the composing room foreman stopped him.

"'You are going to Kent State today, right?' the foreman asked.

"I said, 'Yes.'

"He said, 'I don't think you should go. We're setting headline upstairs, a banner headline for a night final edition, mentioning that four kids were killed at Kent State.'

"About that time, there were a lot of rumors flying around the newspaper, about how many Guardsmen were killed, how many students were killed, the campus buildings burning, but nobody had any hard information, except the people on campus."

And, of course, not everyone on campus cared, or more accurately knew to care, at least in the immediate aftermath of the shootings. One protestor in the thick of the action remembered looking down from Blanket Hill and seeing students playing tennis on courts just to the north of the Commons, blissfully unaware of what had happened between their serves and forehand volleys. In fact, those students were the rule, not the exception on May 4. Only a few thousand of the school's twenty-one thousand students were in any kind of meaningful proximity to the Pagoda, Blanket Hill, or the Commons when those sixty-seven shots were fired.

Barbara Holland was in her apartment a few blocks off campus at 12:24 p.m. on Monday, working on a paper for her neuroanatomy class. "I was totally focused on the paper because I was struggling with it," she said. "I didn't have control over it." Her first real awareness of how her college life had turned upside down came when she and some roommates stepped outside their apartment that evening and got caught in the beam of a National Guard helicopter flying low overhead, imposing martial law.

"The experience was almost post-traumatic," she recalled. "Even though I wasn't there at the shootings . . . it was a really long time before I could let it go."

———

Even the National Guard had trouble getting the story right. Guardsmen controlled the battlefield. They were in radio communication
with one another. They presumably had the training and team discipline to quickly sort through conflicting information. What's more,
they had done the shooting and were in possession of the weapons
fired and of the men who had fired them. And yet they, too, muddled
the facts, along with the local police, who were similarly equipped
with radios and dispatchers and other sources of almost instanta-
neous, in this case, miscommunication.

Guardsmen were, in fact, being brought into Robinson Memorial
Hospital in Ravenna, along with the wounded and dead students,
but they didn't have holes blown out of them. They had been hit by
flying debris—rocks and the like. Only one Guardsman would spend
a night at the hospital: Dennis Breckenridge, who had been among
the shooters at the Pagoda and had passed out afterward from hyperventilation. He was released the next morning. But at least in the
early going, the flow of information made no distinction between the
nicked and panicked and the seriously wounded and dead. The dead,
in fact, were freely apportioned across both camps, more fuel for a
fire that needed no stoking.

Art Krummel was part of a Guard squad doing duty off-campus
when the shootings took place. "The way we found out was when a
police car pulled up the driveway with his lights flashing and said,
'There's been shootings on campus. Get in the car. . . . ' Originally, he
said. 'Several students were killed. A couple of Guardsmen were
killed. There was a shooting, an exchange of gunfire, and it looks like
there is going to be—it's all-out war!"

The police car or cars—Krummel couldn't remember how many
there had been—took the Guardsmen to a hastily set up auxiliary
police station across from a grade school and told them to guard the
driveway into the station. "It was comical," Krummel remembered,
"because we're like these kids kind of standing and watching, and
these cops were big, tough guys armed to the teeth, and we're going
to guard their position. So we stood there, and just kind of envisioned

this horde of students charging over the hill with guns and this whole horrible scene."

It wasn't until parents had claimed all their children across the street and the school building was empty that Krummel and the other Guardsmen began to learn the full story of what had happened on the Kent State campus. By then, the auxiliary police inside the station seemed to be preparing for the all-out war the policeman had earlier predicted.

"I watched these men almost in a—I can't quite describe it—it wasn't a frenzy. It was like an excited anticipation. They had these beautiful leather-and-wood cases that they were opening, and . . . inside [were] these pistol-gripped shotguns that were gleaming, and the grips were beautiful, and these were their personal weapons of control. It was the most chilling thing to see because I didn't have any understanding how these guys [might behave] in a situation like this."

———

The effects of clogged communication and sloppy information flow were being felt beyond Kent, too—sometimes as annoyances, in a few cases with horrible outcomes.

Wendy Miller was in Cleveland on May 4, doing volunteer work for Mayor Carl Stokes, when she heard that one of the Kent State dead was Jeffrey Miller. She had left her brother of the same name that morning back at the College of Wooster, where both were students, an hour's drive from Kent. "It wasn't inconceivable that he had gone there to be part of the demonstration," she remembered. "I was very relieved when I learned he hadn't."

News of the shootings, one Guardsman recalled, "first hit the news back in my family in Pittsburgh. There were special broadcasts— break-ins on television news—that there was gunfire. My mother knew I was on campus, and my father knew I was in the National Guard. They were home. They knew I was working. . . . I tried to get through. We were very limited in our phone calls. I got through to them once, said not to worry about this type of thing. [Then] the message came across in Pittsburgh that three National Guardsmen were shot and killed, and one of them was from Pittsburgh.

"My mother went bananas. Couldn't get through because they shut the phone lines down. Literally, they loaded in the car, and they were coming out here. I was able to get on to a phone—you could call out, but you couldn't call in—and I got ahold of Pittsburgh and said, 'I'm fine. I'm alive. I can't talk,' and hung up."

One of the dead, in fact, grew up in Pittsburgh—Allison Krause, not a Guardsman. Her mother heard the same news, knew her daughter (like the Guardsman) had been involved in the demonstrations, and placed her own calls. Finally, she got through to Robinson Memorial Hospital. Her daughter, she learned, had been dead on arrival.

The Jeffrey Miller who would soon be killed had called his mother, Elaine Holstein, at ten that morning. "He was afraid that I would have heard reports and been frightened," she remembered. "He wanted to assure me he was okay." Driving home from work that afternoon, Holstein heard news reports of the shootings and four deaths. "I entered my apartment, put through my calls, and after what seemed a very long while, a boy answered, and I asked for Jeff. When I told him I was Jeff's mother, he said, 'He's dead.'"

In the nation's capital, the earliest edition of the *Washington Evening Star*—the Republican-leaning daily favored at the Nixon White House—carried a front-page, above-the-fold box headlined "Student, 2 Guardsmen Killed at Kent State." The brief article, distributed by UPI, ascribed the deaths to a "violent campus battle between Guardsmen and 3,000 rioting students."

————

Ray Bye, who had been in charge of the communication center when the shots were fired, joined President White and the top-tier administrators for a meeting after they had returned from their interrupted lunch at the Brown Derby restaurant. "Dr. Roskens [the executive vice president] was more in charge than Dr. White," Bye remembered. "Dr. White was just stunned. I think he was totally shell-shocked."

Not until the next day, May 5, was White able to send off telegrams to the parents of the four slain students.*

KENT, OHIO
MAY 5, 1970
THE THOUGHTS OF MRS. WHITE AND I ARE WITH YOU IN YOUR TERRIBLE LOSS.
AS PARENTS WE ARE FILLED WITH HORROR AND SHOCK.
WE PRAY FOR SUPPORT TO YOU IN THIS HOUR.

ROBERT I. WHITE
PRESIDENT
KENT STATE UNIVERSITY

The somewhat fractured grammar ("Mrs. White and I" instead of "me") and awkward phrasing, especially in the final line, might suggest the emotional pain White was going through. The fact that, by then, the university president could visit his own office only with the blessing of the National Guard must have added further to the burden he faced. Robert White did what he could.

For the parents of the dead, for the wounded, for the protesters in general, such compassion was in short supply in the weeks, even months after the shootings. In Kent, across the state, and even nationwide, the shootings would strain the quality of mercy to the breaking point and, in some cases, beyond.

---

*In a sign of the era, the telegrams were addressed to fathers only: Arthur Krause in Pittsburgh; Bernard Miller in Plainview, New York; Martin Scheuer in Youngstown, Ohio; and Louis Schroeder in Lorain, Ohio.

8

The Age of Hate

Communications cleared up once the Kent State campus was vacated and there were no more frantic calls to gum up the switchboard. But compassion in small and large ways was slow to surface.

Many of the fathers of the Kent State protestors had served in uniform in World War II or Korea. Their mothers had waited at home, fearing bad news, joyful when it didn't come. Now they lived in a world they could barely understand. A generation of rising prosperity, a growing middle class, TV, the recently launched *Sesame Street*, Dr. Spock and Dr. Seuss, greatly enhanced access to higher education had netted this: free love; protest marches; contempt for flag, country, and president; sons and daughters, boyfriends and girlfriends who knew more collectively than any generation ever had and who were, in practical ways of the world, dumb as dirt. The Age of Aquarius had played out in bad clothes, loose tits, shocking language, Woodstock, and protest marches. And now payback had arrived, just as Governor Rhodes had seemed to promise when he talked about eradicating the problem, not treating the symptoms.

Many student demonstrators were differently wired. They had grown up on discord. This was the Loud Generation, not the Silent

125

one. Protest was the way things got done, how you communicated with the powers that be.

"We had protests about everything," said Timothy App, a senior arts major on May 4. "The administration was supposed to build a new arts building, and through some shenanigans on campus, we got pushed back to third place, and we were infuriated. So we had a big protest. A couple hundred of us went to the steps of the administration building. It was the way you got things done then—it was no big deal." The new art center would eventually be built pretty much on the footprint of the burned-out ROTC building.

For their parents, heroism was Audie Murphy valiantly holding off the Germans from atop an abandoned American tank, as described in his best-selling 1949 autobiography *To Hell and Back*.* Their children were more inclined to the worldview of Holden Caulfield, who stormed Pencey Prep with a distrust of authority and a sharp eye for phonies in J. D. Salinger's 1951 novel, *The Catcher in the Rye*. Indeed, Salinger's novel was among the books found in Jeff Miller's room after his death, along with *The Sun Also Rises* and *Lost Horizon*. "My Country, Right or Wrong," now came with a question mark. There was a moral imperative to question authority, including the authority of the Ohio National Guard to ban peaceful assembly.

These were generational forces moving in entirely opposite directions, and the shootings on the early afternoon of May 4 gave them one last violent tug apart. Even almost a half century later, it's shocking to realize just how unmoored so many people became.

Brinsley Tyrrell, who was new to the art faculty that year, recalled a student whose parents refused to allow him in the house after the campus had been cleared. They "screamed through the letterbox at him that they never wanted to see him again—and this was repeated four or five times." That experience, Tyrrell said, was more common than one might hope.

---

*Murphy was awarded the Congressional Medal of Honor for his courage and played himself in the 1955 film version of his book.

"Maybe the saddest thing was three or four days after the shootings, these lost souls started drifting back. . . . They hadn't a clue what to do or where to go or who to talk to. Students would just show up and sit there and cry. That was absolutely heartbreaking. There was so little you could do other than listening."

Chuck Ayers, the student illustrator, asked Dick Bredemeier's help in getting the art supplies he had left behind in the forced evacuation of the campus.* After Bredemeier had fulfilled the request, Ayers showed up at his house and stayed for six hours. The killings, it seemed, compelled either silence or nonstop conversation. Everywhere, emotions had been worn naked.

Once he was cleared off campus, Michael Erwin stopped at the Kent home of a high school classmate. "His mother was kind of like everybody's [mom]. You could go over there, and you could talk to 'mom.' So I stopped there, and she practically threw me out of the house because her husband was at that time the manager of Portage National Bank and I guess the bank had sustained some damage in the activities on Friday or Saturday. This is someone who had always been really unconditional, and she just, you know, booted my butt out."

There were surprises like that all over town. Ellis Berns was "decompressing" at his girlfriend's house that afternoon when her father, also a banker, walked in disheveled from a brawl with a protestor who had torn down a flag in front of his bank. "He was conservative, but . . . he was a true gentleman," Berns recalled, "and he got into a fight with a protestor and got thrown in jail!"

Alan Frank, whose father had arguably saved hundreds of lives back on the Commons after the shooting, went to a friend's house afterward. "His father was a big jock. He said, 'They should have shot more of them.'"

---

*As dean of student activities, Bredemeier was one of the few administrators or faculty members allowed on campus after the shootings.

Laura Davis, who would later return to KSU as a faculty member and be instrumental in the founding of the on-campus May 4 Visitors Center, was already at home that afternoon when her dad returned from work.

"I remember my father coming in the back door, and before his hand even left the door handle, he saw me sitting there, and the first words that came out of his mouth were, 'They should have shot all of them.' And I said to him, 'Don't you realize that one of those people could have been me?'"

"One of the worst things when we got home," Diane Yale-Peabody said, "was the reaction of a lot of people who would look at us and say, 'They should have killed more of you.' How could they say that to us? We were their children, and they were killing us."

Richard Karl Watkins was at a family reunion that summer when a relative began to lecture him angrily about the demonstrations that spring at Ohio State, thinking he was a student there. "I just listened, and then my helpful brother came up and said, 'Oh, he doesn't go to Ohio State; he goes to Kent State.' And which point she said, 'Oh, I wish I would have shot them—if I'd been there, I would have shot them all.'"

Joe Lewis's parents left his sixteen-year-old sister in charge of the other children when they drove to Robinson Memorial Hospital to be with their son, who had been shot in the abdomen and leg. 'She had people call on the phone and say, 'More of the students should have been killed. I hope your brother dies,'" Lewis told an interviewer in 2001. "She should have never had to hear that."

One of the first "get well" cards Dean Kahler opened in his hospital room was filled with the same sort of vitriol—horrible medicine for a just-turned-twenty-year-old who had been on the fringe of the protests and would never walk again.

"Mind you," he said, "it was a small group of people who had these extreme feelings. I took it personally, but I opened up all these dozens of cards that were very supportive." Still, even after he was out of the hospital, he ran into relatives who delivered the same message: "They should have shot more of them."

A letter sent to Bill Schroeder's parents read in part: "There's nothing better than a dead, destructive, riot-making communist, and that's what your son was. . . . Be thankful he is gone."

———

The town-gown divide, which had been widening for a decade, was similarly blown apart by the shootings and their aftermath. On the afternoon of May 4, in the state capital at Columbus, Sylvester Del Corso, the adjutant general of the Ohio National Guard, had issued a statement that Guardsmen had fired on the students only after a sniper had opened fire on them from a nearby rooftop. "Guardsmen facing almost certain injury and death were forced to open fire on the attackers," he explained. Frederick Wenger, the assistant adjutant general, had further explained that the troops "were under standing orders to take cover and return any fire."

Within forty-eight hours, the Guard leadership had backed away from that contention, for multiple reasons. Solid evidence of a sniper never emerged. Moreover, the National Guard manual had a strict protocol for dealing with sniper fire that clearly had not been followed at Kent State. As Robert Canterbury himself told reporters: "Snipers should be engaged only on order and by a single, selected marksman or firing team. Laying down a barrage accomplishes nothing constructive and endangers the lives of innocent bystanders." But the contention was also illogical on its face. Why would Guardsmen respond to a rooftop sniper by firing downhill into the parking lot? The initial statement, though, would long outlive its retraction.

"Regrettable as the outcome of Monday's incident is, those students were violating a lawful order of non-assembly Monday noon but like the infants they are they wanted to see if their bluff would be called," one Kent woman wrote the local *Record-Courier* newspaper.

"However, there was nothing child-like in their cry of 'crush the pigs' as they advanced on the National Guards put there to restore order and protect public property they were bent on destroying."

Added another woman from nearby Diamond, Ohio, in the same space: "I was always under the impression college was very special and took special people to go there. It seems like all the crum-bums go there now and all the real men to Vietnam."

Similar sentiments were expressed to professor and filmmaker Richard Myers in a series of anonymous, on-the-street interviews conducted in the days just after the shootings. "We feel that some of our neighbors—the police, the firemen families—would be without providers now if the National Guard hadn't been here," a well-dressed woman with a son serving in Vietnam told Myers. "Our hearts go out to the parents of those four students, but we feel that the citizens of Kent are just as precious to their families as the students [were to theirs]."

"The students were told to disperse," a woman standing beside her added. "They didn't disperse. . . . What could you do? The students want to run our country. How can they run our country when they can't even obey rules?"

Not all the interviewees and letter-to-the-editor writers were so unforgiving or even disapproving. A middle-aged black man told Myers, "the students have every right to dissent." An older white man said, "Under the stress and strain, I believe both sides were in such a mood that anything could happen. . . . The whole fault lies with the administration of the university itself." A Hiram woman wrote to the *Record-Courier*: "Four innocent students are dead because of a chain reaction and a social philosophy in this country which will keep on killing until everyone accepts the responsibility and makes the effort to stop it."

Nor were what sometimes seemed ad hominem attacks on the dead and wounded necessarily personally intended. Brinsley Tyrrell recalled an employee named Oscar at the lumberyard in Ravenna. "My art students loved him. He broke the rules, cut plywood squares for them, that sort of thing. Yet afterwards, he also said, 'They should have shot more of them.' But he wasn't relating it to the students he knew. He was relating it to this public demonization of the protestors."

Still, if Kent didn't speak with a single voice, there was no mistaking the majority opinion in the weeks after the shootings: In one way or another, the students had brought this on themselves. It was them or us. All that remained was to adjust other facts to fit the story line.

————

"There was a nightmarish quality to the next few weeks," Kent resident Berta Egan wrote in a 1990 "remembrance" to the *Akron Beacon Journal.* "Fear, hate, and animosity toward the student victims rose to paranoic [*sic*] heights. Ugly rumors about imagined venereal disease of the innocent victims, stupid lies about scores of 'commies' and radicals with red bandanas arriving by busloads circulated about the town. Hateful letters attacking the dead and injured students appeared by the score in local newspapers."

Rosann Rissland heard the rumors, too. "Afterward, we didn't hear anything good about the students who were killed. We were told that the coroner said that they had venereal disease and that they were drug addicts and everything. We did not know who they were. We didn't know one was from ROTC or another was an honors' student."

Junior Laura Dressler, whose family lived in Kent, recalled a next-door neighbor who wouldn't go to the university side of town for fear of getting caught up in a riot, even after the campus was evacuated. The shootings were maybe forty-eight hours old when Dressler went to a father-daughter banquet with her dad and found herself sitting across from a high-ranking local National Guard official who kept citing the rock throwing as adequate provocation for what followed.

"I said, 'There really aren't any rocks—there's a nice lawn up in that area, and if they found anything, it would be a few pebbles.' But he said, 'They had specially imported large rocks.' And I thought, well, no. Who's going to import large rocks to a campus and have them sitting in just the right spot for a confrontation like that? But I quit arguing with him. I wanted to have a nice time with my dad."

Berta Egan's house was egged multiple times by passing cars in response to her letter to the editor decrying the killings. The black ribbon that Brinsley Tyrrell tied around a tree in his front garden was slashed and the flowers trampled. Tuesday morning, Lillian Tyrrell gave their two young children permission to play with some other children a few doors down on their street. Maybe fifteen minutes later, both children burst back through the door in tears.

"My daughter was hysterical, and she's holding her brother for dear life and screaming, and his face was just covered in blood. And she said, 'They threw stones at us, Mommy, and I came home!' You could understand why the shootings happened because it could have been an emotional moment. You didn't understand why all your neighbors turned against you . . . how nobody spoke to you, how they crossed the street when you came towards them, how they would phone you up and scream at you on the telephone."

Brinsley Tyrrell remembered walking down Main Street in the days just after the shooting "and having a gentleman sitting on his porch in a rocker train his shotgun on me, follow me as I walked down the street, not doing anything, but very clearly pointing the gun and keeping it there." He also recalled being conscious of lines of sight when he sat in his own living room—moving away from windows, for example, if they offered too easy a shot from the street. That went on for about a month after the shootings, he said.

Dick Bredemeier recalled police advising two high-ranking university administrators, Dave Amber and Bob Matson, to leave town in the days after the killings. "The police thought students might firebomb their houses." Both administrators held their ground.

That sounds like the Wild West of *Gunsmoke* and *Shane*, *Rawhide* and *High Noon*. For several days after the shootings, that's what Kent was, updated for modern times: helicopters at night, Guardsmen and local police patrolling the streets, special deputies, townsfolk ready to take justice into their own hands, while four students laid in the freshly turned earth out at Boot Hill.

———

The dearth of compassion often came with a caveat. "This is all very tragic," a husband and wife wrote to the *Record-Courier*, "yet if this is what it takes to teach law and order to students, then this is the high price that must be paid to keep our country free." In a letter to the editor of the *Akron Beacon Journal*, a woman expressed many of the same feelings: "My heart aches. The tears flow. I was shaken as many other are. When will we learn that laws must be obeyed. It's the nature of everything created. Change cannot come overnight."

The May 4 late edition of the *Record-Courier* that reported the death of the four students also ran a front-page editorial decrying the protests and seeming even to justify the shootings: "The acts of violence in Kent and on campus during the past two days are so serious as to merit the sternest repression." The side-by-side, top-of-the-front-page headlines make for unsettling bedfellows: "4 Kent State Students Killed in Clash Today" and "Universities Must Oust Hooligans." Inside the front section, a poem by a twelve-year-old local girl titled "A Child's Plea" reinforced the paper's implicit editorial stand: "The war in Vietnam is not nearly as bad / As the one you've started with your peace fad. . . . The National Guard has come and things are well in hand. / But look at the disgrace you spread over this land." For Kent State administrators, the editorial stand was particularly hard to ignore: Robert Dix, editor and publisher of the *Record-Courier*, had been president of the university's board of directors since August 1963.

Such responses almost always assumed a collective guilt, whether a shooting victim had been throwing rocks, tossing back tear-gas canisters, or trying to skirt the danger while passing from class to class, and thus a collective justification. By the same cold logic, Jack Kennedy had brought on his own assassination by traveling to volatile Texas, Martin Luther King Jr. by appearing on a motel room balcony in volcanic Memphis, and Bobby Kennedy by campaigning for the Democratic presidential nomination in Southern California, a hotbed of known wing nuts.

The assumption of collective guilt didn't stretch only in one direction, either. Later, after the campus had been closed and students were scrambling to finish the semester, a Guardsman who had joined up to help pay his Kent State tuition went to see one of his professors at an off-campus office.

"I came in to see him, and I said, 'I've missed a test.' And he said, 'Well, why did you miss the test?' And I said, 'Well, I was in the National Guard. I was on active duty.' And he said, 'Were you on this campus, too?' And I said, 'Yeah.' And he said, 'You will *never* pass my course. You will *never* graduate from this university if I have anything to do with it. You *can't* finish this course. You have *failed* this course. And as far as I'm concerned, you shouldn't be permitted back on this campus.'"

Nor were feelings for or against the students or the Guardsmen, Kent State or Kent itself, ever entirely separable from the politics of the moment. The shootings happened early Monday afternoon. Tuesday morning, Ohio Republicans went to the polls to select a senatorial candidate for the November election.

Over the weekend, Robert Taft Jr. had met privately in Cleveland with several Kent State students to assess the situation there and the political consequences of wading into the middle of it somehow. According to John Kelly Jr., Taft's state campaign manager, southern Ohio Republicans wanted Taft to publicly praise the National Guard for keeping order, while up-state supporters were after him to blast Rhodes for calling in the Guard and the Guard itself for strong-arm tactics. In the end, Taft did neither. Private polling a week earlier had shown him with a 7–8 percent lead, roughly what the public polls were showing as well, something like a sixty-thousand-vote cushion, given the likely turnout, with only seven days to go. Better safe than sorry.

Jim Rhodes, on the other hand, had nothing to lose. He'd made his reputation as a law-and-order Republican, and the Guard had been vital to his political success. Since starting his second gubernatorial term in January 1967, Rhodes had called out the National Guard on at least forty separate occasions, more than any other governor in the nation over the same time frame. What's more, the Kent State campus turmoil was proving the exact boost his campaign needed, at just the right moment. On Sunday Rhodes followed up his promise to "eradicate" the problem with a flurry of related proposals: new laws to make it a felony to throw anything at a law-enforcement officer and to provide for immediate dismissal of any student or faculty member involved in a riot. Students expelled under the latter measure would be ineligible to enroll at any other state-run university in Ohio.

In the end, going tough and loud almost worked. Rhodes lost the primary fight by 5,270 votes, half of 1 percent of the 939,934 votes cast. In a single week, Bob Taft's projected lead had shrunk by more than 90 percent. (Taft would go on to narrowly defeat Howard Metzenbaum in the November election.)

———

The further away from Kent State those early responses came, the more they were driven not by personal fear or animosity, but by a sense that the dead and wounded or the shooters themselves were a window into something horribly wrong in the country as a whole. Politics remains the background noise in these letters and telegrams, but the students and Guardsmen start to become faceless players in a morality drama about issues that reach far beyond individual action or anguish.

A California couple wrote on May 6 to Kent State board chairman Robert Dix to express their belief that higher education itself was to blame for the turbulence that had befallen so many universities: "The people's faith in their schools has been shaken to it's [*sic*] very roots by cowardly administrators who have granted amnesty, bowed to Communist demands, and allowed Communist teachers to teach."

In a letter to Mayor Satrom and the Kent City Council, the head of the Department of Psychology at the University of North Carolina at Greensboro wrote that "the killings at Kent State will go down in history as one of the most infamous attacks on defenseless individuals engaged in group protest ever committed in this country." An alumnus of the university and father of a Kent State student telegrammed from Pittsburgh to "demand immediate action against the Hitler youth who are trying to destroy our universities and plunge American into anarchy."

Paul Cameron was serving with the First Infantry Division in Di An, South Vietnam, when he and his unit learned of the shootings via *Stars and Stripes*. Among the comments he recalled: "Way to go, boys! Kill some of those hippies for me, too." Jim Webb, a Naval Academy grad and later a Democratic US senator from Virginia, remembered cheers erupting at the Quantico Marine Base when an enlisted man scribbled, "Kent State 0, National Guard 4," on a blackboard.

On May 4, army captain Hugh Baker was back from his tour of duty in Vietnam, attending the Military Intelligence School at Ft. Leavenworth, Kansas. Shortly afterward, in a course paper titled "The Right to Dissent," he wrote, "The shootings at Kent State and Jackson State College [ten days later on May 14] have become standard jokes. The systematic elimination of the Black Panther leadership without 'due process' has become, for many, a source of pride in the police departments. It is not uncommon to hear such comments: 'I would like to command the next unit that goes on campus, there would be a hell of a lot more than 4 KIA. . . . '

"This country is, of course, built on a system of competition and political diversity, but to compete with student dissidents and radicals

(left or right wing) in a contest of irrationality is not only degrading
to the officer corps, but, in fact, serves to convey to 'the silent majority' a distorted image of the military." His cautionary note, Baker
said, was not universally appreciated at Ft. Leavenworth.

On the West Coast, Neil Young read about the shootings, wrote
down the opening line to a new song—"Tin soldiers and Nixon
coming"—and kept going from there. Within weeks, Crosby, Stills,
Nash, and Young had gathered at the Record Plant studio in Los Angeles to record "Ohio," still etched into the memory of a generation
that spans both sides of the shootings. According to recording engi-
neer Bill Halverson, the finished product took no more than three live
takes. Neil Young would later write that David Crosby broke down in
tears at the end of the session.

———

So it went across the whole range of responses. Murray Vidockler,
president of the Brooklyn-based All State Bus Corporation, wrote
Mayor Satrom on May 5 with tongue grimly in cheek to congratulate
him on creating "a destination for sightseers of the future that will be
as famous as the site of the Boston Massacre. The tourism reception
industry of Ohio should be in your debt." The first Monday in May,
he suggests, "can now be known as Student Massacre Day. . . . If there
is any help that we in the travel industry can help you with in Congress to make this a national holiday, please feel free to call on us."

After the Newark (New Jersey) *Star-Ledger* interviewed Kent State
student Ralph Spielman about the shootings, his father, a New Jersey
drugstore wholesaler, received several threatening phone calls. A Lan-
sing, Michigan, man wrote on May 6 to Mayor Satrom, Kent State
president Robert White, and the president of Ohio State and mayor
of its home at Columbus to compliment them all "on the courage and
conviction that motivated your action when confronted with irre-
sponsible violence in your respective schools, fomented no doubt by
communist agents and by anarchistic thinking people in our midst.

The fact it resulted in the use of fire arms is in our opinion way past due." If he ever opened and read the letter himself, Robert White must have been shocked at its assumption of his complicity in what had happened on his campus.

That same Wednesday, two days after the shootings, White sent a letter to all Kent State University parents, expressing his and the university community's horror at the events of the previous days, their sympathy for the parents of the dead students, and his personal sense of a "frustration never before experienced. Events during those hectic days were quickly taken from our hands. Off-campus security forces assumed command of the University, but, alas, they were unable to quell the forces of violence."

Calm, he wrote, had returned to KSU. He had just received word that Guardsmen were soon to be released from campus duty. Attention was now being focused on reopening the university. But just how hard that was going to be to accomplish can be found in the minutes of the special meeting of the board of trustees of Kent State University held Friday, May 10, the day the Ohio National Guard actually vacated the grounds.

"We have lost our protection," White told the board. "The National Guard has pulled out. The State Highway Patrol is unable to come on campus. . . . We can recruit some deputy sheriffs and off-duty policemen from neighboring areas, [but] we are insecure. State property is insecure on this campus at this moment.

"The Kent Fire Department could be slow in accepting a call from the campus.

"The local situation remains potentially explosive. The past Wednesday night there were 23 arrests downtown—some for carrying concealed weapons.

"We would become a mecca if we were to reopen."

Kent State, it turned out, had been deserted by more than its students. The community of which it was the prime economic engine was ready to cut the university loose, too. So, quite possibly, were the elected state representatives of Ohio. "I think if they'd had a vote in the legislature, they would have turned Kent into a mental institution or something similar—closed the doors for good," Dick Bredemeier said. "The attitude down [in Columbus] was such that we wouldn't have wanted to have that vote."

And that wasn't the end of the problems the school faced, according to its president. "In his opinion," the minutes record, "President White said the national situation is deteriorating." By then, that didn't take a crystal ball to foretell.

9

An Unfortunate Incident

The killings also unmoored the man who had played a key role in the chain of events that brought the National Guard to Kent State: President Richard Nixon.

The decision to extend the war into Cambodia, Nixon's April 30 address to the nation, and the reaction on campuses, in the media, and across the nation had occupied the White House's attention all weekend. There was general agreement that the president's "bums . . . blowing up campuses" gibe at the Pentagon Friday had been an unfortunate moment, but it was broadly consistent with the "line for today" worked out that morning by Nixon, National Security Adviser Henry Kissinger, and White House press secretary Ron Ziegler: "Cold steel, no give, nothing about negotiations," as recorded by Chief of Staff H. R. "Bob" Haldeman in his voluminous longhand diaries.

What's more, the hard line on the war and on protestors seemed to be working. The *New York Times* had slammed the president in its lead editorial on Friday, May 1, calling the Cambodia incursion yet another example of "the military hallucination of victory through escalation." But the *Times* was predictable as far as the White House was concerned. Other press and TV commentators had mostly taken an approving or at least cautious approach to the new war initiative.

Nixon felt so heartened by the response he had received at the Pentagon to his Thursday speech that he whisked the family off to Camp David for the weekend after lunch on the Potomac, aboard the presidential yacht. Internal polling results the next morning further buoyed the president's spirits. He called Haldeman at two that afternoon, with instructions to "let everyone go home and relax." Haldeman declined the offer, though—there was too much to do, and his staff was on a roll.

For Haldeman, the only dark spot on the weekend was a Sunday call from Henry Kissinger complaining that Nixon was being fed too much unsettling information on campus unrest. Kissinger, Haldeman recorded, "is worried [the president] will toss babies to the wolves instead of hanging tight."

By Monday, May 4, maybe with wolves devouring babies in the back of his mind, the White House chief of staff had begun referring to the Cambodia incursion in his diary in all capitals: The Decision, the all-encompassing. "And the repercussions roll on," he began his entry for that day. "Discussed with P the plans for the week. He says he's ready to move to domestic matters, but then keeps coming back to things related to The Decision."

Kissinger and Ziegler were back that a.m., as they were most mornings, crafting a fresh message for the day. Nixon followed that with "some quizzing about follow-up activity, basically *very* calm and undemanding," Haldeman recorded. "Then he went over to [the Executive Office Building] for rest of the day. A long session with [John Ehrlichman] to get caught up on domestic. A nap. Then had me over, reviewed trip plan. Then I told him four students killed at Kent State." And with that, the wheels came off—for the day, for the week, maybe for Nixon's presidency as a whole. Even by his own high standards, Richard Milhous Nixon was headed into the tunnel of the weird.

———

"He's very disturbed," H. R. Haldeman wrote of the immediate aftermath of informing the president of the shootings. "Afraid his decision set it off, and that is the ostensible cause of the demonstrations there. Issued condolence statement, then kept after me all the rest of the day for more facts. Hoping rioters had provoked the shooting, but no real evidence they did, except throwing rocks at National Guard."

The "condolence statement" was only marginally that. The killing of the four students, Nixon said through Press Secretary Ron Ziegler, "should remind us all once again that when dissent turns to violence, it invites tragedy. . . .

"It is my hope that this tragic and unfortunate incident will strengthen the determination of all the nation's campuses, administrators, faculty and students alike to stand firmly for the right which exists in this country of peaceful dissent and just as strongly against the resort to violence as a means of such expression."

All of which left hanging several questions: What is violence? And who had resorted to it at Kent State? The students—four dead and nine wounded, including one paralyzed for life from the waist down? Or the Guard—one overnight hospitalization for hyperventilation? Like many of the residents in and around Kent, the president seemed ready to declare Sandy Scheuer, Bill Schroeder, Allison Krause, and Jeff Miller the victims in essence of their own crime.

In a speech Monday evening to an American Retail Federation gathering in Washington, Vice President Spiro Agnew tread similar ground. "In several recent speeches, I have called attention to the grave dangers which accompany the new politics of violence and confrontation and which have found so much favor on our college campuses," Agnew told his audience, departing from his prepared text. The deaths at Kent State had put an exclamation point on that. Not only were they "predictable and avoidable," Agnew said. They also "make the truth of these comments self-evident and underscore the need that they be said."

Agnew's broad target that evening was a familiar one for him: the purveyors of a "calculated, consistent and well-publicized barrage of criticism against the principles of this nation"—well-educated teachers and government leaders who scorn the "traditions of civility" and "pander to the ignorance and the fears of those who are all too willing to believe that the criminal who throws a bomb at a bank is a hero while the policeman who gets killed trying to stop him is a pig."

In particular, the vice president drew a bead that evening on the liberal Republican mayor of New York City, John Lindsay, one of those men, as Agnew put it, "now in power in this country . . . who cannot cope with tradition, who believe that the people of America are ready to support revolution so long as it is done with a cultured voice and a handsome profile."

Whether or not John Lindsay ever qualified as a revolutionary except in the fevered imagination of the right wing of his own political party is open to question—Lindsay would switch to the Democrats the following year—but the New York mayor did by then have a clear line into Kent State. He had loaned two of his aides to Bob Taft's primary campaign against Jim Rhodes, and those aides would soon fly a Kent State sophomore, Stephen Titchenal, to New York, to appear at several rallies in support of Lindsay's controversial decision to display flags over municipal buildings at half-mast in memory of the dead students at KSU.

———

Spiro Agnew was politically expedient when he was picked to be Nixon's running mate in 1968. A Greek American and veteran of both World War II and the Korean War, voluble and tough-talking, he was governor of an eastern state with southern leanings (Maryland), a useful counterbalance to Nixon's wooden manner and West Coast credentials, but the romance ended once the election was over.

"Nixon's people cut him off right from the beginning," said Victor Gold, who served as Agnew's press secretary during his four-plus years in office. Kissinger, Gold said, looked down on the vice president. Agnew meanwhile thought Nixon "was the coldest man he'd ever met."

"When Agnew came into office," Gold recalled, "he said I want to do this, I want to do that, and then he found out there they weren't going to let him do a goddamn thing. Then he hit on the culture wars and thought this is something I *can* do."

Do *and* succeed at. President and vice president had a similar list of domestic enemies, and serving as Nixon's point man in the culture wars gave Agnew not just a raison d'être but nearly free rein to go after all their mutual villains: Republican "elitists" like Lindsay; the liberal media ("nattering nabobs of negativism" hunkered down in their own "4-H club—the hopeless, hysterical hypochondriacs of history"); academic opponents of the Vietnam War ("ideological eunuchs"); and professional anarchists, "those tomentose exhibitionists who provoke more derision than fear," as he put it in his Monday evening speech to the American Retail Federations.*

Agnew had drawn a sharp line in the sand between the Nixon administration and the student protest movement in an October 19, 1969, speech in New Orleans, four days after the moratorium to end the war in Vietnam brought more than a million demonstrators out into streets all across America.

The young, the vice president said, "overwhelm themselves with drugs and artificial stimulants. . . . Education is being redefined by the uneducated to suit the ideas of the uneducated. The student now goes to college to proclaim, rather than to learn. The lessons of the past are ignored and obliterated in a contemporary contagion known as the

---

*"Tomentose" was vintage Agnew—and probably also vintage William Safire, the Nixon speechwriter and later *New York Times* "On Language" columnist, who contributed many of Agnew's most memorable rhetorical flourishes. From the Latin for "cushion stuffing," it refers literally to the layer of matted hairs on the surface of a plant. The vice president, of course, was extending the meaning to include long-haired war protestors, but the word itself must have been boggling to the retail executives in his audience.

Generation Gap. A spirit of national masochism prevails, encouraged by an effete corps of impudent snobs who characterize themselves as intellectuals."

Agnew was still working that line on the weekend leading up to May 4. "He looked down on the student protestors as a bunch of kids who never had to work, who never went to war, whose parents had given them everything," according to Victor Gold. And he still had the same emblematic "tomentose exhibitionist" in mind. "Agnew blamed it all on Jerry Rubin," Gold said. "The lines he wrote in that New Orleans speech—he was talking specifically about Jerry Rubin."

Rubin, in turn, had taken to baiting Agnew as well. In his April 20 talk at Kent State, the Yippie cofounder had made the battle personal, by introducing into the equation Agnew's daughter, Kim, then a high school student at National Cathedral School in Washington, DC: "Spiro Agnew's family is all f----- up. His daughter was caught smoking pot. She was locked in a bathroom during the march in Washington. We should have marched on Spiro's house." (The transcription is from the administration spy who attended the talk.)

The two might have kept at this for a long time—Agnew was never one to shrink from a fight, and Rubin had perfected the art of tweaking the Establishment and turning the results into theater—but the shootings at Kent State had dismantled the political balance. The broad canvas Agnew liked to work on had suddenly merged with the sinister specifics of Jim Rhodes's Sunday morning press conference—brownshirts, night riders, words and metaphors Agnew never would have used, according to his then press secretary—and the atmospherics now included bodies on the ground, rivers of blood, a skirmish line of Guardsmen with M1s smoking.

What's more, Rhodes's vow to "eradicate the problem" of campus unrest had had, in the short term, precisely the opposite effect. The Kent State shootings added urgency to a national student strike that had been hastily cobbled together after Nixon's Thursday evening address to the nation on Cambodia. The killings also swelled the ranks of those headed to Washington, DC, that weekend for yet another antiwar demonstration on the Mall. As happened at Kent State, moderate students across the nation found themselves suddenly radicalized by the killings; radicals meanwhile had found a new reason to resort to stronger means of protest. All told, more than 450 colleges, universities, and even high schools across the country enrolling some four million students found themselves disrupted by strikes and protests nonviolent and otherwise. Governors in sixteen states would send National Guard units to twenty-one campuses during the week-plus of student strikes, and thirty ROTC buildings would be bombed or burned.

At the University of Washington, an estimated six thousand students swarmed onto Interstate 5 a little before two in the afternoon of Tuesday, May 5, blocking both northbound and southbound lanes for an hour as they marched to the federal courthouse in downtown Seattle to hear speakers decry Nixon and the war. They were back again on I-5 Wednesday, thousands strong, marching down the southbound lanes to the courthouse. On Friday, police turned the express lanes over to the ten thousand university protestors heading to the courthouse one last time—a day of mourning for the Kent State dead.

At Stanford, the home of ROTC commander Colonel Stanley Ramey was hit by three shots. At the University of Wisconsin, students chanting "Remember Kent" marched through the campus and set fire to two ROTC buildings. In Iowa City, University of Iowa students marched on the National Guard armory, set off a smoke bomb in the Old Capitol, and, in the wee morning hours of May 9, torched the on-campus Old Armory Temporary, a military relic of the Second World War. At Princeton University on May 4, nearly four thousand students, faculty members, and staff voted in favor of a strike against the war. Four days of demonstrations at the University of Maryland netted twenty-five arrests and fifty persons injured.

Like other schools nationwide, the University of California, San Diego, campus was crippled by the strike when, on the afternoon of May 10, student George Winne Jr., a former ROTC member and son of a US Navy captain, set fire to a pile of gasoline-soaked rags in his lap as he sat in Revelle Plaza, next to a sign that read "In God's name, end this war." Winne died ten hours later at Scripps Hospital in San Diego.

————

"Big problem today is the whole student disorder situation," Haldeman wrote in his diary entry for May 5. "Not much hard news or specific developments but a lot of planning for strikes and marches for the rest of the week. Reaction very tough to the four killed at Kent State yesterday. All our people trying to figure out how best to handle, and whether [the president] can perform any useful role. . . . Big thing now is to ride out all the crises with a show of cool strength—and no inflammation but no waffling."

On the sixth, the president met at the White House with six Kent State students, all unaffiliated with any campus protest group, all male, all white: Tom Brubach, Dick Cutler, Don Grant, Dean Powell, Don Tretnik, and Sam Trago.

"The Kent State 6 was good group," Haldeman noted, "and meeting went very well. No concrete results. Their main pitch is need for better communication and more student participation in major decisions. Did confirm that Cambodia was not the basic cause."

The good vibrations, however, were only a brief lull in the storm.

"As day went on, concern from outside re campus crisis built rapidly," Haldeman continued in his entry for May 6. "[The president] came to grips with it this aft. Obviously realizes—but won't openly admit—that his 'bums' remark very harmful. He agreed to plan of action—meet [university presidents] tomorrow—press conference Fr. nite—call in all Govs Mon. Wants to hold off on apptg. special commission re Kent State. Feels it may be a mistake—so wait a little. Very aware of point that goal of the Left is to panic us—so we must not fall into their trap."

Kissinger and Ehrlichman came over to the Executive Office Building in the afternoon to talk strategy with Nixon. "K wants to just let the students go for couple of weeks then move in and clobber them. E wants to communicate—especially symbolically." The one thing everyone seemed to agree on was that Spiro Agnew had become a political liability. The president "wants VP to stop saying anything about students," Haldeman wrote on Wednesday. Thursday the seventh he returned to the subject. Nixon "wants VP to avoid any remarks re students, etc.—VP strongly disagrees. I passed the word. . . . VP said he would act only on order of P."

As if to prove his independence, Agnew went on *The David Frost Show* that night and, in the course of a lengthy interview, talked his head off about Kent State, the shootings there, his own culpability as point man of the cultural wars, whether murder was committed in the early afternoon of May 4, whether that murder (if committed) was justified, and whether the dead were—as he and the president had earlier implied—the victims of the collective crime of the demonstrators as opposed to the specific battle rifles of the Guardsmen.

"We know what happened at Kent State," the vice president told Frost. "We know that these demonstrations took place. We know that the ROTC Building was burned. We know that at an airport nearby, light planes were overturned and destroyed. [Damage was done, but no connection was ever made to the antiwar protests.] The fire hoses were cut. Firemen were stoned, and we know that the National Guard were stoned.

"Now, one of the things that is overlooked in that incident is that the Guardsmen—and I don't condone their action; they responded with far more force than they should have—are young people, too, 18, 19, 20 year olds. And if the students are not charged with a high level of responsibility in their conduct, then perhaps we should not impose upon Guardsmen a higher level. They're emotional; they were probably under a great amount of tension. One or two may have lost control, and that caused the tragedy. But we can't say the tragedy occurred because I spoke out against campus violence. That seems to be pushing it a little far."

"What if it is discovered there was no shot fired at [the Guards-men] by a sniper and they just opened fire without a warning shot or anything?" Frost asked a minute or so later. "Not having been fired at in any way, in that sense what is the word for that? Murder?"

"Yes," Agnew answered, "but not first degree. As a lawyer, I am conversant, and I suppose most people who follow the courts are con-versant, with the fact that where there is no premeditation but simply an over-response in the heat of anger that results in a killing, it's a murder. It's not premeditated, but it's a murder, and it certainly can't be condoned. But I would guess that if a very volatile young man got a brick in the neck or in the ribs, he might just blow up and do some-thing like that. The point to remember about that, it seems to me, is that had the rocks not been thrown, there would have been no chance of a killing."

Frost: "And I suppose had the tear gas not been thrown, then the rocks wouldn't have been thrown."

Agnew: "That's right, and had the buildings not been burned and the threatening assembly not been conducted, the tear gas wouldn't have been thrown."

Frost: "I suppose we could go on: Had the President not announced the excursion into Cambodia, maybe the demonstration wouldn't have taken place."

By now deep into what might be thought of as the chaos theory of the Kent State killings—the flicker of the butterfly wings that jolts the lizard that diverts the adder that was going to bite the scientist who ends up curing cancer and so on—Agnew moved on to a morn-ing *Washington Post* column that contended it wasn't right to use a judgment call (Cambodia) to justify the illegal conduct (arson, the ROTC building) that led to the Guard being detailed to the campus, that led to the demonstrations that led to the Ohio Riot Act being invoked, that led to the tear gas, the rock throwing, the skirmish line, and finally the shootings. That argument, though, ignores a judgment call with a much shorter causal string to the killings—the decision to send the Guard onto the Kent State campus in the first place.

————

As far as Richard Nixon was concerned, his vice president wasn't the only loose cannon rolling around the deck of the White House in the wake of The Decision and the Kent State shootings.

On Thursday, May 7, the *Washington Evening Star* reported on a letter that Secretary of the Interior and former (and later) Alaska governor Walter Hickel had just sent the president regarding the need "for communicating w/ young, shutting up Agnew, meeting more w/ Cab. members," as Haldeman recorded it. "P pretty calm about it last nite—pretty cold-blooded today. Feels Hickel's got to go as soon as we're past this crisis." (Hickel lasted until November 25 of that year. He died on May 7, 2010, forty years to the day after the leaked letter surfaced in the *Star*.)

Interior secretaries, though, come and go. Secretaries of state and defense are far closer to the beating heart of a presidency, especially in time of war and the necessary diplomatic initiatives to deal with conflict, and Nixon perceived a problem here as well. Not only had William Rogers, at State, and Melvin Laird, at Defense, failed to phone congratulations to Nixon after his Cambodia address to the nation; now stories were surfacing in the media that they actually disagreed with The Decision. The Hickel "problem" added still more fuel to that fire.

"This led to a rising 'anti-Cabinet' feeling as [the president] thought about it," Haldeman wrote on Thursday. "Went back to deep resentment that none called him after the speech and none rose to his defense on this deal. So he struck back by ordering the tennis court [on the White House grounds] removed immediately."

Rather than heal wounds, a Thursday White House meeting with university presidents—part of Ehrlichman's "symbolic" outreach—had mostly confirmed Nixon and his top advisers' worst suspicions about higher education generally. Nixon "said the Univ. presidents were all scared to death—feels that this now includes the non-radical students—and agrees with Moynihan* theory that the whole Univ. community is now politicized—and there's no way to turn it off. All blame Agnew primarily—then the P's 'bums' crack. General feeling is that w/o Kent State it would not have been so bad—but that even w/o Cambodia there were a lot of campuses ready to blow."

There was also a Friday evening press conference to get through. "An awful lot at stake," Haldeman wrote in his entry for May 8. "Media have built it up very big, and it really is. An awful lot of schools closed, a lot of rhetoric, a major threat of violence, etc." Nixon spent the day at Camp David, working on his briefing book while Haldeman relayed a constant stream of often-conflicting advice. "Everyone feared the P would either be too belligerent and non-understanding of the dissenters, or would be too forgiving and thus lose strength and P leadership." In the end, the president took the middle ground.

He and the students wanted the same thing, Nixon said in response to one question: peace. "They are trying to say that they want to stop the killing. They are trying to say that they want to end the draft. They are trying to say that we ought to get out of Vietnam. I agree with everything they are trying to accomplish." Regarding Cambodia, the action there to date appeared to have bought as much as eight months of additional time for training the Army of South Vietnam to defend the country on its own. The vice president or any member of his cabinet, Nixon assured the reporters crowded into the East Room, is free to dissent: "This is an open administration. It will continue to be."

As for Kent State, the president was waiting for the facts before expressing any opinion about the Guard's conduct, but he was

---

* Daniel Patrick Moynihan, then counselor to the president for urban affairs and later US ambassador to India and the United Nations, and four-term U.S. senator from New York.

personally committed to finding new approaches to containing dissent: "I saw the pictures of those four youngsters in the *Evening Star* the day after that tragedy, and I vowed then that we were going to find methods that would be more effective to deal with those problems of violence, methods that would deal with those who would use force and violence and endangers others, but, at the same time, would not take the lives of innocent people."

"Whole press conference was masterful," Haldeman wrote in his diary. "The aftermath on the White House staff was a mood of great relief and almost exhilaration." Nixon must have felt the same way, too. Before the press conference, he had decreed that he would take no calls; afterwards, he was ready, it seemed, to talk to anyone and everyone. Haldeman and his staff stayed until past midnight handling calls and then had to negotiate their way through soldiers called in to secure the White House grounds in advance of the Saturday demonstrations on the Mall.

"In trying to leave we were jammed in by the troop trucks unloading the Third Army into the [Executive Office Building]. A very strange feeling as the White House and DC batten down for another siege. The buses were being lined up, police all over."

Others had similar experiences. Speechwriter Pat Buchanan remembered running into elements of the Eighty-Second Airborne that night when he went down to the basement of the EOB to buy a pack of cigarettes from a vending machine. Chuck Colson, instrumental in some of the darkest plots of the Nixon years, looked at the troops in the Executive Office Building and the DC Transit buses that ringed the White House nose to nose and marveled at how much like a banana republic the nation's capital had become.

Escape hatches were still available. Camp David was a quick helicopter ride away. But unless Richard Nixon chose to yield the White House to the demonstrators gathering beyond his moat of buses and the just-arriving Praetorian Guard from the Eighty-Second Airborne, for the next twenty-four hours a hundred thousand war protestors would in effect be holding him hostage inside his own well-protected residence. Upstairs in the White House living quarters, though, the president of the United States of America was starting to think outside the box.

———

"The weirdest day so far," H. R. Haldeman began his diary entry for Saturday, May 9. "Started with call from [Ehrlichman] at about 5:00 [a.m.] saying P was at the Lincoln Memorial talking to students."

Nixon, it turned out, couldn't sleep Friday night, and like Spiro Agnew the night before on *David Frost*, he couldn't stop talking either. Between the end of his press conference (nine p.m.) and three thirty the next morning, the White House logged fifty phone calls from the president, one every 7.8 minutes on average, with eight of the calls to Henry Kissinger alone. Shortly after the last call, the president roused his valet, Manolo Sanchez, to ask if he wanted some hot chocolate. Manolo declined, but Nixon wasn't discouraged. Had he ever seen the Lincoln Memorial, the president persisted. Manolo apparently had not, and with that, the adventure was on.

"I said, 'Get your clothes on, and we will go down to the Lincoln Memorial,'" Nixon said, in a version of events he dictated for the record several days later. "Well, I got dressed, and at approximately 4:35, we left the White House and drove to the Lincoln Memorial. I have never seen the Secret Service quite so petrified with apprehension."

With cause. The Memorial sits at the west end of the National Mall, where tens of thousands of demonstrators had already gathered in advance of Saturday's demonstration against the war, against the shootings at Kent State, against most personally and viscerally Richard Nixon himself. But a man on a manic high, as the president almost certainly was, and commander in chief of the world's largest army and his own Secret Service, as he constitutionally was, is not easily dissuaded.

A famous photograph captures the next scene: Nixon in suit and tie, the famous ski-nose profile tilted slightly forward; a handful of sleepy-eyed protestors listening in shock and dull amazement, maybe wondering what drug could have produced such an apparition, as the president reprised his press-conference triumph for the early-morning audience who, stranded on the Mall, hadn't watched a moment of it.

"I said I was sorry they had missed it because I had tried to explain in the press conference that my goals in Vietnam were the same as theirs—to stop the killing, to end the war, to bring peace. Our goal was not to get into Cambodia by what we were doing, but to get out of Vietnam. There seemed to be no—they did not respond. I hoped that their hatred of the war, which I could well understand, would not turn into a bitter hatred of our whole system, our country and everything that it stood for. I said, 'I know you, that probably most of you think I'm an SOB. But I want you to know that I understand just how you feel.'"

That's the president's official account. The protestors would tell an alternate version to the press who descended on them that morning. Nixon had mentioned Vietnam, but when that drew a tepid response, he moved to other matters. What college were they attending? One was at Syracuse University, a chance for the commander in chief to talk about football.* Another was from California—on to surfing.

Both accounts are in keeping with a president obsessed with war matters, battered by Kent State, challenged by small talk (aides commonly fed him three-by-five index cards for such moments), and (credit where it's due) physically brave, but as the sun began to rise around six a.m. and word of the night visitor spread, even Richard Nixon had to acknowledge it was time to leave. Bob Haldeman caught up with the presidential party, which by then included White House aide Bud Krogh, at about six fifteen, but not back at the White House. Manolo had never seen the famous "well" of the House of Representatives either. Having roused security there, the president was sitting in

---

* Under Coach Ben Schwartzwalder, Syracuse University had produced a string of legendary running backs: Jim Brown; Ernie Davis, the first African American to win the Heisman Trophy; and Floyd Little, who graduated in 1967.

one of the House desks as his valet took to the same podium used for State of the Union addresses.

From there, and now with Haldeman and Ron Ziegler in tow, the presidential entourage moved on to the Mayflower Hotel on Connecticut Avenue, five-plus blocks north of the White House, for breakfast. Back at the White House finally and still unable to sleep, Nixon wandered over to the Executive Office Building to greet the soldiers who were just waking up in their sleeping bags on the fourth floor. And so it went the rest of the day, while teeming protestors decried the Vietnam War not many hundreds of yards from the president's south windows: phone calls, the Oval Office, the Executive Office Building, everything but sleep.

"I'm concerned about his condition," Haldeman wrote in his diary later on Saturday. "The decision; the speech; the aftermath—killings, riots, press, etc.; the press conference; the student confrontation have all taken their toll—and he has had *very* little sleep for a long time and his judgment, temper and mood suffer badly as a result."*

———

Five weeks after the Kent State shootings, Richard Nixon authorized a formal study of campus unrest, what became known as the Scranton Commission. Kent State, of course, was a centerpiece. The commission met for three days in Kent—August 19–21, 1970—and

---

*The Nixon administration, of course, ended in disgrace. On August 9, 1974, Richard Nixon became the first and only American president to resign from office. (He was pardoned by his successor, Gerald Ford.) Ten months earlier, in October 1973, Spiro Agnew became only the second vice president to step down. John C. Calhoun had done so in 1832 to take a Senate seat. Agnew's resignation was part of a plea bargain involving criminal charges of tax evasion. White House Chief of Staff H. R. Haldeman would spend eighteen months in prison for his part in the Watergate cover-up, as would John Ehrlichman. But other Nixon administration alumni such as Daniel Patrick Moynihan, Henry Kissinger, Bill Safire, Caspar Weinberger, Peter Peterson, and Pat Buchanan would continue to shape national dialogue and policy for decades afterward.

interviewed a broad range of students, university administrators, municipal and law enforcement officials, and both the adjutant general and the assistant adjutant general of the Ohio National Guard, though no rank-and-file Guardsmen were included. A third of the commission's five-hundred-plus-page final report was consumed by a "special report" on what had happened, and why, on the Ohio campus.

By then, though, KSU had to share the stage with another campus shooting. On May 14, ten days after the deaths and injuries on Blanket Hill, students at predominantly black Jackson State College in Jackson, Mississippi, went on a rampage after rumors circulated that Charles Evers, brother of the slain civil rights icon Medgar Evers, had also been killed. Early on the morning on May 15, Mississippi highway patrolmen reacted much as the National Guard had at Kent State, with a hail of gunfire—150 rounds in twenty-eight seconds, according to Scranton Commission investigators—and with similar results: two dead, twelve wounded. All that was different really was the press and public reaction. White students shot by white National Guardsmen was a man-bites-dog story. Black students killed and wounded by white Mississippi highway patrolmen was just the opposite: dog bites man, an old story deep in the heart of Dixie.

The Scranton Commission report was released on September 26, 1970. Richard Nixon, who had created the commission, finally replied to former governor Scranton in a December 10 letter that ran to 3,600 words, most of them decrying the anarchistic state of higher education and the wantonness of student demonstrators. Kent State and Jackson State were mentioned exactly once, side by side and in passing, in the letter. For those hoping for some sort of legal resolution at the federal level to the complicated issues of who had done what, when, why, and where on May 4 at Kent State, the president's reply was not propitious.

10

Blind Justice

Four people died on May 4, 1970, in the thirteen-second, sixty-seven-shot fusillade at Kent State; nine were wounded. On August 1, 1966, less than four years earlier, fourteen people were killed and thirty-two wounded when engineering student Charles Whitman went on a shooting rampage inside and then from the observation deck of the main administration building on the campus of the University of Texas at Austin. (Overnight, Whitman had also murdered his parents in their sleep.) The first to be hit when Whitman opened fire from the Tower was Claire Wilson, an eighteen-year-old anthropology student then eight months pregnant. Whitman shot her in the abdomen, killing her unborn baby. When eighteen-year-old Thomas Eckman bent down to help his fiancé, Whitman shot and killed him, too. And so it went, person after person, for more than ninety minutes, until Whitman was shot and killed himself by an Austin police officer.

In 2007, thirty-two people died and another seventeen were wounded on the Virginia Tech campus at Blacksburg in two separate attacks launched by senior Seung-Hui Cho over a several-hour period. Between the attacks, the first in a dormitory, the second in an academic building, Cho returned to his own dorm, changed out of his blood-splattered clothes, deleted his email, and removed his computer hard drive. After shooting his final victim, Cho turned his gun on himself.

For sheer horror, of course, neither act begins to equal the December 14, 2012, slaughter at Sandy Hook Elementary School in Newtown, Connecticut: twenty students dead, many of them kindergartners, along with six school staff members before twenty-year-old Adam Lanza took his own life.

The point is this: what happened at Kent State on May 4, 1970, was within perhaps two standard mean deviations of normative school and college violence in America. Newtown, Virginia Tech, UT Austin—those were the true outliers, the massacres. Though often referred to as a massacre, the Kent State shootings don't rise to the "wholesale slaughter" roots of that antique French word, at least in comparison. As with the equally thin and famous Boston Massacre—five dead, six injured—of almost exactly two centuries earlier (March 5, 1770), it's not the numbers that give the Kent State shootings such resonance in our national memory. It's how the four died and nine were wounded, and where and why and for what, that makes this story so enduring a tragedy.

In both instances—Boston and Kent State—the rights of dissent and lawful assembly were at issue. In both, settlement was imposed by gunfire. In both, too, the level of provocation remains a crucial swing vote. Both happened at one of those moments in history packed with dry tinder. All that was needed in either instance was a match and someone willing to strike it. Kent State in 1970 and Boston in 1770 had no lack of volunteers.

But the difference is also significant: in the Boston Massacre, whatever the issues on either side, the scales of justice were promptly employed. That November, eight British soldiers—defended by future president John Adams, among others—stood trial for firing into the crowd. Six won acquittal; two were found guilty of manslaughter, then punishable by death, although the court later reduced the sentences to having their thumbs branded in open court. Their commanding officer, Captain Thomas Preston, had earlier been acquitted of ordering his soldiers to fire. A month later, in December 1770, four civilians were also tried, and also acquitted, of provoking the violence. Beyond the legal resolutions, an ultimate one was imposed by the American Revolution, which removed British rule and soldiers from America's soil.

In the case of the Kent State shootings, such a thorough closure has never been achieved. The American government survives, the Constitution lives on, and the rule of law remains a sacred national principle, but on this case, justice has never been fully tested.

Students died and were wounded at Kent State—that's demonstrable. We know what shot them and in many cases who. We can trace a specific chain of precipitating events back through the efforts to disperse the crowd gathered on the Commons that Monday, through the Sunday night confrontation at the university's main gate, to Saturday's burning of the ROTC building and the arrival on campus of the National Guard, Friday's rampage in downtown Kent, and back beyond that to President Nixon's Thursday night announcement on national TV that the Vietnam War was being expanded into Cambodia.

We have it on the authority of the then vice president of the United States, Spiro Agnew, that murders presumably in the second degree— since he had ruled out first degree in his *David Frost* session—took place on the Kent State campus a little after noon on that Monday in May. While not attempting to establish guilt or innocence, the Scranton Commission condemned both the "violent and criminal acts" of student protestors and the "indiscriminate . . . unnecessary, unwarranted, and inexcusable" discharge of weapons by National Guardsmen. But when it comes to official culpability for the shootings themselves, not a single person involved has ever been convicted of so much as a misdemeanor or even tried solely on the merits of the case as opposed to its technicalities.

The dead, their survivors, the wounded, the shooters, their commanding officers, a host of peripheral players—they all hover still in a kind of legal limbo. That's what makes Kent State so hard to let go.

Portage County prosecutor Ron Kane was quickest to the chase. At a May 15 press conference in the university gym, Kane displayed on several long tables the results of an exhaustive six-day search of the thirty-one now-empty dormitories spread out across the Kent State campus. The haul included a .25-caliber pistol, a light shotgun and some spent shotgun shells, sixty knives of various sizes including machetes, six pellet pistols/BB guns, two cap pistols, and several slingshots, plus hashish pipes, six live marijuana plants, cold remedies, insulin and needles, and a yellow button that read "Dare to Struggle, Dare to Win."

Kane refused to say if any of the guns had been fired, recently or ever, or if charges were likely to be filed based on the items displayed. On the latter point, though, he was treading on thin legal ice. Most of the dorm rooms from which the objects had been confiscated had multiple occupants. Ownership would be hard to establish beyond a reasonable doubt. More to the point, officials had entered and scoured the residences of 8,500 students without benefit of a single search warrant—a patently illegal act, as US District Court judge William Thomas would later rule.

Kane was back in the news two months later, seeking up to $100,000 in state funds to conduct a grand jury investigation of the Kent State shootings and for any trial work that might ensue. The county prosecutor said he had been assured of full cooperation by the FBI, the Ohio National Guard, the Ohio State Highway Patrol, and university and local officials.

Twelve days later, on July 23, the *Akron Beacon Journal* disclosed the contents of a fourteen-page analysis of the Kent State shootings, prepared by the Civil Rights Division of the US Department of Justice and based on fieldwork by the FBI. Among the key points:

- The roughly two hundred demonstrators leading the heckling of National Guardsmen could have been turned back by tear gas or arrests.

- No Guardsman was in danger of losing his life.
- The majority of those wounded or killed could not have been advancing on the Guard's position when they were shot, as witness the fact that nine of the thirteen were hit in the back or side.

In summary, the analysis said, it was unnecessary for the Guardsmen to fire on the students to protect themselves. But the report also contained a key legal distinction: If the crowd was not in a state of riot when the shootings occurred, then the Guardsmen who fired might be liable for criminal prosecution. If the crowd did constitute a riot—even if the riot was of the Guard's own making—then the Guardsmen were protected from prosecution under Ohio law.

Less than two weeks later, Governor Rhodes ordered Ohio attorney general Paul Brown to convene the special grand jury investigation that Ron Kane had requested and to require said jury to produce not only indictments, if appropriate, but also a report on the causes of the upheaval. Rhodes's request in turn freed up state funds to pay for the grand jury proceedings, and on September 15, 1970, a fifteen-member panel was sworn in at the Portage County Courthouse in Ravenna.

One month and a day later, on October 16, the grand jury indicted twenty-five people on charges related to the shooting. All but one of the twenty-five were charged with either first-degree riot (six), second-degree riot (fifteen), or inciting to riot (three), and in some cases to multiple riot charges. Among those indicted for the threshold charge the Justice Department analysis had identified: student body president Craig Morgan; Joe Lewis and Alan Canfora, both wounded in the shootings; Ken Hammond, who had urged a student strike from the top of the Victory Bell just before the Guard moved to enforce its noon crowd-dispersal edict; and associate professor of psychology Thomas Lough.

Five months earlier, Lough had been the most prominent among seven Kent State faculty members named by the Ohio Bureau of

Criminal Identification and Investigation as being "know(n), or suspected to support or aid Activities of Student Activists." Using information provided by the KSU police department, the report called Lough a "known sympathizer with activities on the Kent Campus. . . . He is always around the activists. Reports are that Dr. Lough had taught students how to make fire bombs in his class last year."

Of the Kent 25, as they became known, only one, Helen Nicholas, failed to be charged with a crime that would legally protect Guardsmen from prosecution. Her sole alleged malefaction: interfering with a firefighter.

Along with the indictments, the grand jury also issued an eighteen-page report expressing its collective opinion that the National Guardsmen had acted in self-defense, believing their lives to be in danger from the rioting around them, and laying blame for the campus disturbances and shootings squarely at the feet of those persons "charged with the administration of the University." "Permissiveness," "over-indulgence," and an "overemphasis . . . on the right to dissent" had all started Kent State down the slippery path to its own rivers of blood, the report clearly implied. So apparently had sheer curiosity. "Those who were present as cheerleaders and onlookers, while not liable for criminal acts, must morally assume a part of the responsibility for what occurred," the grand jurors declared.

More than a year of legal maneuvering was to follow. In late January 1971, US District Court judge William Thomas censored Jim Rhodes for instructing the grand jury to identify causes, ordered its eighteen-page report destroyed because it was certain to prejudice a jury, and noted in particular that finding Guardsmen had acted in self-defense essentially declared the dead and wounded guilty of the violence visited upon them.

Nonetheless, Thomas refused to vacate the indictments, subsequent courts agreed, and on November 22, 1971, jury selection began in Portage County Common Pleas Court for the first of the Kent 25 trials. Draconian restrictions would soon be imposed on the trials themselves: no press interviews by the principles; no picketing, parading, or cameras; nothing in short that might reprise the shrill legal circus, a few years earlier, of the Chicago Seven trials. By then, though, the starch seems to have gone out of the state lawyers, jurors, and perhaps even Ron Kane.

The prosecution top-loaded its agenda with what it felt to be the strongest cases—those against defendants Jerry Rupe, Larry Shub, Tom Fogelson, Peter Bleik, and Helen Nicholas. Rupe was convicted of the misdemeanor charge of interfering with a firefighter. The jury failed to reach verdicts on three felony charges: first-degree rioting, arson (the ROTC fire), and throwing rocks at a firefighter. Rupe's six-month sentence was added to time he was already serving on a drug conviction.

Shub pled guilty to first-degree riot charges in return for additional counts being dropped. Fogelson also pled guilty to first-degree riot, the only charge against him. Sentences for both men were eventually trimmed to probation. Charges against Bleik, accused of first-degree riot and arson, were dismissed during the trial. After the case against Nicholas was also rebuffed, Special State Prosecutor John Hayward asked that the charges against the remaining twenty defendants be dismissed, including charges against two defendants who could never be located.

Full of sound and fury, the state's case against the Kent 25 ultimately signified nothing, but the sound and fury might well have been the whole point. "The morbid joke," said Bill Arthrell, "was that . . . the ones they missed with bullets, they got with indictments."

———

The Ohio National Guard was equally quick to respond, but its "fact finding" looked a lot like circling wagons. Weapons had been discharged. Students had died. An inquiry was certain, charges were possible, and from the Guard's point of view, a worrisome model was readily at hand. Eight weeks earlier, the US Army had made public the report of its special investigation into the March 1968 massacre at My Lai—upward of two hundred and perhaps as many as five hundred Vietnamese men, women, and children killed by American forces.

The fact that the panel had recommended bringing charges against twenty-six soldiers, including platoon leader Lieutenant William Calley, who led the slaughter, and twenty-eight officers who had helped cover it up, could not have been lost on the Ohio Guardsmen—grunt privates, noncoms, and officers alike. The more those present at the Pagoda on May 4 could speak convincingly with one voice of the danger they had faced, the sniper fire they were under, the incoming debris that was pounding them, the surer would be both their justification and their defense. United they stood; divided, they could be picked off one by one.

Still, even though the statements they were required to give in the days just after the shootings dovetail at many points, what one carries away from reading them is the overwhelming confusion that swirled around the Guardsmen before and during those thirteen seconds of fury. If there was indeed a riot at Kent State on May 4, it might have been in the Guard's own chain of command, or in their individual perceptions of reality.

"As we were on a hill, several students tried to overrun us," Private Second Class Rodney Biddle wrote. "When that happened, fire broke out. I assumed those who were firing were only firing over the students to drive them back so I fired one round at a 45-degree angle. . . . Several students used very profane language. Green pigs, rotten fascists, and several words I'd rather not write on paper."

Private First Class James Brown, "fourth man in from end on left flank," heard the man on his right flank fire and then fired two rounds of his own forty feet over the heads of the crowd, by his estimation. "I was also hit with rocks and called foul names."

Before he heard an order to fire, Specialist Fourth Class James Farriss remembered at least two verbal warnings being given to students "that they would be fired upon if they didn't keep back." Private Second Class Robert Hatfield "fired because of hearing firing on my right." His fellow private second class, Lonnie Hinton, discharged his M1 "straight into the air" because the students "were all around us and I thought it was the most suitable thing to do at the time."

Officers especially were likely to cite sniper fire as the precipitating event. Captain John Martin wrote: "As Commanding Officer of Company A with approximately 30 troops, we were participating in an action to clear the campus of dissidents when what appeared to sound like gunshots of low caliber were heard coming from the direction of the dormitories." Elements of G Troop 107th Armored Cavalry kneeled and returned fire, Martin continued: "It was not evident to me whether they fired toward the demonstrators or into the air. Fourteen members of my unit thinking that a command to fire had been given fired several shots over the heads of the demonstrators before my officers and I ordered them to cease fire. I did not observe any demonstrators being hit in my area of responsibility."

Lieutenant Dwight Cline had a similar experience: "At approx. 12:55 [actually 12:24] small arms fire broke out on our flank which appeared as sniper fire. The flank unit of which the majority were G Troop 107th Armored Cavalry took up kneeling positions and returned fire at onrushing students. The members of our unit for the most part refrained from firing. However, several heard one of the commanders of the flank unit yell 'fire.' Some of our people thought this meant them; thus a few rounds were fired into the air. Many rounds hit at my feet no more than 30 yds to my front. They may have been fired by someone other than our men."

Lieutenant H. R. Fallon wrote almost the same thing: incoming small-arms fire, the command "fire" shouted from down the flank, and so forth, except in Fallon's account rounds were going into the ground no more than twenty-five feet in front of him. In his statement, Second Lieutenant Randall Leeper cited the patchwork nature of the entire operation: units drawn from multiple venues, unfamiliar leaders, a broken chain of command: "While in a line formation, confusion, due [to] a quick job of coordination and a number of people directing, may have caused more fire than was necessary."

Captain Ronald Snyder and his men from Company C were holding the position on the far side of Taylor Hall, at the top of the hill, when shooting broke out at the Pagoda. "At this time, I saw two students (male) stumble into the cement roadway and fall down bleeding. I then took a squad of men and moved forward to try and recover the downed students. Upon checking the two students closer, it became obvious that they were dead. We then tried to recover the bodies but were unable to, due to the students throwing rocks and trying to beat us with their hands. . . . The reason I knew the downed students were dead beyond any doubt is because of my experience as a coroner's investigator in my civilian job."

While "fired into the air" is the common currency of the Guard statements, all shots, obviously, did not disappear harmlessly into the ether. Some enlisted men at the Pagoda freely admitted to shooting into the crowd of students, even to targeting specific ones. "One shot fired into air," Ralph Zoller noted. "One shot fired at leg of demonstrator." James McGee did the same: two shots in the air, one at a demonstrator's leg. Barry Morris "fired into the mob in self-defense." James Edward Pierce "fired in self-defense at unknown individuals." Larry Shafer fired "one over heads of mob and four times at the demonstrators in self-defense."

As for provocation, McGee wrote that he and his fellow Guardsmen were under constant barrage as they reclimbed Blanket Hill from the practice field. "We had our backs to the students. That's when the rocks were the worst. . . . I was hit many times by rocks, once by a brick. When we got to the crest of the hill, I was running. The students were very close. The order was given to turn around. I turned. The students were approximately 30 feet away still moving ahead fast. . . . At this time, I was very frightened. The only thing I could think of was being shot with my own rifle."

Pierce likewise remembered the barrage increasing as the Guard retreated back up the hill toward the Pagoda. "We were down on our knees and attempting to utilize the trees for cover when they just made a massive charge. They were also at our rear. I felt the total group was hitting us—4,000—and all of a sudden everyone was firing."

Barry Morris wrote: "I was being pelted from three sides all during the retreat. By the time we reached the buildings at the top of the hill, the students were only approximately 20 to 30 feet away. When reaching the hill, most of the men were looking back and saw how close they were and how fast they were coming. At that point I heard gunfire to my left, looked and saw an officer firing, and drew my pistol, dropped to cover, and fired two shots into the mob where the most of the rocks were coming from."

Ralph Zoller drew a chart on his statement to show how, in his memory, the Guardsmen had been trapped front and back. "The students kept throwing and coming towards us. I fired my second shot at the leg of a male student, coming towards us and throwing." Larry Shafer, as noted earlier, could see Joe Lewis's right hand—with an extended middle finger—but not his left. Maybe he had a weapon in it, or a brick, something heavier, or what have you. Shafer estimated the distance between himself and Lewis when he fired at twenty to thirty feet.

Specialist Fourth Class William Earl Perkins wrote, "By the time we got to the top of the hill, we had over a thousand people going to do the best they could to prove to the student union they would kill anything that stood in their way of running the world the way they wanted it to be run. The people had moved all around us. Within 25 feet from my end. I was being hit from every point of my body in such a manner that in Roman days they put people to death."

———

What a panel of peers might have done with these exact provocations was nearly put to the test. On December 18, 1973, a federal grand jury met in Cleveland to consider the Kent State shootings. Approximately 180 witnesses appeared before the grand jury. The eight

Guardsmen known to have wounded or killed students refused to testify, but their previous statements to multiple interviewers—the Guard itself, the highway patrol, the FBI, and a previous state grand jury—were closely compared to one another and to extensive photographic evidence, including a jittery ninety-second, eight-millimeter film taken by student Chris Abell from the fifth floor of Wright Hall, about a third of a mile distant from the shootings.

The results were damning, according to a March 8, 1974, memorandum from Robert A. Murphy, chief of the Criminal Section of the US Department of Justice, to Assistant Attorney General J. Stanley Pottinger. The photographs, Murphy wrote, "demonstrate, conclusively, that no National Guardsman was about to lose his life—the only possible justification for the shooting by the subjects." The Guard, Murphy wrote, was not surrounded. The twenty to thirty feet Shafer remembered turned out to be twenty yards. Guardsmen had a clear route back to their staging ground by the burned-out ROTC building.

Eleven of the sixteen men in Troop G, under the command of Captain Raymond Srp, had acknowledged firing their weapons, but Srp himself had told investigators, "I was right in the middle of it and felt no danger." At the most, fifteen students might have been within eighty-five feet of the Guardsmen when they fired, and none of them was moving toward the Guard. Only one Guardsman required medical treatment for being hit by a rock, an injury received back on the football practice field.

Nor were accounts consistent across even narrowly separated intervals. On May 7, 1970, William Earl Perkins told the FBI, "I fired all eight rounds of my clip into the air. . . . I am sure all of my rounds were fired into the air and none into the crowd." A month later, in a June 9 statement to the Ohio State Highway Patrol, Perkins acknowledged that his last three rounds had been fired "straight ahead of me, my rifle waist high. I figure that my rounds would have been chest high or above." The one constant in all of Perkins's accounts is that he felt his own life and the lives of his troops to be in danger.

Three weeks later, on March 29, 1974, the grand jury indicted Perkins, McGee, Pierce, Morris, Zoller, Shafer, and two other Guardsmen—Matthew McManus and Leon Smith—on charges of violating the civil rights of the dead and wounded students.

At the trial, which began on October 21, the US Justice Department lawyers brought forth thirty-three witnesses and 130 exhibits, mostly photographic, to show that the "riot" that supposedly justified the shootings had posed little actual threat to the Guardsmen on Blanket Hill. Jurors also traveled to Kent, from the federal courthouse in Cleveland, to tour the site. Less than three weeks after the trial began, on November 8, 1974, US District Court judge Frank Battisti ruled that the government had failed to prove that the Guardsmen had willfully deprived the dead and wounded of their civil rights—the threshold charge in this case—and acquitted the eight defendants of all charges against them. In the end, a statute created as a counterbalance to the all-white justice of the Deep South was not equal to the nuances involved in the Kent State shootings.

By then, too, the immediate physical evidence of the alleged crime—the M1s that accounted for the bulk of violence—were long gone. On November 14, 1973, the Ohio National Guard informed the FBI that its entire stock of 12,906 M1 rifles had been shipped via Railway Express to the Letterkenny Army Depot in Chambersburg, Pennsylvania, almost two years earlier. According to the FBI memo-for-the-file, the Guard further told the bureau that it "maintains records for only three fiscal years and there is no way to check serial numbers of weapons issued to individual Guardsmen."

One more Ohio National Guard document needs mentioning. On June 8, 1970, a month to the day after the Guard marched off the KSU campus, its commanding officer, Brigadier General Robert H. Canterbury, filed his after-action report with the chief of the National Guard Bureau in Washington, DC.

The deployment to Kent State had involved, at its prime on May 4, 1,317 Guardsmen, Canterbury noted. Total military equipment deployed during the occupation of the campus and town included eighty-six half-ton trucks, nineteen three-quarter-ton trucks, twenty-two weighing in at 2.5 tons, and eleven five-tonners; seven APC M113s, the fully tracked armored personnel carriers used to bust through heavy jungle growth in Vietnam; three M106s, the M113 adapted for mortar launchers; five armored-command vehicles; five OH-13 and three OH-23 helicopters, the Sioux and the Raven respectively, both multipurpose light copters; four UH-19 Chickasaw helicopters and one of its more powerful cousins, the UH-34 Choctaw; and two each of the fixed-wing Cessna 01-A and De Havilland U6A.

Little wonder that the Guard's presence on the ground and in the air so overwhelmed both the campus and Kent itself. It was massive, in men and machinery. But what is in many ways most memorable about Robert Canterbury's report are the final two items on his list: "Problem Areas and Lessons Learned" and "Recommendations." Beside both, the highest-ranking National Guard officer at Kent State University on May 4 typed: "None." Of all the thousands of pages of documentation spawned by the shootings, there may be no sadder testament than those two "nones."

———

The FBI and Ohio State Highway Patrol beat the bushes harder than anyone. The FBI had an uncontested federal crime—arson of the ROTC building—to sift through in addition to the May 4 mayhem. The highway patrol had more resources on hand and local ears to the ground than anyone else. Between them, they amassed some eight thousand pages of investigative documents (FBI) and five thick books of background materials (highway patrol) that suggest they left no stone unturned, no innuendo unrecorded, and no blind alley untraveled.

On May 6, 1970, for example, the FBI's Cleveland office teletyped Director J. Edgar Hoover with the news that, while searching the body of Jeff Miller, the Ohio State Highway Patrol "found small scrap of paper which had telephone number 'six seven three seven five nine' and words 'communication center.'" The highway patrol quickly traced the number to 237–1/2 North Water Street in Kent and, later on the fourth, Kent police obtained a search warrant, arrested several people at the address for curfew violations, and during a search of the premises uncovered a letter from Abbie Hoffman, dated April 30, in which he urged [name blacked out] to "above all build the conspiracy in your back yard that will defend our growing nation." But what officials had been hoping to discover—evidence of a well-financed and highly sophisticated communications center—was nowhere to be found.

The same teletype informed FBI director Hoover, who had asked that news about the shootings be relayed directly to his desk, that negatives of photos taken of the demonstrators at Kent State were on their way to Washington by separate communication.

The next day, still busy, the Cleveland office sent an "urgent" teletype to its fellow offices in Albany, Baltimore, Buffalo, Cincinnati, Newark, and Pittsburgh, seeking help with locating and interviewing witnesses to or those who might have participated in the attack on the Kent State ROTC headquarters. "Campus was closed May Four, Last by Ohio National Guard and students were evacuated," the teletype reads. "Cleveland therefore setting out leads to have possible witnesses located and interviewed by home addresses."

Among the leads: two students, one from Toledo and the other from Pittsburgh, who had been treated at the Campus Health Center the evening of May 2 for "cuts on hands" and another who had been seen for "wound to left knee"; a Rochester, New York, student who "reportedly discussed" the ROTC burning while being treated for hearing loss on May 4; another student who "reportedly has info about hippie-type individuals in Volkswagen on KSU campus night of burning"; and yet another person who "telephonically advised" that a fellow student "can identify a KSU professor, who encouraged students to demonstrate and threatened [their] grades if they did not."

Two weeks later, Cleveland was informing Headquarters that, according to a blacked-out source, "WILLIAM K. SCHROEDER, KSU student who was shot to death during a confrontation with the Ohio National Guard (ONG) on 5/4/70 . . . had previously expressed doubts about the place of ROTC on campus and had considered fleeing to Canada to break his contract with the ROTC." Among the possible crimes listed in the header of this memo: sabotage, sedition, destruction of government property, and, under the Civil Rights Act of 1968, interference with a federally protected facility.

A May 10 FBI memo further advises that "[name blacked out] advised that a group of three students reported to [name blacked out] that they could testify to the fact that ALLISON KRAUSE had a weapon in her possession at the time of the shooting, May 4, 1970."

For a full month after the shootings, Lillian and Brinsley Tyrrell received no mail. "It was very strange," he recalled. "No bills, no anything. Some people wanted to rent our garage. They drove up the driveway to ask about it, but we were renting the house. If you walked downtown, strange, hippie people wanted to buy you drinks and talk. . . . Then all of a sudden, we got a flood of mail, everything that had been held back."*

English professor Lew Fried, like Tyrrell new to the faculty that year, also fell under FBI scrutiny. "They were very nice. They knocked on the door and asked if they could come in. They told me President Nixon is interested in what I have to say, and within two minutes, I knew that they knew everything about me. The first thing they said was on such-and-such a date did so-and-so ask you for a mechanical pencil? I was floored. That had happened, and I knew they were sending me a message. Don't lie. We know everything."

And so it went for months and months of the same, alternately intriguing, frightening, and rumor-ridden, and often highly specula-

---

*Brinsley Tyrrell had been arrested multiple times in his native England while taking part in antiwar protests directed at America.

tive. The Scranton Commission, for example, chose to ignore completely thirdhand accounts of Allison Krauses' possessing a weapon.

The highway patrol meanwhile was committing to its files a spectacularly uninformative report of an interview with Mary Ann Vecchio, who had vaulted to instant front-page fame as the mourner kneeling beside Jeffrey Miller's lifeless body.* Far from proof that outside agitators were crawling all over May 4, Vecchio appears to have been just another midteen loose in the world in 1970, without much awareness of what was going on around her.

The third youngest of six children, Vecchio ran away from her parents' home in Opa-Locka, Florida, in February 1970, made her way to Atlanta (although she wouldn't say how), and from there "bummed" her way to Youngstown, Ohio. Roughly two weeks before the shootings she traveled from Youngstown to Kent for the first time "for the purposes of frequenting a discotheque, known as J.D.'s. At that time, she was not aware of any student or non-student extremist political action or agitation at Kent State University."

On Friday, May 1, Vecchio and, in her words, "two other chicks hitched a ride" back to Kent, again headed for J.D.'s, and arrived just in time to see a student arrested in front of the discotheque for intoxication, the beginning of a long night of rampage and response. She awoke the next day about three in the afternoon, at the house of "friends" she refused to identify, and spent that night and the next day shuttling between campus and her temporary home.

At 12:24 p.m. on May 4, when the Guardsmen turned and fired, Vecchio fell, rolled down the hill behind her, and then saw Jeff Miller bleeding out on the road near her. She ran to him, she told the interviewer, knelt, and had just raised her hands when photographer John Filo made her the nationally recognized iconic image of dissent and death at Kent State.

---

*The interview took place at the Marion County Juvenile Detention Center in Indianapolis, where she was being held by juvenile authorities pending the arrival of her parents.

After the shootings, Vecchio learned of the free bus service being offered to students, who had been ordered off campus, and caught a ride to Columbus, where she stayed five days, including participating in demonstrations over the four killed at Kent State and the "thing in Cambodia."

Vecchio, the report said, "was asked specifically concerning the Young Socialist Alliance (YSA) and Students for a Democratic Society (SDS), however, she advised she had never heard of such organizations." The report concluded with a physical description of the interviewee: white, female, five feet eight, 155 pounds, with brown hair and eyes. Vecchio's birthdate is recorded as December 3, 1954, a year and a day before she was actually born, in Palermo, Sicily.

———

Another commonality that binds together the FBI and OSHP investigative efforts: Terry Norman. Indeed, Norman winds through the entire saga of the Kent State shootings like an urban myth, or maybe connects like a missing link.

What's known about Norman can be summarized from a June 1970 statement he voluntarily made to the Ohio State Highway Patrol. Born Terrence Brookes Norman on April 30, 1949, he was by the spring of 1970 a twenty-one-year-old Kent State junior majoring in criminal enforcement. For several years, Norman had also been earning freelance money by photographing campus antiwar radicals and other extremists and selling the negatives to the Kent State police. In mid-April 1970, just at the time Jerry Rubin visited the school, Norman said he struck a similar deal with another "agency" he wouldn't name but is most likely the FBI, probably through the Bureau's Akron office. Norman also owned a gun—a .38-caliber Smith & Wesson Model 36, nickel-plated, with a two-inch barrel, custom grip, and trigger shoe.

On May 4, as he had been doing all weekend long, Norman was photographing demonstrators. His Smith & Wesson .38 hung ready to cross-draw in a semishoulder holster on his left side, concealed by a lightweight sport coat and loaded with "four rounds of Super Val and one of Armor Piercing," he told the interviewer. Norman had also brought along a gas mask. He was, by his estimate, 150 to 200 feet south of the skirmish line when the Guardsmen opened fire. He was heading toward the campus police station shortly afterward when he was set upon by incensed demonstrators.

"Somebody ran toward me and grabbed my gas mask with one hand and my camera with the other. . . . Somebody at the time yelled, 'He's a pig photographer!' Also someone grabbed my left arm and tried to pull me to the ground. Again at that time, someone yelled, 'Kill the pig! Kill the pig!' Someone then clipped me behind the knees, and I fell down. Then someone said, 'Stick the pig!' This meant to me that someone had a knife. At that time, I drew my weapon."

That's when Bill Barrett, the Kent State alumni publications editor, came on the scene:

"There were maybe a dozen students standing in almost a semicircle, and they were all looking at one photographer who was standing there, facing them by himself, and he had a pistol in his hand. And they were shouting different things. Some were saying he shot somebody, or he's going to shoot somebody. There was a lot of confusion. . . .

"He was backing off a step or two and threatening. He had a camera around his neck; he had a gas mask on, wearing a sport coat, carrying a camera bag. I was right on the end, and I looked at him, and it was just like the Guardsmen that I had seen a few minutes earlier. His eyes were as big as dollars. And I thought, *Oh my God, if these kids take one step towards him, something's going to happen here.* . . . I yelled, 'Put that goddamn gun away!' And he looked at me, and I don't know whether he recognized me or not, but he said, 'If I do, they'll kill me.' And I said, 'Yeah, and if you don't, you'll kill somebody.' . . . At the same time, on the other end of this semi-circle of students, I saw a guy standing over there wearing a suit and carrying a briefcase, a black man, and he was yelling at him from the other side, saying the same thing, 'Don't do anything; put that gun away.'"

Just about that time, Barrett recalled, Norman ripped off his gas mask and began racing downhill toward the Guard lines. Barrett and the black man—Harry Reid, a graduate student—took off after him, both shouting to warn people that he had a gun. They were still shouting when Norman ran right through the Guard lines, with Barrett and Reid still behind him.

"When we got through the lines," Barrett continued, "I saw some of the campus police, and Terry Norman was standing there. He was bent over with his hands on his knees like he was trying to catch his breath, and I yelled, 'He has a gun!' and they kind of looked at me, and then finally [campus policeman] Harold Rice came along, and he knew Terry Norman because he called him by name. And he said, 'Terry, do you have a gun?' And he straightened up and kind of nodded, and Harold Rice told him, 'Let's have it. Take it out. Easy.' I remember him . . . reaching in with two fingers and pulling that gun out and handing it to Harold Rice. My next recollection was that Harold Rice took the gun and looked at it and sniffed it, and said that it hadn't been fired. He seemed pretty certain about it."

Others recall that moment differently. Newsman Fred DeBrine of Cleveland's WKYC-TV told *Tampa Tribune* reporter Janis Froelich in 2006 that he was watching as Rice passed Norman's gun on to campus detective Tom Kelley:

"Kelley yelled, 'My God! He fired it four times. What the hell do we do now?'

"Shaking, Terry said, 'I had to shoot. They were trying to kill me.'"

In a statement dated August 9, 1973, National Guard Second Lieutenant Richard L. Day seconded DeBrine's account. On May 4, 1970, Day's unit had remained at the base of Blanket Hill to protect some vehicles while the bulk of the force moved up the hill, separating to go around Taylor Hall. Day was still there when Norman came racing through the Guard lines and handed his pistol to a "civilian official." "This officer stepped back from the young man and toward me," according to Day. "He rolled the cylinder to the side of the pistol and remarked that there were 'four spent cartridges' in the cylinder."

The space between the two versions is critical. If Barrett's memory is accurate and complete, then Norman's clash with his fellow students is just another piece of the shocked and angry aftermath of the shootings, even if he was waving a pistol. If DeBrine and Day have it right *and* if the four shots were fired prior to the Guard opening up on the students, then Norman's four spent cartridges might explain the sniper fire many Guardsmen claimed to have heard and the four possible "shots" heard on the audiotape that surfaced in 2007—although, as noted earlier, those four shots precede the actual fusillade by more than a minute.

That potential has kept the Terry Norman story alive ever since and wrapped it in further allegations and speculation—that, for example, the FBI for mysterious reasons ignored multiple efforts to bring the Norman matter to its attention; that Norman had indeed fired his gun before the shootings but was able to reload on the fly afterward; that he had actually shot a person, never identified; even that Norman's alleged four shots were intentional, to provoke and justify the fusillade that followed. In addition to exonerating the National Guard from responsibility for the shootings, that last allegation also tends to drag the Kent State shootings down the rabbit hole of a conspiracy theory that connects Norman via his supposed FBI ties with J. Edgar Hoover and ultimately places responsibility for the four deaths at the feet of Richard Nixon. Filmmaker Oliver Stone among others is said to favor this interpretation. For his part, Terry Norman gives no interviews, but Janis Froelich reported in her *Tampa Tribune* article that Norman had told relatives across the years that he was indeed the one who launched the tragedy of Kent State.

But here's a further problem from a legal point of view: Terry Norman may not be a reliable witness. As a student, he had cards printed up to support his claim that he worked for the Brookes Detective Agency, after his middle name. According to relatives, he pictured himself as something of a James Bond figure, a law enforcement wannabe. Harold Rice said the same: Norman went out of his way to hang around with campus police. He also liked to imply that he was working for a "higher authority" without actually naming it. He once flew a girlfriend to Washington, DC, presumably on tickets provided by the FBI, and had her sit on a park bench across from the old FBI headquarters in the Department of Justice building on Pennsylvania Avenue while he disappeared inside for forty-five minutes. Maybe he met with J. Edgar Hoover himself. Maybe he took the tour instead, including the famous shooting range downstairs. Who knows? But a good rule of thumb is that the more hints one drops about connections with "higher authorities," the less likely such connections actually exist.

Norman's postcollegiate career poses problems as well. After Kent State, he did serve on the DC police force for a dozen years, but not without controversy. In September 1973, he lost permission to carry a gun and make arrests and was transferred from the narcotics squad to a desk job. Things went south from there. In the 1990s, while employed by the document management firm Anacomp Inc., Norman manipulated false invoices to steal $675,000. He pled guilty to various counts of mail fraud and money laundering and spent three and a half years in the federal prison system. In a court of law, a competent prosecutor likely would have chewed Terry Norman's story to pieces, but like so much else with the shootings, this part of the saga was never weighed on the scales of justice.

———

Even if he is not the golden thread that pulls the Kent State shootings together, Terry Norman did manage, at least obliquely, to get the case reopened. Richard Day's account of Norman's gun and its supposed spent cartridges ended up, via another Guard officer, in the hands of Senator Birch Bayh of Indiana, who had taken an interest in the case. Bayh, in turn, pressured the Justice Department, which had put Kent

State on ice, and Attorney General Elliot Richardson, soon to resign in the famous Watergate-related Saturday Night Massacre, ordered the case reopened, leading to the indictment of the eight Guardsmen. When that case was dismissed by US District Court judge Frank Battisti in November 1974 on the grounds that the prosecution had fallen short of threshold requirements, the Justice Department closed its books for good on Kent State, but the case would live on in the legal system for another half decade.

Arthur Krause was at the center of the civil litigation that finally brought closure of a sort to the Kent State shootings. His daughter, Allison, had been dead only five weeks when Krause filed two suits: one for $2 million in the Portage County Court of Common Pleas against the State of Ohio, the other for $6 million in federal court against Governor Rhodes, Ohio National Guard adjutant general Sylvester Del Corso, and Robert Canterbury, the Guard Mission Commander at Kent State, for "intentionally and maliciously disregard[ing] the lives and safety of students, spectators and passersby, including Allison Krause."

Simultaneously, Krause was pressing the White House and Justice Department to empanel a federal grand jury to consider filing criminal charges in the case. In February 1971, White House aide John Dean addressed Krause's persistent efforts in a memo-for-the-file. If the Justice Department was not going to satisfy Krause's demand for a grand jury, Dean wrote, the decision should be made public as soon as possible. "An announcement by the government that the grand jury will not be convened could very likely provoke demonstrations this spring on the campuses and the longer we wait to announce that decision the more likely we will have a more celebrated incident upon the announcement of the government's actions."

If Arthur Krause ever did read the memo, the political calculation behind Dean's thoughts on the timing of the grand jury decision must have enraged him. James Michener's account of the shootings—*Kent State: What Happened and Why*, published in spring 1971—certainly had that effect. "Michener kept calling the murders and wounding an accident as if trying to convince himself that it was right when he knew it was wrong and more than an accident," Krause replied to a questionnaire sent as part of a class project at Kent State. Krause also maintained that Michener had "put me up for ridicule by his intimation that a father speaking out at the murder of his daughter is to keep silent so as not to destroy his dignity."

Other families of the dead students followed Arthur Krause's lead in bringing damage actions against Governor Rhodes, the Guard leadership, Guard officers and enlisted men, and even Kent State president Robert White for, as one suit put it, "intentionally, recklessly, willfully and wantonly" causing the Guard deployment on the Kent State campus and ordering Guard members to commit acts that resulted in the four deaths. But all the suits kept coming up against the same barricade: Rhodes, White, and the other plaintiffs contended that they were being sued in their official capacity as agents of the state and that the damage actions were therefore against the state and thus barred by the Eleventh Amendment.

District and appeals courts agreed: the doctrine of sovereign immunity extends not only to states, they held, but to its officials. In December 1973, the case rose to the attention of the US Supreme Court, and on April 17, 1974, the court issued its verdict. By an 8–0 vote, with William Douglas sitting out the decision, the Court ruled in the plaintiffs' favor. Even a governor, when he acts "in a manner violative of the Federal Constitution . . . is subjected in his person to the consequences of his individual conduct."

A year later, in May 1975, the civil case known as *Krause v. Rhodes*, which by then had consolidated all the previous suits and added to the plaintiffs the wounded as well as the families of the dead, opened in Cleveland before a federal jury. Named as defendants, in addition to Rhodes and Kent State president Robert White, were twenty-seven current and former Guardsman. The amount sought was $46 million, but on August 27 of that year, after thirty-three hours of deliberation, the Cleveland jury acquitted the defendants on a 9–3 vote, finding, much as previous juries in the criminal trials had, that those killed and wounded on May 4 had not been the victims of "wanton misconduct or of the negligence of some or all of the defendants."

Still, the case soldiered on, looking for a fresh legal opening, and in September 1977, Krause and the other plaintiffs found another hole. Citing misconduct on the judge's part in the earlier proceedings, the US Court of Appeals ordered a retrial. That was never held, but sixteen months later, in January 1979—more than eight and a half years after the shootings—*Krause v. Rhodes* was finally settled in the only place it probably ever could have been brought to conclusion: out of court. The twenty-eight defendants—Robert White, by then, had been cut loose from the suit—agreed to and individually signed a statement that read in full:

> In retrospect, the tragedy of May 4, 1970, should not have occurred. The students may have believed they were right in continuing their mass protest in response to the Cambodian invasion, even though this protest followed the posting and reading of an order to ban rallies and an order to disperse. These orders have since been determined by the Sixth Circuit Court of Appeals to have been lawful.
>
> Some of the Guardsmen on Blanket Hill, fearful and anxious from prior events, may have believed in their own minds that their lives were in danger. Hindsight suggests that another method would have resolved the confrontation. Better ways must be found to deal with such confrontations.
>
> We devoutly wish that a means had been found to avoid the May 4 events culminating in the Guard shootings and the irreversible deaths and injuries. We deeply regret those events and are profoundly saddened by the deaths of four students and wounding of nine others which resulted. We hope the agreement to end this litigation will help to assuage the tragic memories regarding that sad day.

For their part, and for agreeing to forgo all future claims against any of the defendants, the plaintiffs were awarded $675,000—1.5 percent of the $46 million they had originally sought, and all footed by the taxpayers of the State of Ohio. After $50,000 was deducted for attorneys' fees and $25,000 for out-of-pocket expenses—the Court's determination—plaintiffs divvied up the remaining $600,000.

The bulk of that—$375,000—went to Dean Kahler, still using a wheelchair today, with a .30-caliber round lodged in his spine. Joe Lewis, shot twice, received $42,500; Tom Grace, $37,500; Donald Scott MacKenzie, $27,500; and John Cleary, $22,500. The other wounded and the estates of Sandy Scheuer, Bill Schroeder, Jeff Miller, and Allison Krause received $15,000 each.

Something, in short, for everyone, and maybe as much closure as the case will ever receive.* But like all the court proceedings and the many investigations and commissions that preceded it, *Krause v. Rhodes* failed to answer the foundational question that haunts the Kent State shootings to this day: What happened?

---

* The out-of-court settlement in *Krause v. Rhodes* didn't end the case. In 1981, the US Court of Appeals for the Sixth Circuit heard arguments from Steven Sindell, the original counsel for twelve of the plaintiffs, that the $50,000 the District Court had allotted for attorneys' fees improperly invalidated his contract for a 33–1/3 percent contingency fee. A year later, the Appeals Court was back on the case, considering "certain public disclosure orders" imposed by US District Court judge William Thomas. In ruling against Sindell, the Appeals Court noted that "the record in this case is a long and torturous one."

11

Plan B

The Kent State shootings are one of those events that cry out for a villain, a smoking gun (figuratively—there were plenty of literal ones), someone to step forward and take the blame, even a deathbed confession. Some had pinned their hopes, with reason, on Sergeant Myron "Mike" Pryor who stands with .45 pistol leveled, seemingly leading Troop G as it fires from the Pagoda, in another of Kent State's memorable photos.

Pryor proclaimed his innocence, under oath, on multiple occasions. The sudden wheeling at the Pagoda had taken him by surprise and forced him to a forward position, where "I could have been shot by the men behind me, very easily." Neither just prior to nor doing the shooting had he raised his hand in any way. His .45 pistol, he said, was held in a "standard forward position" with the slide back so it couldn't be fired, and though he had "aimed in the general direction of the crowd," he never even bothered to push a magazine into the handle and load his weapon.

Others saw it differently. Photographer John Filo, soon to take the famous photo of Mary Ann Vecchio, was both a hunter and familiar with the .45, having fired an automatic version of the weapon at a range. He testified in 1975 that during the thirteen seconds of mayhem he had watched Pryor shooting repeatedly at the crowd in the parking lot.

"[It] appeared to me that he was firing the gun, just a recoil and firing down the hill."

"You actually saw the recoil?"

Filo answered in the affirmative.

Pryor's account is further compromised by the fact that his weapon that day went missing after the shooting and was quite possibly not the same gun that he eventually identified as the .45 he had been carrying on May 4. But Mike Pryor died in August 2002 without baring his soul, if indeed there was anything to cleanse.

Others favor Major Harry Jones as Kent State's smoking gun. In a 1974 deposition, Captain Raymond Srp said Jones had ordered the kneeling skirmish line on the practice field. Later, in trial testimony, Srp testified that while on the practice field, he also heard Jones say to the protestors words to the effect that, "Come on. I will fix you!" A spectator watching the action on the practice field through binoculars from the balcony of Taylor Hall told investigators that he had seen an officer fire a single shot from a .45-caliber pistol over the heads of nearby rock throwers. Jones was the only officer present who carried a pistol—a .22-caliber Beretta automatic, not a .45—and indeed a .22-caliber shell casing was found the next day near the edge of the field, but Jones denied under oath firing his pistol on the practice field or any other time on May 4.

Jones was old-school, hard-nosed. All weekend long he had shown minimal patience with the protestors. If Mike Pryor didn't cue the shooting with his pistol, the theory goes, Harry Jones did so with his baton. But Jones and his baton also played a key role in bringing the firing to a close—not because the Guard had no right to defend itself, but because the firing "was indiscriminate. I had heard no order to fire . . . [and] I did not observe anyone firing at the Guardsmen. If I had, I would not have stopped it." Reconciling such actions and attitude with direct culpability for the shootings themselves seems a stretch.

Maybe some day resolution will magically arrive. Terry Norman will suddenly appear on national TV, clutching the four spent cartridges that sparked the thirteen seconds of mayhem, or we'll hear from the repentant prankster who lit the firecrackers that were mistaken for gunfire or from one of the Guardsmen who took part in an alleged secret huddle on the football practice field, during which Jeff Miller, Alan Canfora, Allison Krause, and others were targeted. The Kent State shootings are going on half a century old. Students and Guardsmen alike are heading into those years when one has to decide to die with secrets or greet whatever lies ahead with a conscience cleansed by confession. But odds are that even if such a moment should come to pass, the effect will be more spectacular than explanatory.

The Kent State tragedy resulted, of course, from specific rounds squeezed off by specific Guardsmen with the specific effect of killing and wounding specific students. But the tragic outcome was also the end point of a cascade of failures and misjudgments that piled up one on top of the other until the shootings were in some ways almost inevitable. Every party to the violence—the university, the town, the governor, the hard core of students who led the demonstrations, the National Guard—had a strategy, or at least a purpose in mind. But no one, it seemed, had bothered to think beyond that point, to what would happen if the initial approach didn't work or was rendered inoperable for practical reasons or because circumstances had spun out of control. At Kent State that first weekend in May 1970, everyone seemed to have a Plan A. Plan Bs, however, went fatally AWOL.

————

The university did, in fact, have a contingency plan in place and well rehearsed in the event campus unrest accelerated to the point where outside law enforcement had to be summoned to contain the violence. When that actually happened, though, school officials were looking in the wrong direction for help, according to Dick Brede- meier, then the dean of student activities.

"I was pretty proud of our planning for this, and it turned out it was totally useless simply because the National Guard was called in as backup. We expected it to be the highway patrol. We spent a lot of time with the highway patrol talking about this, talking about communication. It was clear the National Guard didn't want communication, didn't want to be bothered by it."

Ray Bye, who would end up alone in the communication center when the shootings took place, also cited the lack of any effective interface between university officials and the National Guard. The two "were like ships passing in the night. There was no coordination on the Guard's part with us, and we had no ability to coordinate with them." The ultimate aftermath of that failure, four dead and nine wounded, Bye said, "is a classic example of how the worst mistakes in any organization happen when communication goes awry."

In his appearance before the Scranton Commission, Robert White testified time and again to how out of the loop he and other university administrators were as the weekend events churned toward a midday Monday showdown. No one—not the National Guard, not Mayor Satrom, not the governor's office—had contacted White (by phone, since he was still in Iowa) or any other administrator prior to the Guard's Saturday night arrival on the Kent State campus. The few moments White had alone with Jim Rhodes when he did return midday Sunday left White with no doubt that the Guard controlled the campus and that its brief was to keep the school open and running at all costs. It was the Guard, not White or any other administrator, that decided to ban all assemblies peaceful or otherwise; the Guard, not White or any other administrator, that determined a "crowd" would be wherever three or more were gathered.

As White put it in a 1975 deposition, "I came to feel that all parties, all governmental bodies had a feeling that it was up to them to take control of the situation, that the university officials were not crucial or significant."

Clearly, this wasn't the situation the university had prepared for. "The highway patrol," Dick Bredemeier said, "would have just waited the students out, I'm convinced. That was how they approached it." The Guard did precisely the opposite—took the reins into its own teeth and pressed the students at every turn. And when the Guard did that, the university had no alternative strategy to fall back on.

Part of that failure can be traced to Kent State's larger chain of command. For all the autonomy conferred by academic freedom and other traditions, the university was a state school: its buck stopped at the governor's desk, not at its own front door. Part, too, lay in the very nature of the man at the top of the university's internal hierarchy: Robert White. By all accounts, White was a laissez-faire president, far more inclined to committees than dictates from on high. He had come up through the education school. One longtime faculty member referred to him as Kent State's last "teacher president." By most accounts, too, he was widely liked. Professors gave him a standing ovation at the first general faculty meeting held after the shootings. Ray Bye, among others, talked of the pain of seeing White's postpresidential years consumed by depositions and court appearances.* But on that first weekend in May 1970, once White had returned to campus, his senior staff seems to have been as much concerned with shielding him from the conflict as involving him in it.

To have not even contacted White on Sunday night to inform him that protestors were waiting for him and Mayor Satrom at the school's front gate; for the university president and his top staffers to be absent from the campus at noon Monday, when the dance of death began in earnest; for the president never to inquire (as he testified before the Scranton Commission) whether the M1s being carried all over his campus were loaded with live ammunition; for the resolution of the postshooting crisis back on the Commons to have fallen largely on the broad shoulders of one geology professor with no help from the university's senior leadership—these things can all be explained away

---

*White resigned as Kent State president in February 1971, effective that September.

in their small details, but collectively they represent a vast abdication of responsibility that finally has to be laid at Robert White's own feet.

White, Brinsley Tyrrell said, was "a sweet guy. He really believed in teaching, and he was very democratic. But he was hopelessly outgunned by this. He hadn't a clue. My guess is that none of the senior staff wanted to claim any responsibility at all, so they just bowed out. . . . It was just terrible."

Jerry Lewis, who like Tyrrell would spend virtually his entire career teaching at Kent State, put it succinctly: White "was the wrong man in the wrong place at the wrong time"—with almost predictable results.

"We were young and naïve in feeling protected and feeling that we had rights and were going to be heard," former student Martha Dishman recalled in a 2010 interview, "but the lack of leadership at the governor's level and the military level and the presidential level— there was no leadership at all exhibited. . . . For us, it was traumatic to be unprotected, but for them, it was a huge failure not to be able to manage a crisis." Robert White, she said, "was nowhere to be found." He did nothing to present "a calm face or to combat what had happened to his campus."

Timothy App, then a senior art major and now a professor at Maryland Institute College of Art in Baltimore, extended that criticism to the senior staff as a whole: "My sense is that they so didn't want this to be happening that they didn't step in and try to do anything about it. It's a state university. The governor of the state calls in the National Guard. What do you do? You defend the campus, and they didn't do that."

———

The university at least had the opportunity to set events on a different course as the weekend wore on. A show of force by the campus police at the ROTC building Saturday evening, a brief appearance by

President White during the Sunday night standoff between Guardsmen and students, a Monday morning summit meeting between senior administrators and the most hard-core demonstrators, even a noontime address by the university president at the Commons where students had gathered—who knows what might have turned the tide or spread a steadying influence over events quickly spinning out of control? All we can know for certain is that *not* doing any of those things didn't work.

In theory, two other key players in the drama—the City of Kent and the governor's office—had similar elasticity, but in practical terms, both were left with virtually no room to maneuver once the National Guard arrived on the Kent State campus.

LeRoy Satrom, the Kent mayor, died in 2004 without ever saying publicly if he had acted in haste only to repent at leisure, but from the moment in the very early hours of Saturday morning when he placed his call to the office of Governor Rhodes, Satrom set in motion a process that turned not only the campus but his own city into a war zone. The helicopters overhead kept Kent residents as well as Kent State students awake Saturday and Sunday night. Their searchlights illuminated children's and grandparents' beds along with dorm rooms. The full-tracks and half-tracks and armored personnel carriers ground equally down campus streets and community ones. The bulk of the Guard force was never on campus; it was spread across Kent city and the roads leading into it.

Such an overwhelming military presence inevitably suggested to the people of Kent a dire military threat just on the other side of the campus walls. Rumors about that threat—snipers, stashed guns, a sophisticated communications center secreted somewhere in a student rental, "outsiders," LSD-tainted drinking water, vigilantes racing down the sewers to bomb Kent's one-site shopping—all this became the common currency between the occupied and their occupiers. Fevered imaginations were commonplace, from backyard parties when a roofer first cried down "Oh, my God! My God, they've killed the

Guardsmen!" to inside the gas masks of Guardsmen retreating up the back side of Blanket Hill. And once that genie was out of the bottle, there was not a single thing Mayor Satrom could have done about it except phoning the same office he had called early Saturday morning and pleading that the dogs be called off. By Monday morning, though, that was equally impossible. In the whole panoply of Kent State players, no one was more wedded to his own Plan A than Jim Rhodes.

Rhodes, Timothy App contended, "called out the Guard in the knowledge that it was not well trained in riot control and that the prejudice against students opposed to the Vietnam War was rampant all over Ohio. We were angry, but the citizens of Kent were furious. And the news media kept portraying it that way: 'Who do these students think they are?'"

We can't read Jim Rhodes's mind at this distance in time, but both assertions are quite likely on the money. Ohio was heavily represented both in the battlefield in Vietnam and still today on the walls of the Vietnam War Memorial. Only five states—California, New York, Texas, and Pennsylvania—suffered more fatalities. Feelings ran high all across the state. As for the effectiveness of the Ohio Guard's riot-control training, one has only to look at the results on May 4— although that's a story more complicated than training alone.

Jim Rhodes was also following a political path well established in California by Ronald Reagan in his successful 1966 gubernatorial campaign against Pat Brown and by S. I. Hayakawa in building the conservative base that would eventually land him in the US Senate. Hayakawa had famously unplugged a set of loudspeakers in the midst of a student strike at San Francisco State University, not long after becoming the school's president in 1968. For his part, Reagan had taken his stand against hippies, liberals, antiwar protesters, free-speech advocates, dirty dancers, and a good deal more at the University of California, Berkeley. "If it takes a bloodbath" to end campus violence, he said on April 8, 1970, less than a month before Kent State, then "let's get it over with, no more appeasement."

Rhodes would later claim, under oath, that he had "no knowledge" that Guardsmen were carrying loaded weapons when they went onto the Kent State campus, but if so, one suspects the reason is that he didn't want to know. Rhodes was of the same mindset as Reagan and Hayakawa, and his timing could not have been more fortuitous. Kent State had fallen into his lap exactly when he needed it most, on the weekend before a Senate primary election in which he was trailing by roughly sixty thousand votes. Even had he seen the train wreck coming on Monday, the governor had no way to back away from his position without forfeiting all the electoral ground he had made up by bringing the Guard to Kent State and vowing to keep the university open and running.

With the university administration hors de combat, the City of Kent occupied by the military and consumed by its own fears, and the governor's office with eyes locked straight ahead on Tuesday's primary vote, brokering a way out of the swirling vortex at Kent State fell to the principal antagonists: the students and the Guard. And by Monday midday, neither group had any capacity to alter its course: the students because they lacked effective leadership, the Guard because it lacked the same.

———

Maybe because for the hard core of protestors Plan A was so simple—provoke and react, provoke and react, provoke and react—it seemed to many people deeply nuanced and complex.

"They gave us much more credit for being organized than we really were," Diane Gallagher remembered. "I think it was part of the government's paranoia at the time because they credited us with organizational skills that we really didn't have. It was very grassroots, very spontaneous, very whimsical at times.

"I had a boyfriend at the time of the shootings whose apartment had been busted into. It was [occupied by my boyfriend] from Ohio, a student I believe from Ethiopia, and a Jew from New York City.

That combination brought attention, and they went into his apartment and destroyed many things because they thought the apartment,
on Water Street, was the headquarters of the organization. There was
nothing there except three people with I'm sure some political leaflets
and everything, but there was no telephone system. There was not
anything to create the kind of fear that was in this country."

By midday Monday, though, the very success of Plan A and the
lack of any organizational infrastructure undergirding it had exposed
a gaping problem. Guardsmen were frazzled. Anger had been largely
transferred from the abstraction of a war in Southeast Asia to the National Guard's heavy-booted presence on the Kent State campus. Lo-
calization had intensified emotions and drawn a much larger circle
into the fray, and now students and Guardsmen were ready to con-
front one another at a major crossroads of college life. Everything was
in place except one very big thing: What happens next? For that, students had no organized answer, largely because the entities best
equipped to provide leadership at this crossroads moment in the university's history had been banned from campus a year earlier.

"At Kent from the mid-'60s up until the spring of 1969, there
were a number of organizations, including Students for a Democratic
Society, that had been the structure of the radical movement," said
Ken Hammond, a prominent SDS member in the two years before
the university shut the organization down. "These were organizations
that would book rooms on campus for meetings or for films or to
have a speaker come in. They did the day-to-day work of managing
the movement."

All that went into steep decline in the spring of 1969, Hammond
said, when SDS's charter was revoked following its dustup with conservative students and campus police.

"By the winter of '69–'70, SDS was gone; some of the people
from the Student Mobilization Committee had moved on. A lot of
people who had been active in the previous years backed away from
things. . . . There weren't chartered organizations, and there weren't

structures remaining in place that would have allowed us in May of 1970 to really effectively organize and manage the situation. Things happened so fast. There was no organization in place through the weekend. People were just reacting, and the situation was spinning out of control very rapidly."

On Monday morning at about ten a.m., forty to fifty students, Hammond among them, gathered at the student union to discuss how to get control of the situation and turn it, in his words, "in a more positive direction."

"Everyone recognized there was a lot of anger, a lot of outrage, a lot of energy flowing, but what was going to happen? We burned the ROTC building, we fought with the cops and the National Guard, but where was that going? We couldn't agree among ourselves. Some people wanted to cancel the rally, but how are you going to do that? We didn't have an effective mechanism—we didn't have a bullhorn or a P.A. system. Our ability to manage it, to organize it, to give some structure and direction was minimal. When we got out there at noontime on the Commons, the situation was beyond redemption. . . . We didn't have any discipline. We didn't have any organization sufficient to cope with a couple thousand pissed-off people. It was beyond our ability."

That left the task of coping with several thousand pissed-off people to the one entity that appears to have lacked not only a Plan B but any capacity to conceive of one: the Ohio National Guard.

———

"The Guardsmen had a right to a chain of command, and they didn't have a chain of command," said Jerry Lewis, one of the most active of the antiwar faculty members. Just how confused that chain of command was can be seen in the testimony of Robert Canterbury during a November 1974 deposition in *Krause v. Rhodes*, back when that case was still in its relative infancy.

"Who was in command of the troops on the Commons at [mid-day Monday]?" one questioner asked.

"The 145th Infantry senior officer, Major Jones," Canterbury answered. "It would have reverted to him because the acting commander stayed in the command post. Then, the Lieutenant Colonel, Colonel Fassinger, who actually was the ranking commander."

Later in the deposition, the question comes up again in a slightly different configuration: "Who was the senior officer on the Kent State campus on May 4, 1970?"

Canterbury: "I was."

Question: "Did you consider yourself in command?"

Canterbury: "No."

Question: "Let's try to get that clear. You were not in the chain of command?"

Canterbury: "That is correct."

Question: "As the highest ranking officer, did you have any kind of authority?"

Canterbury: "To issue missions to the commanders, and to develop missions, and to affect the coordination with the authorities."

Question: "Who was in command that day?"

Canterbury's answer: Colonel Fassinger commanded Troop G of the Second Squadron, 107th Armored Calvary Regiment, and Major Wallach commanded Companies A and C of the First Battalion, 145th Infantry Regiment. According to Canterbury, Fassinger was the one who issued both the initial order on the Commons to fire tear gas—after having "talked to me about that"—and the subsequent order to vacate the practice field "based on instructions from me."

And so the dialogue goes, reflecting the traditional military distinction between mission and field commanders, while also veering off time and again toward the theater of the absurd. Canterbury was the highest-ranking officer on the field, in charge of issuing missions as the confrontation progressed, but by his own testimony he was not in the chain of command and had no "knowledge" of who if anyone might have given an order to lock and load M1s. When it came time to pull out the bullhorn and order students to disperse, Canterbury first sent Sergeant Rice, of the campus police, to do the job because "we were there in an assistance role" to the university. Yet in his role of "affect[ing] the coordination with authorities," Canterbury had systematically cut the university out of all decision making. What's more, the highest-ranking officer on the field was, as noted earlier, in civilian clothes just like the faculty marshals, for example, but without their robin's-egg-blue armbands. Little wonder Guard troops were confused.

"No one really knew who was in charge," Larry Shafer told an interviewer in 2001. "The skirmish line consisted of a mishmash of Guardsmen and officers," Rudy Morris added. "The control was diminished considerably." The mishmash of officers did react quickly and decisively once the firing had begun, but by then the barn door was wide open.

The Guardsmen who were sent up Blanket Hill that day also had a right to expect that their mission would be backed up by decent intelligence and that they would have been equipped with the proper tools to do their job. Neither was the case.

Canterbury testified in his November 1974 deposition that he didn't learn until ten that morning that there was to be a noon rally on May 4. By then, the campus radio station had already taped for rebroadcast Barclay McMillen's nine a.m. class, warning students to stay away. True, Canterbury did not return to the campus from out of town until late Sunday evening—he might have been slow out of bed the next morning—but this left the person charged with shaping the Guard's mission only two hours to contemplate both his troops' response and the terrain over which they would be operating.

As for the tools to do the job, the results were disastrous. By noon Monday, the tear-gas canisters available to the on-campus Guard contingent were a countable quantity. The fourteen-mile-an-hour prevailing wind held steady. It could not have been hard to calculate that the effectiveness of the gas in dispersing the crowds would be compromised and the supply of canisters would quickly grow thin in anything like a prolonged confrontation, both of which are exactly what happened.

That left Guardsmen with mostly bayonets and battle rifles armed with live ammunition to control an ever-more restless crowd—in other words, they could blow holes in people from a distance if they felt sufficiently threatened or they could try to knife and slice them if their position was about to be overrun. Shotguns loaded with birdshot, snarling dogs, rubber bullets (first employed in 1970 by British forces for riot control in Northern Ireland)—almost anything would have done the job less lethally, but the Guard was using army surplus, and what army surplus had in abundance was M1s.

Guardsmen also had a right to adequate training to do the job they were called to do—and students had a right to expect that as well. Here, too, the entire system seems to have come up woefully short. Larry Shafer had been a Guardsman since November 1965, but he testified that he had never trained with an M1 and never been told to lock and load one until that weekend at Kent State. The first time he ever fired an M1, he said, was at 12:24 p.m. on Monday, May 4, directly at Joe Lewis.

Other Guardsmen had to make up instant responses to what were often almost surreal circumstances. In a 1975 deposition, Rudy Morris remembered pointing his M1 "at a colored guy, tall, wearing bright clothes with a medium Afro haircut. . . . He was jumping up and down, what appeared to look like military calisthenics or any kind of calisthenics, jumping jacks, yelling 'Shoot me, motherfucker! Shoot me!'"

"Did you shoot at him?" Morris was asked.

"No."

The National Guard in 1970 was, of course, a mishmash of its own: a mix of active-duty veterans keeping a hand in the game, factory workers and students looking for some extra money, weekend warriors, and young people seeking to avoid service in Vietnam—not a fail-safe proposition but an almost certain one. Only 6,140 Guardsmen saw duty in Vietnam, of the roughly 2.6 million military personnel who served within South Vietnam's borders, and only 101 died there, less than 0.0002 percent of total US fatalities.

Inevitably, readiness for a mission like Kent State's was all over the place, as was experience with hostile crowds. Training also can never be the same as the real thing, seen from inside a gas mask, with the occasional incoming rock or other projectile, under a rain of curses. But the Guard's own standard operating procedures relied on nuanced judgment calls under such circumstances, and those judgment calls were not well honed.

"Was the situation at the time of the shooting which you personally observed in your opinion as senior officer with great experience—did that situation warrant the giving of the order by the officer to fire?" General Canterbury was asked during his 1974 deposition.

"Not in my opinion."

"Why?"

"Because I think every officer has an obligation under those conditions to be as restrained as he can be, and to take it right down to the last possible split second before he takes that kind of action. . . . I think for that matter it was something every individual out there could have considered."

"That includes the enlisted personnel, does it not?"

Canterbury: "That includes everyone out there." Four and a half years after the fact, though, is a little late to be urging last-split-second caution.

Finally, the Guardsmen sent into the fray on May 4 had the right to a coherent strategy and an achievable mission. Both are hard to discern in the wreckage of those twenty-four minutes. To disperse the crowd that confronted his force on the Commons at noon Monday, Robert Canterbury invoked the Ohio Riot Act, ordered the crowd to scatter, and, when they didn't, directed his troops up Blanket Hill, splitting them to either side of Taylor Hall. As they had been doing all weekend long, the students broke apart, moved on, and then flowed back together like water.

Thus, at the top of the hill and "hoping with all my heart" that this would be the end of it, Canterbury instead confronted yet another crowd and, like an automaton, marched his men downhill to disperse it—and straight into a near cul de sac, a strategy one suspects advised in no military manual in any language. From there, an even greater air of sour inevitability began to hang over everything until, almost back to the crest again, Guardsmen turned and fired, and the crowd was at long last scattered, running in many cases (so they thought) for their lives. And then remarkably enough, back at the far end of the Commons and facing a new and even more volatile crowd, the senior officer present ordered—what else?—that the crowd be dispersed.

"It's almost as though we were put together in such a way that we were destined to fail," Rudy Morris said in 2001. "And Lord knows, how we failed."

Larry Shafer, who shot Joe Lewis twice during the barrage, put it more simply in a 1980 interview with the *Akron Beacon Journal*: "If that general had had his head out of his ass, he never would have put us in that situation."

Catastrophic decisions, though, even a cascade of them, don't pull triggers. People do that.

———

In trying to piece together what happened on the Kent State campus at 12:24 p.m., Monday, May 4, Dick Bredemeier could not get around the way the shooters turned in formation. "I have some military experience," Bredemeier told me—he'd been commander of his Army Reserve unit while starting his career at Purdue University in Lafayette, Indiana. "It's impossible for me to believe that activity wasn't coordinated. I don't know by whom or by what or by how . . . but I would have been proud of my unit if they could have done that. I couldn't get them to do that much and coordinate that well in the armory.

"If there was a sniper shot, and they all heard it at the same time coming from the same direction, they could have turned and fired without command. For a while, I believed that was what happened because that was the only thing I could think of. I didn't believe any officer could have given that command. . . . But the FBI and Scranton report concluded that there was no sniper, no firecracker, anything like that. In the absence of a trigger, it seems to me that something had to cause it."

Then he added: "If they hadn't turned before firing, I might not be sitting talking with you. They were facing in my direction."

Timothy App also brought military experience to his observations. As a high schooler, he had been in Junior ROTC. Today, he's active as a commander in Civil War reenactments and collects vintage weapons, including the M1. "I knew formations then," he said. "I knew the M1 rifle backwards and forwards. I knew how to disassemble it, clean it, and put it back together. I was close enough to the Pagoda that I could see them turn in formation and fire. . . . Anybody in the military, in formation, doesn't do anything without being given orders. They don't do anything. It wasn't immediately clear to me, but afterwards, I realized that they had been given orders to fire."

In 1975 court testimony, student photographer Howard Ruffner described the moment just before the shooting as a kind of staged tableau.

"All of a sudden a line of Guardsmen turned almost in unison, it seemed. It was just like one unit turning. . . . Some kneeled or at least dropped down lower than the others, and I saw weapons pointing in every direction from down to the ground to right up in the air. It was almost like a—I don't know—just a display of weapons."

Ken Hammond was near to the practice football field when a dozen or so Guardsmen went down on one knee and trained their weapons on the students.

"I saw [Myron Pryor] go around to this small group, Troop G, they all had their gas masks on. And he went up to each guy—maybe nine, ten, eleven guys—and tapped on their helmets. And they eased off part of their gas masks, and he said something to each of them.

"It has always been to me crystal clear that he said something like, 'Okay, when we get up to the top of the hill, we're going to give these punks a lesson,' or words to that effect, because that's the crew that when they got to the top of the hill, they did that. They turned. He brought his arm down with the pistol, and then they all fired. It wasn't a panic reaction. It wasn't, 'Geez, we're cornered. Let's defend ourselves.' It was an orchestrated act. . . .

"These were some scared kids. They were just like us—they were young, they didn't want to go to Vietnam. They were macho. They were out there. We'd been yelling at them, they were all pumped up, and I think this little group just lost their shit."*

"The most parsimonious explanation," Jerry Lewis told me, "is that you had a group of soldiers who were poorly led. They didn't know who their noncoms were; they didn't know who their fellow soldiers were or who were their officers. And they were being yelled every name in the book, which is not a capital crime.

"A few of these guys decided to take things into their own hands and said, 'Okay, we're going to end it and show what we can do.' They fired high, but they didn't bother to tell their fellow soldiers what they were going to do."

The two-stage firing theory—one coordinated and high, the second reactive and into the crowd—is far from fail-safe. Alan Canfora, for one, is convinced that he was hit "in the first second" of the fusillade, but at that distance (seventy-five yards away), the bullet that struck Canfora in the wrist would have arrived in about a tenth of a second, ahead of the sound of the shot itself. Furthermore, time is

---

*Myron Pryor, it should be noted, denied under oath that he had said anything to the kneeling guardsmen on the practice field.

notoriously hard to gauge in panic situations, both in the moment and in memory. But a two-stage process does help pull many parts of the story together.

As we've just seen, multiple eyewitnesses with knowledge of military formations have noted the precision with which the shooters turned at the Pagoda, even though they were tightly bunched and carrying nine-pound battle rifles with fixed bayonets. That suggests premeditation, not a last-minute order or a spontaneous reaction to what they mistook as incoming fire.

Multiple eyewitnesses have also noted that Guardsmen fired almost to a man downhill into the parking lot when the pressure so many claim to have felt was coming mostly from the side. Firing over the heads of the students in the parking lot might well reflect a plan hatched earlier on the practice field and executed at the Pagoda. A second wave of shooters firing where they thought their fellow Guardsmen were aiming and instantly zeroing in on known or threatening targets—Joe Lewis with his hidden hand, Alan Canfora with a black flag, darting Jeff Miller, distinctive Allison Krause—would constitute a final communications failure to cap a fatal slew of them.

Days after the shootings, Kent State police chief Donald Schwartzmiller told the *Los Angeles Times* that he had heard two volleys so close to one another that they could easily have been mistaken for a single burst by inexperienced ears. "It appeared to me the first volley was aimed high. There was a slight, very slight hesitation," between the two, he said. The second was "lower" in its aim.

Brinsley Tyrrell answered the same "What happened?" question more broadly: "I think there was complete incompetence by everybody in authority, every single person as far as I could see. It left the students leaderless, but in a sense it also left the Guard leaderless. They were being asked to do stupid things. They had been brought up to believe that when they told people to do things, people would do them, and they weren't doing them. I've always thought some of the Guardsmen lost their tempers and fired. I don't think it was an organized plot."

Dean Kahler is now retired, but he spent much of his adult life teaching American history and civics. I asked him what he had told his students about Kent State.

"Many had never seen anyone in a wheelchair teaching," he answered. "In the first couple days, the questions started to arise. 'Well, how did you get hurt, Mr. Kahler?' 'You born that way?' That was the teachable moment.

"I explained to them why students were upset around the country, that it wasn't just Kent State. In the days after April 30, lots of universities were having lots of turmoil . . . but people had better restraint at other places. People didn't have a governor who was running for the US Senate, who was trailing in the polls, who was used to leading all the time, whenever he ran for anything, and he was desperate. I didn't go any further than that he was desperate.

"I explained to them, you guys are all hunters. You know what happens when something is rustling in the brush behind you. You turn around. You load your weapon, and you wait until you get a shot—until the pheasant or quail flies out. You're deliberate. You're intentional. Then I show them the pictures, and I tell them it's up to you to decide, and they're just amazed. They can't believe it."

The shooting, he said, "was very intentional. They've got bayonets on those rifles. You have to know how to turn with them. It looked very deliberate."

———

When I met Dean Kahler at Kent State during the forty-fifth commemoration of the shootings, I was struck by how serene he appeared. So many speakers were fevered. Conspiracy theories abounded. Nixon was the enemy, far more than Jim Rhodes. May 1970, it seemed, had never ended. And here was someone who had taken his last step forty-five years ago that weekend, someone who had borne the weight of what he considered "intentionality" for two-thirds of his lifetime. How did he manage, at an event like this, to be so much at peace?

"I can't vouch for others," he told me. "All I can do is vouch for myself. When the doctor is telling your parents, pray for an hour, and then after twenty-four hours of praying an hour at a time, pray for the next twenty-four hours and the next twenty-four hours. . . . I heard it from the doctors as well. I was just extremely lucky, and I'm extremely thankful to be alive."

12

Paradise Lost

Murvin Perry, then director of the School of Journalism, told an interviewer in 2008, "I think there was terrible naïveté on the part of students who thought that they could rampage through the town, trash buildings, and get away with it. If you engage in civil disobedience, you take the consequences."

That's one way of looking at what happened at Kent State over that long first weekend in May 1970: action and responsibility had come unhooked. Somewhere between the August 1963 March on Washington (250,000 strong and maybe 75 percent black, Martin Luther King Jr.'s majestic "I Have a Dream" speech) and the August 1969 rain-drenched, dope-soaked "Aquarian Exposition . . . of Peace & Music" that we know today as Woodstock (400,000 strong and overwhelmingly white), civil disobedience had become a generational right and bad behavior risk-free. And anyone who didn't like what a decade of protest had morphed into or into whose hands it had fallen could pretty much (as Jerry Rubin might have put it) fuck off, even National Guardsmen with M1s and fixed bayonets.

The Age of Aquarius played out in free love and a Day-Glo rainbow, but when it came to the Vietnam War, the choice was all white or black: with us or against us. The same can be said of many of the war's defenders—"My Country, Right or Wrong," is not a nuanced response either—but they weren't staging student strikes, taking over administration buildings, casting a pall over homecoming parades by following beat-up hearses down Main Street. Even those sympathetic to the cause sometimes had trouble embracing the messengers.

Vita Semeraro was a supervisor in the registrar's office when anti-war activism was at its peak at Kent State. She remembered seeing an American flag being burned on campus: "For my generation, that was a terrible atrocity." On another occasion, Semeraro was sitting at her desk when protestors hurled a bottle through a twenty-foot-high window behind her, showering her and her typewriter with glass. Many times, she said, "we had to stand out in the parking lot with no coats on in cold weather or bad weather—just grab your purse and go because there was a bomb threat in the building.

"As time went on," she recalled, "I realized they had a message, and someone should listen. . . . At one point in time, I felt so strongly for these young people and their message that I even walked in the Vietnam parade in Washington, D.C. . . . I'm proud that I did walk with them. I later lost a nephew in Vietnam, 19 years old, that I had raised after his mother died. He got out of a helicopter, was shot down, and never saw actual duty. He laid in the swamps for five days before he was found. So I know the heartache. I also know the heartache that the parents must feel over these children. . . . To have their lives snuffed out so early was a terrible tragedy. It shouldn't happen to anyone."

As for the National Guard, Semeraro said later in the interview, "I don't know what I would have done in their situation. I wouldn't like to have had rocks thrown at me. I wouldn't have liked to have plastic bags of urine thrown at me. I wouldn't have liked to have had plastic bags of fecal matter thrown at me. I think I would have wanted to defend myself. . . . But I still think that our young people had a tremendous message to give to our nation, and I just wish that it could have been said in a way that no lives were lost."

Maybe everyone wishes that. The shootings were senseless, and the hatefulness of so many of the early responses has largely faded into the background noise of an overwrought era in American history.

Yet apart from the ways in which the message was delivered at places like Kent State, the right of "the people peaceably to assemble, and to petition the Government for a redress of grievances" is enshrined not just in the Bill of Rights, but in the very first amendment to the Constitution, before the right to bear arms, before protection against unreasonable search and seizure and against cruel and unusual punishment. That right of peaceful assembly and the other First Amendment guarantees related to religion, free speech, and the press were clearly at the forefront of the Founders' concerns, and at noon on Monday, May 4, when the National Guard began its march across the Commons, the Kent State students across from them and on the surrounding hills were peaceably assembled by any measure, whether or not they were in violation of the Ohio Riot Act.

"I think there was a great deal of naïveté on the part of the students," Brinsley Tyrrell said. "I think the students all believed in the Constitution and their rights, and couldn't believe that no one was taking any notice of those rights. In a more sophisticated place, this might not have happened. The students would have known more, and the police would have known more."

That same naïveté, or lack of sophistication, or whatever one chooses to call it might also have played a key role in Governor Rhodes's decision to send the National Guard to Kent in the first place, according to Jerry Lewis. "He could justify putting a major commitment—over nine hundred troops—into Kent State because we were a less prestigious university." KSU gave Rhodes a chance to have his campaign cake—please the law-and-order right of his own party by cracking down on student hooligans—without having (in theory) to worry about the sort of entangling response he might have drawn from students at a place like Ohio State or from influential Buckeye alumni. As Brinsley Tyrrell suggests, though, it might have been the very naïveté Rhodes hoped to exploit that made Kent State so ripe for the tragedy that was to unfold as Monday wore on.

"Kent was a rural college. It brought together a lot of white kids who were idealistic, maybe naïve, hopeful," said Lafayette Tolliver, one of the leaders of the Black United Students. "We made sure our members stayed far and clear of the Commons. A lot of our members came from the Akron and Cleveland areas. They had a knowledge of what it means to be on the wrong end of police brutality. But you tell that to a white student who has never been involved with police misconduct, kids who think that the police are their friends—I can see how they would let down their guard, not take this seriously. 'They shoot other people; they don't shoot us.'"

One of those rural, naïve, idealistic, hopeful white kids the Guardsmen did shoot was Dean Kahler.

"I'd been hunting since I was sixteen years old," he said. "I took the NRA safety course. I learned there was only one time you could assume and not make an ass out of you and me, and that's when you see a weapon. You see a weapon, and you always assume it's loaded. *Always.* I had no naïveté, no concept, no illusions that these weapons were not loaded. My naïveté was that [the Guardsmen] were there to protect us."

————

The Kent State shootings also occurred at one of the most turbulent crosscurrents in our national history. A gaping generational divide, opposing interpretations of patriotism, the democratization of higher education, the tail end of a decade of assassinations (Kennedy, King, Kennedy) and race riots (Detroit, Watts, DC), the general collapse of comity, and not least of all (but maybe not most important) the most divisive war in modern American times were all in play that Monday noon when the Guard moved out across the Commons and students braced for whatever lay ahead.

As the spring of 1970 progressed, Jerry Rubin and Spiro Agnew became the rhetorical face of that vast societal division—Rubin from the left, metaphorically slaying parents; Agnew from the right, prattling on about tomentose exhibitionists. Jim Rhodes added a more sinister spin to the word flow at his Sunday morning press conference with his talk about eradicating the problem rather than treating the symptoms. ("Eradicate," from the Latin for "torn up by the roots.") Over that fateful weekend in May, Robert Canterbury, the senior National Guard officer on the Kent State campus, talked about teaching Kent State students the meaning of law and order.* Canterbury's boss, Major General Sylvester Del Corso, it's also worth remembering, was an ex officio member of Jim Rhodes's cabinet. Students added their own incendiary rhetorical flourishes: "Kill the pigs." "Stick the pigs." Fuck this and fuck that.

Emotions were raw and grew rawer still as the weekend progressed. "The Guard's attitude was that these guys are wrong," Dick Bredemeier remembered. "They're traitors. They have the audacity to question the government. As a state, we were operating as undemocratically as any of the students were."

Stephen Titchenal was called to testify before the Portage County Grand Jury that fall, in part about the extensive tapes he had recorded during the weekend of protesting. "I remember . . . listening to my tapes and 'One, two, three, four, we don't want this fucking war.' I almost felt like, for some people, that's enough justification to shoot somebody right there. That was part of what the polarization was all about, just the idea that you're either on one side or the other. It was a scary time with all of that."

"If you disagreed with the Vietnam War and you had long hair, you were clearly the enemy," Jerry Casale said. "You were on the fringe. You were disenfranchised. You were a target." The Guardsmen,

---

*At his September 1974 deposition, Canterbury said he didn't remember any such statement.

of course, were targets, too—not only of curses but of stones and other projectiles, some dangerous, some disgusting. By midday Monday on Blanket Hill, whatever firewalls had previously existed between protestors and Guardsmen broke down completely. Think of crossing two wires without adequate insulation.

"Anyone with any intelligence should have looked and said, Somebody's going to get shot here sooner or later if we let this go on," Guardsman Art Krummel told an interviewer. "The campus should have been closed. There should not have been this ongoing confrontation with armed people."

As another Guardsman who was in the thick of the action put it, "These men weren't put here to kill people. They weren't brought here to wound and maim, to take life away. They joined the Guard to get out of Vietnam. . . . They were people from Ravenna who worked in the factories or taught school or whatever they had to do. They were from all walks of life. No one came here and said, 'Let's go kill some of those damn college students.'"

And yet they did.

————

Robert White took eloquent note of all this at his Tuesday, May 5, press conference: "I hear lunacy on one side and frightening repression on the other, and I don't hear from that traditional center position that says, Let us discuss fully and without limits, let us study fully and without limits, and let us come to a decision and a conclusion within orderly processes, which are in the themselves subject to orderly change. What I hear instead are those who say, Let's have such and such without order and those who say, Let us have order without discussion. . . . If I'm frustrated over something, I'm justified in taking extreme steps. If I don't like what I hear, I'm justified in stifling that person."

White was right—that was what the last decade of divisiveness had come down to, a binary moral world. He acquitted himself well in that press conference, in what must have been horrible circumstances for him. But his comments, the student taunts, Agnew and Rubin's posturing—it was all just words until Monday, May 4, 12:24 p.m., when rhetoric was converted into deeds, in some cases irreparable ones.

"I always believed that Kent was the period at the end of the sentence for the '60's," said Ellis Berns, who would punctuate his own May 4 and maybe the '60s by throwing his army fatigue shirt caked with Sandy Scheuer's blood at a Guardsman. "It was at that point when things became quite real. I know there was Jackson State and students killed, but Kent was like the exclamation mark. It was the point where things started to change."

"Kent State was not just Kent State," said Bill Arthrell, he of the napalmed dog stunt that had so enraged locals and even alarmed KSU faculty members. "Kent State was a symbol of everything and indicative of everything." And he might have added, a distillation of everything as well, because Kent State on that early afternoon of May 4 is where all the raging waters of the 1960s, bad and good, evil and sublime, flowed together for one brief, horrible moment.

———

"I turned a corner that day," Timothy App said of May 4. "I wasn't asleep at the wheel, but I didn't consider myself a radical. But that did radicalize me, and it was because of the way things were handled, the intentionality, the fact that there were never any charges brought."

App was one of tens of thousands, probably millions similarly affected. Student deferments had created a four-year war-free zone from which to protest the war. The draft lottery of December 1969 had effectively exempted half the male population of America from involuntary military service. Kent State brought the war closer to home. It made protest more visceral, and the shock of its outcome broadened the base of resistance.

"It had an immediate transformative effect on the entire country," Dick Bredemeier told me. "In some ways, we have James Rhodes to thank for getting us out of Vietnam. . . . Within a year, a member of our board of trustees, George Janik, was marching in Washington against the war."

Vearl Mathis Harrington, class of 1971, credits her own commitment to public service and activism to what she witnessed on her campus at the start of May 1970 and to the "should-have-shot-them-all" responses waiting for her when she returned to New Jersey after the campus was closed down. "I found out what it was like to be hated, just for being there on campus," she recalled. "Years of defending myself and Kent made me, the non-political girl from NJ, take a stand on things in the world. It was a different world then when children's opinions didn't count in the adult world, but when the children got cut down in cold blood, it gave the United States a wake-up call."

There were even benefits in unusual places to be tallied. Peter Thoren—a fourteen-year-old Washington, DC, high schooler in May 1970—told me that his most abiding memory of the Kent State shootings was of a demonstration held a few days afterward, during a student strike at American University. "It was crazy," he said. "The police had fired tear gas, and everyone was dousing their shirts in water and using them to soothe their eyes. I was doing the same, but I was doing my best to see what I could through my tears because women were walking around with no shirts or bras on. Three days after Kent State is the first time I ever saw for real a woman's naked breasts. I couldn't wait to get to college!"

We do, after all, remember the things that are contextually important in our lives, but it's also easy to idealize the aftermath of the shootings—to create a scenario in which these four didn't die and these nine were not wounded in vain. The facts might argue otherwise.

"The mainstream was that they should have killed more," Ellen Mann said, "but you know what? They didn't need to kill more because just killing four white students, four white kids, was enough to stop the whole anti-war movement."

"One of the consequences that was rather apparent was that there weren't any further demonstrations," recalled John Guidubaldi, then a professor in the Education Department. "It was like all of sudden people realized this was a deadly game. This was not a panty-raid kind of mentality. This was not something that could be done on a whim without regard to consequences; the consequences were indeed dramatic and severe. I think it was a sobering moment nationally to see that we could have an occasion where the youth of our country were actually killed by the military units that were there to preserve the peace. . . .

"I saw other consequences. I saw financial consequences. I became the chairman of the Early Childhood Department here at Kent State. I saw our enrollment plummet. The Early Childhood Department relied heavily on female enrollment, and a lot of people decided they weren't going to send their females to Kent State University and subject them to this kind of potential trouble."

May 4, Bruce Dzeda said, "put paid to the whole idea of student activism all over the country. I remember hearing that afternoon, on the Commons, kids saying stuff like, 'That does it. I'm not going to stay interested in politics. Who gives a damn about this world? All they're going to do is shoot you anyway. We can't change anything. I'm just going to worry about my own interior furniture.' On the spot, people turned inward, and the war in Cambodia and the war in Vietnam, all those other raging disputes became less and less important. . . . If you want to know when the sixties died, they died on May 4th, 1970, right there, at 12:24 in the afternoon. That was it. The curtain came down."

Brinsley Tyrrell put it very simply: "Everything you believed in just went poof."

The shootings, Lew Fried said, were "a catastrophic event that ruptured every expectation of your life."

Life magazine reporter John Pekkanen, who arrived on campus within hours of the shootings, quickly decided to focus his reporting on Bill Schroeder. "I talked to his roommates, friends, guys who knew him," Pekkanen told me. "The feeling of fear was just endemic. It was all over the place. Everybody was touchy and scared, even his roommates. One of them wouldn't give me his name. He said, 'If I want to get a job at General Motors in five or ten years, and my name is in this story . . . ' He was just really frightened."

"Innocence" is the word that keeps getting used in interviews and in memory. "Idealism" might do just as well, or maybe some combination of the two, a word that captures at the same time that dual sense of preexperience and endless possibility—not quite an Edenic future but one less clouded by mean calculations. "Surprise" enters in as well, the way mindsets and worldviews collapsed so quickly. What happened at Kent State had been building for a long time, but the shootings happened on the turn of a dime.

Mary Homer, a Kent resident, was attending Davey Junior High in 1970. "Cambodia was crazy. Nixon was crazy. The students thought everything was crazy. In turn, the University administration, the governor, and the police thought that the students were crazy and uncontrollable. Kent lost a lot then, and it will never be the same. This Midwestern town lost its innocence."

Paul Beckwith, also a student at Davey Junior High, felt much the same, as if the shootings had compacted all the miseries of the 1960s and delivered them to his own door. "I remember in elementary school when President Kennedy was assassinated and the only quiet school bus ride I ever had home. I remember seeing photographs of the fire hoses and the police dogs in *Life* magazine during the civil-rights demonstrations. I remember the film footage of the riots in Watts. To me, at *that* time in my life, the Kent State shootings were a hybrid of those events plopped right down in the most unlikely of all places, my own quiet little northeast Ohio backyard."

For Martha Dishman, what happened on May 4 amounted almost to a sudden fall from grace. "I think everybody who was there and participated in that time, they all lost their innocence, and we were in the least likely place for this to happen. If it had happened at Columbia or Berkeley, people would have said, 'What would you expect?' But for it to happen at Kent. . . . "

It did, though, indelibly. Jeanne Anderson, a junior in 1970, remembered Dorothy Fuldheim, a popular and fiery Cleveland TV news anchor of the time, saying that on May 4 Kent State "joined the world." But it wasn't just the university. Many of the school's students also joined the world of adults on that day, torn out of youth by what they had witnessed. In a 2000 interview, Robert Pescatore remembered thinking in the immediate aftermath of the shootings: "Is this the way maturity is? You get hit all of a sudden with it?"

––––––––

In ways subtle and direct, the Kent State shootings have helped to shape the world of American politics and sensibilities ever since. In his memoir, *The Ends of Power*, H. R. Haldeman speculates that the shootings were "a turning point" for Richard Nixon, the "beginning of his downfall slide into Watergate"—not because he was grief-stricken for the dead but because J. Edgar Hoover couldn't deliver him the "outside agitators" that had orchestrated the demonstrations and finally provoked the National Guard into firing. On May 8, for example, John Ehrlichman informed the Justice Department that same-day copies of all field reports on Kent State were now to be delivered to the president as well as Hoover.

"I saw that Nixon had given up on the intelligence and investigatory agencies such as the FBI to help in his battle to quell the national uproar [over the Cambodia invasion] and bring the war to a satisfactory close," Haldeman wrote. "As far as he was concerned, the FBI was a failure. . . . It hadn't found Communist backing for the antiwar organization which he was sure was there. In sum, it had done nothing to help him."

From there, according to Haldeman, the path led through Daniel Ellsberg and the 1971 leaking of the Pentagon Papers to the creation of the secret White House Plumbers group—"Plumbers" because its brief was to fix "leaks"—and eventually to the June 1972 break-in at the Democratic National Committee's Watergate headquarters and, more than two years and one presidential election later, to Richard Nixon's resignation from the office of President of the United States.

Maybe, but that's a long string of assumptions. If Haldeman is right, though, this analysis comes with a heavy dose of irony because the Kent State shootings also helped to so radicalize the Democratic Party at a national level that its next presidential candidate, George McGovern, suffered one of the worst landslide defeats in American history. To borrow from the late four-term Louisiana governor Edwin Edwards, the only way Nixon could have missed out on a second term was to be "caught in bed with either a dead girl or a live boy," and even that was no sure bet.

Kent State's role in the creation of the so-called Silent Majority is far more certain. Nixon's team had been playing with the phrase in speeches since the fall of 1969, but they found intellectual justification in Ben Wattenberg and Richard Scammon's demographic-based best seller *The Real Majority*, published in early 1970. The average voter, the two argued, was "unyoung, unpoor, and unblack" and less interested in progressive causes than law-and-order issues. Wattenberg and his partner had aimed their book at fellow Democrats, urging them to tailor their message to what they called the "middle-aged, middle-class, and middle-minded," but Republican strategists were in a far better position to react, and a May 9 demonstration in New York, where municipal flags were still flying at half-mast to honor the Kent State dead, handed them their moment.

As perhaps a thousand war protestors, mostly students, set out through the Wall Street area, counterdemonstrators organized by the

Building and Construction Trades Council of Greater New York and joined by construction workers on their lunch break, stormed through police lines, pummeled the students with fists, hard hats, and crowbars, and marched straight on to Gracie Mansion, the official residence of Mayor John Lindsay, where they forcibly raised the American flag back to full height. That evening, Nixon phoned congratulations to Peter Brennan, head of the Trades Council, and invited him and other union leaders to the White House, where they presented the president with his own ceremonial hard hat.*

Chuck Colson would call the subsequent photo ops a "seminal event" in launching a five-term string of Republican presidents, broken only by the troubled four years of Jimmy Carter, but the key to the whole package might be the quintessential "average voter" first identified by Wattenberg and Scammon and targeted by Colson and others: a forty-seven-year-old homemaker who lives with her machinist husband just on the outskirts of Dayton, Ohio—exactly the sort of person, demographically and geographically, whose son or daughter might have been attending Kent State University on May 4, 1970, and who, if so, almost certainly longed for law and order as she waited for the phone lines to clear up so she would know that her child was not among the wounded or slain.

———

The Kent State shootings left behind a memorable anthem, but they also estranged multiple generations not only from activism but from caring or even informing themselves about the issues that activism used to feed on, according to Jerry Casale.

"We did exactly what they wanted us to do," Casale told me. "We were willing victims. They understood that any activist group, not

---

*Peter Brennan would be back, as secretary of labor, in Richard Nixon's second term.

just SDS, would be outraged over the expansion of the war into Cambodia without an act of Congress. This was before the full effects of de-evolution in the culture. Students were informed, and students were civic-minded, and students could discuss issues. This was when there could still be outrage over the Constitution's being usurped. Today, everybody would just scratch their heads while they were going to get their frappuccino. 'What's the big deal?'"

Devo—the band that Casale founded at Kent State in 1972 with his brother Bob, Mark and Bob Mothersbaugh, and Alan Myers— drew its name from the "de-evolution" described above, the reverse progress of humankind of which, Casale argues, the shootings were a defining moment.

Again, maybe, but there's a second way to look at this. The violent opposition to the Vietnam War and the particular violence of May 4 also played a major role in ending the draft and thus insulated students and young people generally from many of the issues that had spurred such activism in the 1960s. Waging war today is a matter of finding the right price point at which sufficient numbers of young men and women will be tempted to risk their lives in service to their country. Arguably, too, it's a matter of fostering economic conditions—underpaid and underemployed youth, hyperexpensive higher education—that make military service an attractive choice. What's apparent, though, is that American troops have been in combat somewhere in the world almost continually since November 2001 with barely a whimper from the campuses that led the opposition to the Vietnam War.

May 4 shocked the nation, even the world, but it also reset the bar on what is tolerable in this country in the interface between public and private forces. In early May 1963, the Birmingham, Alabama, commissioner of public safety, Bull Connor, became internationally notorious for using water cannons and snarling dogs to break up street demonstrations organized by the Southern Christian Leadership Conference and peopled largely by children, some as young as six years old. Anyone who lived through that time is likely to have the film footage still seared in memory. Seven years almost to the day later, the Ohio National Guard managed to make Bull Connor's crowd control techniques look not only efficient but humanitarian.

Water cannon for M1s? Leashed Dobermans for bayonets? Anyone who was on the back side of Blanket Hill or in the Prentice Hall parking lot at 12:24 p.m. on May 4, 1970, would have made that trade in a New York second. After a decade of increasing permissiveness, the shootings at Kent State delivered a different message: the grown-ups were back in charge, and they weren't taking any crap.

Sometimes what happened at Kent State seems in danger of losing its own story line. In the years immediately afterward, the university mostly wanted the memory of the shootings to go away. Enrollment dipped sharply. Academic programs and faculty had to be trimmed back. Legislators were still angry. State funding for higher education was based on full-time enrollment, and even with its reduced numbers, Kent State was still a large school and Columbus was locked into the funding formula. Without that, Dick Bredemeier said, the school might have had to shut down. "They had to give it to Kent. That saved us."

A 1977 plan to build a new athletic center not quite on but very near the site of the shootings was met with fierce opposition, mostly led by those who had been at the school seven years earlier. Eventually, the administration backed away and chose another site. Commemorations of the shootings tended to be fractious, sometimes in the extreme. The university tried to limit them to every five or ten years, without success. More bitter controversy followed—including over the size and nature of a permanent memorial and the propriety of parking cars where four students had been shot dead.

All that, though, is largely in the past. Probably no American university has ever embraced its darkest hour more successfully than Kent State has over the past decade or more. The May 4 Visitors Center that opened in 2010, under the direction of Laura Davis and the late

Carole Barbato, is a model of its kind, reminiscent in its emotional impact and its exhibits (though at a smaller scale) of the Birmingham Civil Rights Institute and Museum—Bull Connor's snarling dogs large as life at one and the National Guard with gas masks and fixed bayonets menacing at the other.

Jeff Miller's antiwar poem is on display at the Visitors Center, as is a drawing done jointly by Miller and Sandy Scheuer and a photo of Allison Krause helping to hold a huge banner as she "joins millions worldwide for a moratorium to halt the war in Vietnam." For balance, there's also a quote from a student at the Maryland high school Krause had attended the year before she was killed: "People bring up this thing about this chick who was killed at Kent. They were all out mourning her death. Flying the flag low. GIs have been shot. Why wasn't the flag lowered then? They're in there fighting to keep the flag up."

Also available: a self-guided tour of the Commons and Blanket Hill, with explanatory plaques along the way and an eloquent narration by Julian Bond. In the Prentice Hall parking lot, four spaces are now taken up by memorials to the four who died there: Miller, Krause, Scheuer, and Bill Schroeder.

The university library holds a vast archival collection on the shootings, including more than 120 (and growing) oral histories collected over the last thirty years—and from which this book has benefited immensely. Beyond the school, Alan Canfora, wounded on May 4, has amassed his own rich treasure of primary sources and insights into what happened and why. The online May 4 "Truth Tribunal," launched in 2010 by Allison Krause's sister, Laurel, and filmmaker Emily Kunstler continues to hunt for new leads that might explain in a binding way why twenty-eight National Guardsmen fired sixty-seven rounds into a parking lot crowded with students.

But the shootings will be half a century old in 2020, and memory is always an uphill struggle. Winona Vannoy was a physical education instructor at Kent State in 1970. Later she would go on to be director of intramurals and campus recreation. "I have told parts of this story to students recently, and all have expressed great surprise that students had any part in causing the 1970 tragedy. Their typical comment is 'I just thought students were partying and got shot.'" That interview was in 1990.

I was standing at the Pagoda on May 4, 2015, studying lines of sight, trying to imagine what the Guardsmen saw through their masks, when I was joined by a father and his daughter, just finishing her freshman year at Kent State. She was vivacious, obviously bright, and she seemed amazed to be discovering these artifacts, like ancient ruins, scattered across the center of her campus. Down in the parking lot, gray- and white-haired men and women, some in tie-dye T-shirts, were explaining to their grandchildren why this parking space had been set aside for Allison, that one for Bill, and on down the line—the oral tradition at work.

Meanwhile, eBay still had up for auction a last few of the "vintage" Kent State sweatshirts that had been briefly offered for sale the previous September by Urban Outfitters—the ones meant to look as if they were splattered with blood and riddled by gunshots, available online only for $129.

"It was never our intention to allude to the tragic events that took place at Kent State in 1970 and we are extremely saddened that this item was perceived as such," Urban Outfitters claimed as it withdrew the sweatshirts from sale. The red stains were the product of natural discoloration, the company explained; the holes, of regular wear and tear. Right. Also pigs fly. But this is what so often happens to memory when commercialism gets hold of it: everything gets cheapened, lives included.

"If we don't help people remember, if the students on campus today put this behind them, then it's going to happen to them, and it's going to happen to their children and it's going to happen to my children, and those four people would have died for nothing," Diane Yale-Peabody said. "I can't accept that."

AFTERWORD

Kent, Ohio, and what was once South Vietnam are roughly 8,500 air miles apart, separated by twelve time zones—eleven when daylight savings is in effect in the United States. Yet on that early afternoon of May 4, 1970, there was much to pull the two places together.

Four Kent residents had already been killed in the war in Southeast Asia, including Frank John Picelle, who would have turned twenty-two that May 4, and Mark John DeFrange, whose brother Timothy was a senior at Kent State and whose father, Nick, died at Robinson Memorial Hospital just as the wounded were being wheeled in.

Vita Semeraro in the registrar's office had helped raise a nephew who was killed almost the moment his feet hit the ground in Vietnam. Ellen Mann, the high schooler standing by Joe Lewis when he was shot twice, had a brother who had just been drafted and a stepcousin among the Guardsmen who did the shooting. Student William Derry Heasley, who had been one of the first people on the Commons that morning and who would later sit under a tree and cry after coming across the body of Jeff Miller, had served in the navy in Vietnam. Fellow student Albert Van Kirk, who helped treat some of the wounded, had spent nearly nine months in country as an army infantry soldier. Another student, who chose to remain anonymous, had arrived at the demonstrations wearing a hat his brother had taken from a dead Viet Cong. His brother, he said, had survived the war only to become an addict and die fifteen months after returning home.

Vietnam veterans and Kent State students alike found themselves branded not for who they were but for where they had been. Drafted after college and assigned to an army missile crew, Ronald Sterlekar had to wait three months for a security clearance because he had been a campus leader at Kent State. The summer after the shootings, Richard Karl Watkins applied for a job at a canning factory in Napoleon, Ohio. "I filled out the form, and the woman read that I was going to Kent State, and she goes, 'Are you a Communist?'"

———

Suffering was mass-produced in Vietnam, drawn out over an almost unbearably long time frame. At Kent State, the violence was custom-fit, compacted into a single, intensely violent instant in time. Over the nearly eleven years of the Vietnam War, roughly three American military personnel were wounded every hour, and one American killed every two hours. At Kent State, four Americans died and nine were wounded in only thirteen seconds.

How do you compare statistics like that, or experiences like that, other than to say that all the lives snuffed out in both places, all the ones disrupted and compromised by injuries, all the people who still can't let go of what they lived through are important. They matter— to individuals, to survivors, to the American story, to the American legacy.

We have to try to see events in both venues through the eyes of those who couldn't—or wouldn't—turn their eyes away from them. We have to put ourselves inside those names on the wall in Washington that memorializes the Vietnam dead and inside the gas masks of the Guardsmen who had heard the Ohio Riot Act read so often that they saw danger through every eye porthole. We have to imagine (if we weren't there) the disbelief when what seemed to be a threatening gesture proved a lethal one. *Pop! Pop! Pop! Pop!* It's amazing still that what might have been blanks or firecrackers or some sort of audio trick were so quickly recognized for what they were—live and lethal ammunition racing faster than the speed of sound. What college course fully prepares you for that?

We also have to try to feel as best we can what the families of Allison Krause, Jeffrey Miller, Bill Schroeder, and Sandy Scheuer must have felt when they first learned their loved one—brother, sister; son, daughter—had been shot to death: a student killed by National Guardsmen on an American campus, the unthinkable come true.

———

In an exact legal sense, what happened at 12:24 p.m. on Blanket Hill might have been murder in the second degree, as Spiro Agnew told David Frost. More likely, it was manslaughter voluntary or otherwise, but finding a jury that would have convicted the Guardsmen of that crime seems unlikely, even without procedural roadblocks. Trial juries both respect the laws they are called on to interpret and treat them with a heavy dose of common sense, and common sense would tell just about anyone that the Guardsmen called to duty at Kent State that weekend were poorly trained in crowd control, miserably led over the twenty-four minutes that preceded the shootings, and armed with precisely the wrong tools to complete a nearly impossible mission.

That the Guard was there at all was the result of an early-morning call that never should have been made. Students and outsiders behaved poorly, in some cases criminally, in downtown Kent on the night of Friday, May 1. Cambodia was an incentive. Way too much beer was probably just as big a reason. Windows never should have been smashed. This was a charged moment in American history; the air was fraught with rumors of worse to come.

Whatever the insult, though, Mayor LeRoy Satrom, an estimable man in other regards, overreacted when he phoned the office of Ohio governor James Rhodes in the wee hours of Saturday morning, and Rhodes, when he learned of the call, saw an opening he could run through all the way to the US Senate—a deus ex machina for a man then trailing badly in the polls, with a May 5 primary looming. But all that is background noise, ultimately, to the Kent State shootings and the larger horror of Vietnam. People died who should not have on both fronts, the almost permanent one in Southeast Asia and the instant one in Northeast Ohio. Empty spaces opened in hearts that had once been full. Everyone affected can count the ways in which both experiences etched lifetime scars.

Here, though, is a final thought: The best thing that could happen for those who still carry the Kent State shootings or the Vietnam War gratingly close to their hearts is to get beyond who did what when. In an interview during the twentieth anniversary commemoration in 1990, Janice Marie Wascko talked about an earlier speaker who had vowed she would never forgive. "It tore my heart out. I'll never forget, and I think there are real important lessons with this. But if there's no forgiveness, there's no healing, and the murder goes on forever."

Amen.

NOTES

Quotations in this book are primarily drawn from four sources, designated as follows:

ACLU: The ACLU (American Civil Liberties Union) of Ohio Kent State Project Records. This collection—now in repository at the Yale University Library Division of Manuscript and Archives—contains a wealth of documents, including depositions and testimony, related to the long legal aftermath of the shootings. Sources are identified by request box number.

IWA: Interview with author. Original interviews conducted for this book.

M4C: The May 4 Collection, over three hundred cubic feet of archival materials available through the Special Collections and Archives division of the Kent State University Libraries. Again, sources are identified by request box number.

OH: The Kent State Shootings Oral Histories project, founded in 1990 by Sandra Perlman Halem and available online through the Kent State University Libraries Department of Special Collections and Archives at www.library.kent.edu/special-collections-and-archives/kent-state-shootings-oral-histories-0. The histories are searchable by subject, narrators' roles, and narrators' names.

One further note on quotations: Most come from raw transcriptions, my own and others. In a number of instances, I have taken the liberty of removing without ellipses interjections, false starts, and other rhetorical quirks that are commonplace in conversation but hard to get around on the printed page. In no such case have I altered intended meaning. Brackets are used when I insert a word or words to improve clarity.

PROLOGUE: MAY 4, 1970—SOUTH VIETNAM

1   *On May 4, 1970:* Background information on American fatalities on
     May 4, 1970, including comments by survivors, is drawn primarily from
     The Vietnam Veterans Memorial: The Wall-USA, www.thewall-usa.com.

3   *An online photo shows:* See www.mtmorrisfire.com/history.html.

3   *Theologies of Memory: Time and Eternity in the Far Country* (Malden, MA:
     Wiley-Blackwell, 2010), 214.

3   *In a blog entry:* See Richard T. Edwards, "Vietnam—It Happened on May
     4th, 1970 over Firebase Nancy," 4th Battalion, 77th Field Artillery AFA
     (blog), May 20, 2011, 4thbattalion77thfieldartilleryafa.blogspot.com/2011
     /05/it-happened-on-may-4th-over-firebase.html.

1. "WE HAVE TO SAY 'F---' EVERYWHERE"

6   *Seated at his nearly empty desk:* Richard Nixon, "Address to the Nation,"
     YouTube, 4:59, www.youtube.com/watch?v=rDSsDBieVGE.

8   *"There were maybe 500–600 students:* Rob Fox, OH.

8   *Kent State president Robert White would later:* The Report of the President's
     Commission on Campus Unrest (Washington, DC: US Government Printing
     Office, 1970), 239.

9   *Many Kent students assumed:* Richard Karl Watkins, OH.

10   *"All the organizations:* Timothy App, IWA.

10   *J. R. Hipple:* J. R. Hipple, IWA.

12   *"all you rebels, youth spirits:* The "Yippie Manifesto" in its entirety can be
     found at faculty.atu.edu/cbrucker/Amst2003/Texts/Yippie.pdf.

13   *"Kent State is a super prison.":* The complete notes taken by the administra-
     tion spy are available at Kent State University Administrative Office papers,
     Box 127B, M4C.

14   *Less than two weeks after:* William G. Arthrell, OH.

14   *Also in the crowd was Glenn Frank:* Jerry Lewis, IWA.

15   *Chuck Ayers, who would go on:* Chuck Ayers, OH.

16   *"The town hated the students:* Lew Fried, IWA.

16   *Spring 1968 "saw a big change here,":* Ruth Mulvihill papers, Box 87, M4C.

17   *Federal law enforcement officials:* Anonymous Kent resident, OH.

18   *Carol Mirman was a senior:* Carol Mirman, OH.

19   *As would happen sixty hours later:* Diana Gallagher, OH.

19   *At about the same time:* Hipple, IWA.

20   *Even after the shootings:* LeRoy Satrom papers, Box 8, M4C.

22   *Even the motorcycle gangs:* Ronald Sterlekar, OH.

23   *"The most important fact:* Richard Bredemeier, IWA.

23   *"It was almost like if you said:* Lafayette Tolliver, IWA.

23   *"He said he actually started:* Peter Jedick, OH.
24   *"There were disorderly incidents:* Report of the President's Commission, 243.

2. BURN, BABY—BURN

25   *More than half a decade:* For more on attacks on campus ROTC buildings, see Joseph A. Fry, "Unpopular Messengers: Student Opposition to the Vietnam War," in *The War That Never Ends: New Perspectives on the Vietnam War*, ed. David L. Anderson and John Ernst (Lexington: University Press of Kentucky, 2007), 219–243.
27   *"You'd better watch: The Report of the President's Commission on Campus Unrest* (Washington, DC: US Government Printing Office, 1970), 244.
27   *The university also activated:* Jerry Lewis, OH.
28   *Carolyn Mallon Fair:* Written Narratives and Commentaries 1970–2003, Box 101, M4C.
29   *Kay Jankowski left her dorm:* Commission on KSU Violence records, Box 193, M4C.
31   *Student senator Rob Fox:* Rob Fox, OH.
31   *Arthur Koushel, a sophomore:* Arthur Koushel, OH.
31   *Gerald Casale, cofounder:* Gerald Casale, IWA.
31   *Lafayette Tolliver agreed:* Lafayette Tolliver, IWA.
31   *Others see a much less sinister inattention:* Ray Bye, IWA.
32   *Like actions, though, inactions:* Timothy DeFrange, OH.
32   *That same night, Rosann Rissland:* Rosann Rissland, OH.
32   *An anonymous Ohio National Guardsman:* Anonymous Guardsman, OH.
33   *In a 2007 interview:* Ronald Snyder, OH.
35   *Denny Benedict, a freshman in 1970:* Denny Benedict, OH.
36   *An Ohio National Guardsman and Kent State student:* Anonymous Guardsman, OH.
37   *"We were told point-blank:* Steven Sharoff, IWA.
38   *At just about the same time, Art Krummel:* Art Krummel, OH.

3. NIGHT OF THE HELICOPTERS

42   *"Sunday morning, I went in at nine:* Ray Bye, IWA.
42   *One Guardsman recalled waiting:* Anonymous Guardsman, OH.
43   *However much Friday night's rampage: The Report of the President's Commission on Campus Unrest* (Washington, DC: US Government Printing Office, 1970), 251; Federal Bureau of Investigation Kent State Shootings records, Box 132, M4C.
44   *"We had been downtown:* Ken Hammond, IWA.
44   *Rather than prima facie evidence:* Brinsley Tyrrell, IWA.

44 *"They would bring the crowds to us:* Anonymous Guardsman, OH.

45 *"What was clear to me:* Albert Van Kirk, OH.

45 *In their Saturday night senatorial:* All quotes are from the *Columbus Dispatch* coverage of the debate, May 3, 1970.

46 *"We have seen here at the City of Kent:* Press conference transcript, Charles A. Thomas papers, Box 64D, M4C.

47 *Governor Rhodes and Kent State president: Report of the President's Commission*, 255.

48 *"He says, 'I don't know.':* Richard Bredemeier, IWA.

49 *At an earlier meeting to organize:* Jerry Lewis, IWA.

49 *Sunday afternoon, still believing:* Jerry Lewis, OH.

49 *Jim Sprance, a junior in 1970:* Jim Sprance, OH.

50 *Diane Yale-Peabody, a sophomore:* Diane Yale-Peabody, OH.

50 *"Anywhere you went:* Ellen Mann, OH.

50 *Ray Bye felt the same:* Bye, IWA.

50 *Jim Vacarella, a junior that spring:* Jim Vacarella, OH.

51 *A few days earlier, Ralph Spielman:* Ralph Spielman, IWA.

51 *John Panagos, then a new professor:* John Panagos, OH.

51 *Allison Krause, another of the four dead:* "Allison Krause: Shot & Killed on May 4, 1970," May 4 Archive, www.may4archive.org/allison_krause.shtml.

52 *"At best," one Guardsman remembered:* Anonymous Guardsman, OH.

52 *The schoolyard, too, left little room:* Scott Swan, OH.

52 *The students who left Kent State on Friday:* Joseph Sima, OH.

53 *Eldon Fender, a freshman education major:* Eldon Fender, OH.

53 *William Derry Heasley, a Kent State student:* William Derry Heasley, OH.

53 *"We were trying to make it:* Janice Marie (Gierman) Wascko, OH.

54 *"Looking back, people kept saying:* Murvin Perry, OH.

54 *Faculty wife Lillian Tyrrell:* Lillian Tyrrell, OH.

54 *For its part, the university:* Panagos, OH.

56 *The scene at Prentice Gate:* Denny Benedict, OH.

57 *Thirty years later, Rob Fox:* Rob Fox, OH.

57 *Jim Vacarella recalled standing:* Vacarella, OH.

57 *Many Guardsmen, too, were reaching:* Anonymous Guardsman, OH.

58 *The same, of course, can be said:* Henry Mankowski, OH.

58 *John Cleary, who would be shot:* John Cleary, OH.

58 *Ellis Berns, a nineteen-year-old undergraduate:* Ellis Berns, OH.

4. *DANSE MACABRE*

59 *The previous three days had amounted to:* Joe Lewis's recollections are included in the Emmy-winning documentary *Kent State: The Day the War Came Home* (Single Spark Pictures, 2000).

61   *Part of the problem was proximity and fatigue:* Box 4, Vol. 5, ACLU.

61   *Worse still, the fast-approaching noon rally:* Box 5, Vol. 6, ACLU.

62   *In the many investigations that were:* The Report of the President's Commission on Campus Unrest (Washington, DC: US Government Printing Office, 1970), 260–261.

63   *"Guards were there in front:* Joseph Sima, OH.

63   *Laura Dressler, also a junior:* Laura Dressler, OH.

63   *Brinsley Tyrrell arrived:* Brinsley Tyrrell, IWA.

63   *Barclay McMillen was among the teachers:* See Barclay D. McMillen papers, Box 131, M4C, and McMillen's class lecture, www.kentstate1970.org /timeline/may4th1970.

64   *Diane Yale-Peabody's class:* Diane Yale-Peabody, OH.

65   *At the same time, Jim Vacarella:* Jim Vacarella, OH.

65   *Freshman Dean Kahler:* Dean Kahler, IWA.

65   *"The street was just filled:* Robert Pescatore, OH.

66   *By the time Lowell Zurbuch:* Lowell Zurbuch, OH.

66   *John Snediker was making sales calls:* "Remembering May 4" responses from readers, *Akron Beacon Journal*, Box 74, M4C.

66   *Suzanne Irvin left her journalism class:* Box 101, M4C.

67   *Peter Jedick ran into a woman:* Peter Jedick, IWA.

67   *William Derry Heasley was in the midst:* William Derry Heasley, OH.

67   *In an on-campus interview:* Anonymous Guardsman, OH.

69   *"Reading the Riot Act to students:* Kahler, IWA.

69   *"Somebody decided to clear the area,":* Denny Benedict, OH.

69   *"These were not 2,000 people hell-bent:* Heasley, OH.

71   *"People were saying:* Rob Fox, OH.

72   *"My purpose," Canterbury would later testify:* Report of the President's Commission, 268.

72   *The "mob," as he referred to it:* Benedict, OH.

72   *Jerry Casale once described the Guardsmen:* Gerald Casale, speech at the commemoration of the fortieth anniversary of the shootings, Kent State University, May 4, 2010, clubdevo.com/component/content/article/53 -uncategorised/79-gerald-v-casale-of-devo-on-kent-state-shootings.

72   *Carol Mirman was among those:* Carol Mirman, OH.

73   *Randy Gardner, who would be shot:* Randy Gardner, OH.

73   *Rob Fox said much the same:* Fox, OH.

73   *Ronald Sterlekar was equally unimpressed:* Ronald Sterlekar, OH.

74   *"When you pick all of these ingredients:* Art Krummel, OH.

74   *"There was taunting and jeering:* Naomi Goelman Etzkin, OH.

75   *"start whacking us over the head:* Michael Erwin, OH.

75   *"It was the classic Battle of the Bulge strategy:* Gerald Casale, IWA.

76   *"I got down to the first floor:* Chuck Ayers, OH.

5. BLOOD LIKE A RIVER

77 *The M1 Garand battle rifle:* Information on the M1 Garand comes from various sources, including Wikipedia. I'm particular indebted to my neighbor and friend Jeremiah "Joe" Blatz, who maintains an extensive library on weaponry and munitions.

78 *Of the twenty-eight rounds:* A chart showing all the rounds fired, distance traveled, impact point, and so forth is available in the *Akron Beacon Journal* Kent State Shootings collection, Box 208, M4C.

79 *Steven Grudzinski was waiting:* Steven Grudzinski, OH.

80 *Alan Canfora, prominent in the demonstrations:* The quote is from John Cleary, OH.

80 *Joe Lewis was also 20 yards away: Kent State: The Day the War Came Home* (Single Spark Pictures, 2000).

80 *He said that while he could clearly see:* Larry Shafer, *Kent State.*

80 *Ellen Mann, then attending high school:* Ellen Mann, OH.

81 *"Something had to happen at the top:* Rudy Morris, *Kent State.*

81 *He said that he distinctly heard a shot:* Albert Van Kirk, OH.

81 *Canfora, who has identified the words "right here,":* Alan Canfora, IWA.

82 *Rudy Morris, one of the retreating Guardsmen:* Box 18, ACLU.

82 *What's more, not everyone who was within eyesight:* Gerald Casale, IWA.

83 *According to audio engineers:* Canfora, IWA. For more on the Strubbe tape, including an enhanced audio version, see "DOJ Refuses to Reopen Kent State Shootings Case," YouTube, 2:52, April 30, 2012, www.youtube .com/watch?v=d1GdbZuhWvI.

83 *"Several of us were lowering our weapons:* Anonymous Guardsman, OH.

84 *Jeffrey Miller—twenty-one years old, five-foot-six:* Autopsy reports for all four fatalities can be found in Box 208, M4C.

85 *Freshman Eldon Fender was watching Miller:* Eldon Fender, OH.

85 *John Filo, the student photographer:* Box 20, ACLU.

86 *"I'd never seen blood like that:* Carol Mirman, OH.

87 *"I'm extremely afraid that I'll be classified:* The complete letter is at Biographical Information of Victims of Kent State Shootings, Box 99, M4C.

88 *"The impact of the bullet:* Henry Mankowski, OH.

88 *"I remember I had my arm:* Ellis Berns, OH.

89 *The Scheuers arrived at Robinson Memorial Hospital: Kent-Ravenna Record-Courier,* May 5, 1970.

89 *Martin Scheuer would later tell a reporter:* See "Sandy Scheuer, Shot & Killed on May 4, 1970," May 4 Archive, www.may4archive.org/sandy _scheuer.shtml.

89 *"Two of the students were killed:* Richard Bredemeier, IWA.

90 *"As I drove through Kent:* Timothy DeFrange, OH.

91   *Ralph Spielman also thought the Guardsmen:* Ralph Spielman, IWA.

91   *Ronald Sterlekar remembered everyone:* Ronald Sterlekar, OH.

91   *William Derry Heasley, who had served in the navy:* William Derry Heasley, OH.

92   *Jeff Miller was also the first person:* Chuck Ayers, OH.

92   *As he wandered through the parking lot:* Mankowski, OH.

92   *"After the immediate shots were fired:* Arthur Koushel, OH.

93   *"When I saw him:* Diane Yale-Peabody, OH.

93   *"May 4 is like Passover:* Janice Marie (Gierman) Wascko, OH.

93   *"Everything seemed bigger in 2010:* Casale, IWA.

94   *"I remember the Guard . . . :* Carol Mirman, OH.

94   *"Hundreds of people were falling:* Morris, *Kent State.*

94   *In a February 1975 deposition:* Rodney Biddle deposition, Box 12, ACLU.

94   *"The closest Guardsman was:* Bill Barrett, OH.

95   *"big, hulking guy, crew cut:* Brinsley Tyrrell, OH.

95   *"a very tall bear of a student:* William Derry Heasley, OH.

95   *"It got totally quiet:* Anonymous Guardsman, OH.

95   *"Those Guardsmen came down:* Jim Vacarella, OH.

6. ONCE TO EVERY MAN AND NATION

97   *"You have to remember:* Brinsley Tyrrell, IWA.

98   *"People who were not radical:* Arthur Koushel, OH.

98   *"You have to imagine what everybody felt:* Eldon Fender, OH.

98   *"You felt like you were invincible:* Rob Fox, OH.

98   *Another protestor who requested anonymity:* Anonymous Student 2, May 4, 2010 interview, OH.

98   *"They were going to go down and battle:* Jim Vacarella, OH.

99   *"There was a point in time when General Canterbury:* Ronald Snyder, OH.

99   *"I was telling the students to sit down:* Steven Sharoff, IWA.

101   *"I realize now this man was blithering to save our lives:* Janice Marie (Gierman) Wascko, OH.

101   *"I don't care whether you've never listened:* An audiotape of Glenn Frank's plea is available at Kent State 1970, www.kentstate1970.org/timeline/may4th1970.

101   *Frank, she said, was:* Diane Yale-Peabody, OH.

102   *"We were really pissed:* Vacarella, OH.

102   *"I was in the Student Center, just finishing up lunch:* The quotes here and on the following pages are from Alan Frank, IWA.

103   *None of this heroism, however:* The full text of Glenn Frank's letter is available at "The Survivors," May 4 Archive, www.may4archive.org/survivors.shtml.

104   *"They wanted everybody to leave:* Denny Benedict, OH.

105 *"So I parked my car:* Bruce Dzeda, OH.

105 *"was actually almost more scary:* Stephen Titchenal, OH.

105 *"You hear a distinctive wailing:* Gerald Casale, IWA.

105 *"almost in a state of shock,":* Ellis Berns, OH.

106 *"I remember saying:* Chuck Ayers, OH.

106 *Janice Marie Wascko, who had earlier screamed:* Wascko, OH.

106 *That feeling was widespread:* Jeanne Anderson, OH.

107 *"I wasn't running:* William Forrester, IWA.

107 *"We decided that the cops or the Guard:* Ken Hammond, IWA.

107 *Ellen Mann, the high school student:* Ellen Mann, OH.

107 *Jim Vacarella was wandering around:* Vacarella, OH.

108 *"We went into the campus, trying to get somewhere:* John Pekkanen, IWA.

108 *Albert Van Kirk, who had medic training:* Albert Van Kirk, OH.

109 *Robert White would later tell the Scranton Commission:* A transcript of White's testimony before the commission is in Box 127B, M4C.

109 *Meanwhile, students had to make do as best they could:* Koushel, OH.

109 *Kathy Bye's parents lived in Miami:* Kathy Bye, IWA.

110 *"I sat down at dinner:* Naomi Goelman Etzkin, OH.

110 *"I saw two soldiers that I'd met:* Koushel, OH.

111 *Janice Marie Wascko was sitting:* Wascko, OH.

111 *Chuck Ayers had to flash:* Ayers, OH.

111 *"They said, 'Okay, we'll be right back:* The complete lyrics of "Everything Is Beautiful" can be found at www.lyricsmode.com/lyrics/r/ray_stevens /everything_is_beautiful.html.

7. "OH, MY GOD! THEY'VE KILLED THE GUARDSMEN!"

113 *A little after midday, Rosann Rissland:* Rosann Rissland, OH.

114 *Faculty wife Lillian Tyrrell was heading across campus:* Lillian Tyrrell, OH.

114 *Mary Homer, then thirteen years old:* Mary Homer, OH.

115 *Kent resident John Whyde:* John Whyde, OH.

115 *A daughter of a Kent police officer:* Anonymous resident, OH.

116 *"The radio kept talking about a Fifth Column:* Brinsley Tyrrell, IWA.

116 *"I was in a luncheon with:* From White's testimony before the President's Commission on Campus Unrest, Box 127B, M4C.

117 *According to faculty member Jerry Lewis:* Jerry Lewis, IWA.

117 *"The center was on the second floor:* Ray Bye, IWA.

118 *"We were all just eating:* Laura Dressler, OH.

118 *Bill Forrester was in the student union:* William Forrester, IWA.

118 *Martha Dishman and a friend:* Martha Dishman, OH.

118 *At one o'clock that afternoon:* Mike Williams, OH.

119 *Barbara Holland was in her apartment:* Barbara Holland, IWA.

120 *Art Krummel was part of a Guard squad:* Art Krummel, OH.

121 *Wendy Miller was in Cleveland:* Wendy Miller, IWA.

121 *News of the shootings, one Guardsman recalled:* Anonymous Guardsman, OH.

122 *The Jeffrey Miller who would soon be killed:* Elaine Holstein's account is included in *Kent State: The Day the War Came Home* (Single Spark Pictures, 2000).

122 *Ray Bye, who had been in charge:* Bye, IWA.

123 *Not until the next day, May 5:* White's telegram can be found in Box 127B, M4C.

8. THE AGE OF HATE

125 *The Age of Hate:* The chapter title is borrowed from *The Age of Hate: Andrew Johnson and the Radicals*, George Fort Milton's 1930 history of Reconstruction.

126 *"We had protests about everything:* Timothy App, IWA.

126 *Brinsley Tyrrell, who was new to the Art Faculty:* Brinsley Tyrrell, IWA.

127 *Once he was cleared off campus:* Michael Erwin, OH.

127 *There were surprises like that all over town:* Ellis Berns, OH.

127 *Alan Frank, whose father had arguably saved hundreds of lives:* Alan Frank, IWA.

128 *Laura Davis, who would return to KSU:* Davis's account is included in *Kent State: The Day the War Came Home* (Single Spark Pictures, 2000).

128 *"One of the worst things when we got home:* Diane Yale-Peabody, OH.

128 *Richard Karl Watkins was at a family reunion:* Richard Karl Watkins, OH.

128 *Joe Lewis's parents left his sixteen-year-old sister:* See *Kent State.*

128 *One of the first "get well" cards Dean Kahler:* Dean Kahler, IWA.

129 *A letter sent to Bill Schroeder's parents read:* See "Bill Schroeder: Shot & Killed on May 4, 1970," May 4 Archive, www.may4archive.org/bill _schroeder.shtml.

129 *"Guardsmen facing almost certain injury:* Kent-Ravenna Record-Courier, May 5, 1970.

129 *"Snipers should be engaged only:* Robert Canterbury's comments to reporters can be seen in *Confrontation at Kent State*, a film by Richard Myers with Pat Myers, Jake Leed, Mary Leed, Robert Ohlrich, Carla Ohrlich, Mel Someroski, and Mike Tarr (1970, black and white, 43 minutes).

129 *"Regrettable as the outcome of Monday's:* Reactions to the shootings from the general public are drawn largely from four sources: *Kent-Ravenna Record-Courier*, May 5–9, 1970; *Confrontation at Kent State*; "Remembering May 4"

responses, *Akron Beacon Journal,* April 29, 1990, Box 74, M4C; Robert C.
Dix May 4 papers, Box 212, M4C; Box 8, M4C; and Box 101, M4C. Specific exceptions follow.

130   *Nor were what sometimes seemed ad hominem attacks:* Brinsley Tyrrell, IWA.

131   *Rosann Rissland heard the rumors, too:* Rosann Rissland, OH.

131   *Junior Laura Dressler:* Laura Dressler, OH.

132   *"My daughter was hysterical:* Lillian Tyrrell, OH.

132   *Brinsley Tyrrell remembered walking down Main Street:* Brinsley Tyrrell, OH.

132   *Dick Bredemeier recalled police:* Richard Bredemeier, IWA.

134   *"I came in to see him:* Anonymous Guardsman, OH.

136   *Paul Cameron was serving:* Box 101, M4C.

136   *Jim Webb, a Naval Academy graduate:* The Webb anecdote is cited in Myra
      MacPherson, *Long Time Passing: Vietnam and the Haunted Generation,* new
      ed. (Bloomington: Indiana University Press, 2002), 37.

136   *On May 4, army captain Hugh Baker:* Hugh Baker, IWA.

137   *On the West Coast, Neil Young:* For more, see "The Story of 'Ohio," Rock
      Hall Blog, May 17 [2014?], rockhall.com/blog/post/crosby-stills-nash
      -young-ohio-kent-state-shooting.

137   *After the Newark (New Jersey):* Ralph Spielman, IWA.

138   *That same Wednesday, two days after:* White's May 6 letter can be found in
      Box 8, M4C.

138   *Calm, he wrote, had returned to KSU:* Minutes of the May 10 special meet-
      ing of the board can be found in Box 127B, M4C.

9. AN UNFORTUNATE INCIDENT

141   *The decision to extend the war into Cambodia:* All excerpts from Haldeman's
      journals are taken from a copy of the original longhand notes obtained by
      Charles A. Thomas and available from Box 64B, M4C. Where necessary for
      clarity, I have converted Haldeman's shorthand to full words. The journal
      entries for May 4–10, 1970, can also be found in H. R. Haldeman, *The
      Haldeman Diaries* (New York: Putnam, 1994), 159–164.

143   *The "condolence statement" was only marginally that:* Richard Nixon, "State-
      ment on the Deaths of Four Students at Kent State University, Kent, Ohio,"
      The American Presidency Project, May 4, 1970, www.presidency.ucsb.edu
      /ws/?pid=2492.

143   *In a speech Monday evening:* New York Times, May 5, 1970, 17.

144   *"Nixon's people cut him right off from the beginning:* Victor Gold, IWA.

145   *Agnew had drawn a sharp line in the sand:* See Spiro T. Agnew, *Collected
      Speeches of Spiro Agnew* (New York: Audubon Books, 1971), 55.

146   *Agnew was still working that line:* Gold, IWA.

149 *"We know what happened at Kent State:* Quotes from the Frost-Agnew exchange are taken from Appendix 2 of I. F. Stone, *The Killings at Kent State: How Murder Went Unpunished* (New York: New York Review, 1971), 139–140.

152 *There was also a Friday evening press conference:* Richard Nixon, "The President's News Conference," The American Presidency Project, May 8, 1970, www.presidency.ucsb.edu/ws/?pid=2496.

154 *"I said, 'Get your clothes on:* For more on Nixon's visit to the Lincoln Memorial, see Tom McNichol, "I Am Not a Kook: Richard Nixon's Bizarre Visit to the Lincoln Memorial," *Atlantic*, November 14, 2011, www.theatlantic.com/politics/archive/2011/11/i-am-not-a-kook-richard-nixons-bizarre-visit-to-the-lincoln-memorial/248443, and "New Nixon Tapes Reveal Details of Meeting with Anti-War Activists," *PBS Newshour*, November 25, 2011, www.pbs.org/newshour/bb/white_house-july-dec11-nixontapes_11–25. (The latter site includes an audiotape in which the president explains the visit.)

157 *The Scranton Commission report was released:* For the full text of Nixon's letter, see Richard Nixon, "Letter to the Chairman, President's Commission on Campus Unrest, on the Commission's Report," The American Presidency Project, December 12, 1970, www.presidency.ucsb.edu/ws/?pid=2844.

10. BLIND JUSTICE

163 *Five months earlier, Lough had been:* Box 208, M4C.

164 *Along with the indictments:* For the entire special grand jury report, see J. Gregory Payne, "Appendices," May 4 Archive, 1997, www.may4archive.org/appendices.shtml.

165 *"The morbid joke,":* William G. Arthrell, OH.

166 *"As we were on a hill, several students:* This and the other Guardsmen statements that follow, except as noted, can be found in Box 64D, M4C.

169 *Specialist Fourth Class William Earl Perkins:* Box 6, Vol. 9. ACLU.

170 *The results were damning:* Department of Justice May 4 Investigation records, Box 122X, M4C.

170 *Eleven of the sixteen men in Troop G:* Box 64D, M4C.

170 *Nor were accounts consistent across:* Box 6, Vol. 9, ACLU.

171 *By then, too, the immediate physical evidence:* Box 132, M4C.

171 *The deployment to Kent State had involved:* Canterbury's entire after-action report is available in Box 64D, M4C.

172 *The FBI and Ohio State Highway Patrol beat the bushes:* The FBI memos cited here can all be found in Box 132, M4C.

174 *For a full month after the shootings:* Brinsley Tyrrell, OH.

174 *English professor Lew Fried:* Lew Fried, IWA.

175 *The third youngest of six children, Vecchio:* Box 132, M4C.

176 *What's known about Norman:* Norman's statement to the Ohio State High-way Patrol is available in Box 132, M4C.

177 *That's when Bill Barrett:* Bill Barrett, OH.

178 *Others recall that moment differently:* Janis Froelich, "Kent State—A New Look," *Tampa Tribune*, April 30, 2006, kent.state.tripod.com/janis.html.

181 *Simultaneously, Krause was pressing:* John Dean's memo for the file can be found in Charles A. Thomas papers, Box 64B, M4C.

181 *If Arthur Krause ever did read the memo:* Carl Moore Papers, Box 72, M4C.

183 *"In retrospect, the tragedy of May 4, 1970:* Judge William K. Thomas's Settlement and Dismissal Order, www.library.kent.edu/special-collections-and-archives/settlement-and-dismissal-order-page-3. A contemporaneous "Statement by the Students Wounded and by the Parents of the Students Killed at Kent State University on May 4, 1970" can be found in Virginia Lee Heidloff-Reichard papers, Box 22, M4C.

11. PLAN B

185 *Pryor proclaimed his innocence:* Box 4, Vol. 3, and Box 9, ACLU.

185 *He testified in 1975:* Box 20, ACLU.

186 *Others favor Major Harry Jones:* Box 4, Vol. 3, and Box 12, ACLU.

186 *But Jones and his baton also played:* Box 9, ACLU.

188 *"I was pretty proud of our planning for this:* Richard Bredemeier, IWA.

188 *Ray Bye, who would end up alone:* Ray Bye, IWA.

188 *As White put it in a 1975 deposition:* Box 19, ACLU.

188 *Clearly, this wasn't the situation:* Bredemeier, IWA.

190 *"a sweet guy:* Brinsley Tyrrell, IWA.

190 *"was the wrong man:* Jerry Lewis, IWA.

190 *"We were young and naïve:* Martha Dishman, OH.

190 *"My sense is that they so:* Timothy App, IWA.

192 *Rhodes, Timothy App contended:* App, IWA.

193 *Rhodes would later claim, under oath:* Box 5, Vol. 6, ACLU.

193 *"They gave us much more credit:* Gallagher, OH.

194 *"At Kent from the mid-'60s:* Ken Hammond, IWA.

195 *"The Guardsmen had a right:* Lewis, IWA.

196 *"Who was in command of the troops:* Box 64D, M4C.

196 *According to Canterbury, Fassinger was the one:* Box 4, Vol. 5, ACLU.

196 *And so the dialogue goes:* Box 64D, M4C.

197 *"No one really knew who was in charge":* The Larry Shafer and Rudy Morris quotes are from *Kent State: The Day the War Came Home* (Single Spark Pictures, 2000).

198   *Guardsmen also had a right to adequate training:* Box 3, ACLU.
198   *Other Guardsmen had to make up instant responses:* Box 18, ACLU.
199   *"Was the situation at the time of the shooting:* Box 64D, M4C.
200   *"It's almost as though we were put together:* See *Kent State.*
200   *Larry Shafer, who shot Joe Lewis twice:* John Dunphy, "Guardsmen Ends 10-Year Silence on KSU," *Akron Beacon Journal*, May 4, 1980, www.may4 archive.org/accounts.shtml.
200   *In trying to piece together what happened:* Bredemeier, IWA.
201   *Timothy App also brought military experience:* App, IWA.
201   *"All of a sudden a line of Guardsmen turned:* Box 20, ACLU.
202   *"I saw [Myron Pryor] go around:* Hammond, IWA.
202   *"The most parsimonious explanation:* Lewis, IWA.
202   *Alan Canfora, for one:* Alan Canfora, IWA.
203   *Brinsley Tyrrell answered the same:* Tyrrell, IWA.
204   *"Many had never seen anyone in a wheelchair:* Dean Kahler, IWA.

12. PARADISE LOST

207   *Murvin Perry, then director of the School of Journalism:* Murvin Perry, OH.
208   *Vita Semeraro was a supervisor in the registrar's office:* Vita Semeraro, OH.
209   *"I think there was a great deal of naïveté:* Brinsley Tyrrell, IWA.
209   *"He could justify putting:* Jerry Lewis, IWA.
210   *"Kent was a rural college:* Lafayette Tolliver, IWA.
210   *One of those rural, naïve, idealistic:* Dean Kahler, IWA.
211   *Emotions were raw and grew rawer still:* Richard Bredemeier, IWA.
211   *Stephen Titchenal was called to testify:* Stephen Titchenal, OH.
211   *"If you disagreed with the Vietnam War:* Gerald Casale, IWA.
212   *"Anyone with any intelligence:* Art Krummel, OH.
212   *"These men weren't put here:* Anonymous Guardsman, OH.
212   *Robert White took eloquent note:* Box 64D, M4C.
213   *"I always believed that Kent:* Ellis Berns, OH.
213   *"Kent State was not just Kent State:* William G. Arthrell, OH.
213   *"I turned a corner that day:* Timothy App, IWA.
213   *"It had an immediate, transformative effect:* Bredemeier, IWA.
214   *Vearl Mathis Harrington, class of 1971:* Box 101, M4C.
214   *There were even benefits in unusual places:* Peter Thoren, IWA.
214   *"The mainstream was that they should have killed:* Ellen Mann, OH.
215   *"One of the consequences:* John Guidubaldi, OH.
215   *"put paid to the whole idea:* Bruce Dzeda, OH.
215   *Brinsley Tyrrell put it very simply:* Tyrrell, IWA.
215   *"a catastrophic event:* Lew Fried, IWA.
216   *"I talked to his roommates:* John Pekkanen, IWA.

216   *"Cambodia was crazy:* Mary Homer, OH.
216   *"I remember in elementary school:* Box 101, M4C.
217   *"I think everybody who was there:* Martha Dishman, OH.
217   *remembered Dorothy Fuldheim:* Jeanne Anderson, OH.
217   *"Is this the way:* Robert Pescatore, OH.
217   *"beginning of his downfall slide:* H. R. Haldeman, *The Ends of Power* (New York: Dell, 1978), 151.
218   *"caught in bed with either:* This and other colorful Edwin Edwards quotes can be found at www.brainyquote.com/quotes/authors/e/edwin_edwards .html.
219   *"We did exactly what they wanted us to do:* Casale, IWA.
221   *"They had to give it:* Bredemeier, IWA.
223   *"I have told parts of this story:* Winona Vannoy, OH.
223   *"If we don't help people remember:* Diane Yale-Peabody, OH.

AFTERWORD

226   *"I filled out the form:* Richard Karl Watkins, OH.
228   *"It tore my heart:* Janice Marie (Gierman) Wascko, OH.

SELECTED BIBLIOGRAPHY

PRINT BOOKS

Barbato, Carole A., and Laura L. Davis, eds. *Democratic Narrative, History, & Memory*. Kent, Ohio: Kent State University Press, 2012.

Caputo, Philip. *13 Seconds: A Look Back at the Kent State Shootings*. New York: Chamberlain Bros., 2005.

Davies, Peter, and the Board of Church and Society of the United Methodist Church. *The Truth About Kent State: A Challenge to the American Conscience*. New York: Farrar, Straus and Giroux, 1973.

Eszterhas, Joe, and Michael D. Roberts. *13 Seconds: Confrontation at Kent State*. New York: Dodd, Mead, 1970.

Haldeman, H. R. *The Haldeman Diaries: Inside the Nixon White House*. New York: Putnam, 1994.

Haldeman, H. R., with Joseph DiMona. *The Ends of Power*. New York: Dell, 1978.

Michener, James A. *Kent State: What Happened and Why*. New York: Random House, 1971.

Payne, J. Gregory. *Mayday: Kent State*. Dubuque, IA: Kendall/Hunt, 1981.

The Report of the President's Commission on Campus Unrest. Washington, DC: US Government Printing Office, 1970.

Stone, I. F. *The Killings at Kent State: How Murder Went Unpunished*. New York: A New York Review Book, 1970.

E-BOOKS

Taylor, Charles A. *Blood of Isaac*. speccoll.library.kent.edu/4may70/IsaacOne.htm.

———. *Kenfour: Notes on an Investigation.* speccoll.library.kent.edu/4may70/kenfour3.htm.

———. *The Scales Overturned.* speccoll.library.kent.edu/4may70/scales.html.

(Taylor's unpublished books, all available through the Kent State University Libraries May 4 Collection, are especially valuable for their footnotes and embedded links.)

FILM AND VIDEO

Allison. Directed by Richard Myers. Black and white, 10 minutes. 1970.

Confrontation at Kent State. Directed by Richard Myers. Black and white, 43 minutes. 1970.

The Day the Sixties Died. Directed by Aaron Matthews for PBS. Color, 60 minutes. 2015.

Fire in the Heartland: Kent State, May 4th, and Student Protest in America. Directed by Daniel Miller. Color, 86 minutes. 2010.

Kent State: The Day the War Came Home. Directed by Chris Triffo. Companion DVD to *13 Seconds* by Philip Caputo. Color, 47:32 minutes. Single Spark Pictures, 2000.

WEBSITES

alancanfora.com. Resource-rich website of one of those wounded at Kent State. Alan Canfora has been an indefatigable researcher of the shootings.

dept.kent.edu/sociology/lewis/lewihen.htm. This website is the home of "The May 4 Shootings at Kent State: The Search for Historical Accuracy," a thoughtful and provocative essay by Jerry M. Lewis and Thomas R. Hensley.

kent.edu/may4. An introduction to Kent State University's excellent May 4 Visitors Center.

library.kent.edu/special-collections-and-archives/may-4-collection. The gateway site for the Kent State University Libraries' rich and vast collection of resources: print and photo archives, oral histories, bibliographies, and more.

may4archive.org. This extensive site is the work of J. Gregory Payne, another tireless researcher of the shootings. Payne's play *Kent State: A Requiem* honors the lives of the four dead students.

web.library.yale.edu/mssa. Gateway site for the online guide to the ACLU of Ohio Kent State Project Records.

ACKNOWLEDGMENTS

Writing is mostly a solitary act, but books are often group efforts, and this one is no exception. The Kent State University Libraries May 4 Collection, which includes an excellent digital archive and the exemplary Kent State Shootings Oral Histories project, is an immensely valuable resource, and public services librarian Amanda Faehnal guided me through it with great skill and infinite patience. Many thanks.

Thanks, too, to those who took the time to relive for my edification what were often painful memories. Their names can be found in these pages. Indeed, this book wouldn't exist without their help. Let me here mention just a few of the very many to whom I am forever grateful: Alan Frank, whose father certainly saved lives on that awful day of May 4, 1970; Dean Kahler, grievously wounded in the shootings; Dick Bredemeier, who dissected events with a surgeon's precision; and Timothy App, Brinsley Tyrrell, Ken Hammond, and Jerry Casale, who recalled that long weekend with wisdom and passion.

Alan Canfora, also wounded in the shootings, has spent decades researching the causes of the shootings and amassing a vast, publicly accessible archive of May 4 materials. Any book about the subject necessarily builds on his work. Any book also has a ready foundation in the meticulous investigation of the President's Commission on Campus Unrest, better known as the Scranton Commission. Working at a feverish pace, the commission produced within four months of the shootings a report that remains admirable today for its thoroughness and clarity. The ACLU of Ohio Kent State Project Records, in repository at Yale University's Sterling Memorial Library, has also preserved a valuable legal record of the many court cases spawned by the shootings. Thanks to the ACLU and Yale for that.

My agent, David Patterson, connected me with editor Bob Pigeon, and Bob has proved perfect at the role: wise, patient, and encouraging, with a fine eye for detail. The faults of this book are mine. Without Bob's counsel, there would be far more of them.

Friends also have played a central role in *67 Shots*. Joe Blatz walked me through the subtleties of the M1 Garand. H. Baker, Chip McConville, and Tom Stouffer helped me see the Kent State shootings through the eyes of Vietnam War veterans. Ken DeCell got me in touch with Ray and Kathy Bye. Sandy Stoddart connected me with J. R. Hipple; Mary Layton, with Bill Forrester; Georgia Sherlock, with Walt Wagner; David Means, with Jerry Casale. My daughter, Ihrie London, reminded me that Timothy App, one of her favorite teachers at Maryland Institute College of Art, had been a Kent State student in 1970. In addition to giving generously of his time, Timothy suggested I contact one of his teachers from back then: Brinsley Tyrrell. These webs of connections went on and on, and extended my own reach exponentially.

Friends and family also provided enormous encouragement, helped fill in missing pockets of knowledge, or made a call on my behalf. Thanks to Brewster and Mary Ellen Willcox, Ben Lamberton, Winslow McCagg, Dick Victory, Jay Sumner, Larry Van Dyne, Bill Mead, Abby Addis, Joyce Young, Bob Stieg, John Lewis, Nancy Graham, Jon London, Xan Hamilton, my son and business partner, Nathan Means, and others too numerous to name here. As always, the real burden of writing this book has fallen to the person closest to me—my wife, Candy, without whom none of this would have gotten done.

Howard Means
Millwood, Virginia

INDEX